THE
St Louis - San Francisco
TRANSCONTINENTAL RAILROAD

The Thirty-fifth Parallel Project, 1853-1890

THE
S͟T LOUIS - SAN FRANCISCO
TRANSCONTINENTAL RAILROAD

The Thirty-fifth Parallel Project, 1853-1890

by H. Craig Miner

The University Press of Kansas/Lawrence/Manhattan/Wichita

© Copyright 1972 by the University Press of Kansas
Standard Book Number 7006-0081-7
Library of Congress Catalog Card Number 76-163197
Printed in the United States of America
Designed by Fritz Reiber

TO MARTIN M. POMPHREY
an enlightened businessman

PREFACE

To the procession of success stories which constitute most of the published material on transcontinental railway enterprise, the history of the St. Louis–San Francisco project provides a welcome contrast. When there is no golden spike, no opening excursion, no junketing congressmen, and when the businessmen involved must face the transitory nature of a boom psychology from the wrong end, then and only then does self-deception concerning the stakes of the enterprise become impossible. This, combined with the element of high tragedy involved in the confrontation of the relatively ethical managers of this road with the relatively unethical managers of certain competitors, gives the study a kind of drama not found in smoother waters.

The St. Louis–San Francisco transcontinental was the serious continental railway which was longest before the public eye. It was one of the first routes to be seriously considered and the last great trunk line to resolve its fate. As a result it experienced and was forced to deal with changes in the public temper which the Union Pacific, pushed to completion in a mere seven years, could not. Men died of old age working on it and men spent careers working on it. Five corporations ran the cycle from organization to bankruptcy, the Indian nations through which it ran evolved from primitive agriculturalists to sophisticated industrialists—and still the project remained incomplete. To our age this enterprise, lacking a history until now, is the most unfamiliar of the transcontinental lines; to the nineteenth century it was an old friend.

As in every work of this size it is impossible to acknowledge all the help I received. But special thanks are due to Martin Pomphrey of the St. Louis–San Francisco Railway Company, Carl White of J. & W. Seligman and Company and William Cox of the Atchison, Topeka and Santa Fe Railway Company. These men not only gave encouragement but made available to me the corporate records upon which this study is largely based. It is my hope that this book might encourage scholars to don overalls, sharpen their craft of translating faded handwriting, and seek out the corporate vaults and warehouses where much of the history of the United States is housed. Special thanks also to Robert G. Athearn of the University of Colorado who as my doctoral adviser did his best to steer me away from endless exposition of trivia and toward the balanced treatment of significant themes for which his own railroad volumes are justly known. Last I wish to acknowledge the continuing inspiration of my association with William E. Unrau of Wichita State University, first as my teacher, now as a colleague, and always as a friend.

H. CRAIG MINER
Wichita State University

CONTENTS

ILLUSTRATIONS

1

A HAUNTED JOURNEY

The usual silence in the forest along the Mississippi River was broken sharply in the first days of June 1853 by the noisy passage of the steamboat *Norma*, southbound for Fort Smith, Arkansas. Aboard the vessel everything was extremely civilized. Lavish meals were served, announced by a bell, and the accommodations were described by one of the passengers as "gigantic, splendid, and convenient." Yet it was apparent that the *Norma*'s passengers were more meditative than average travelers, and some exhibited melancholy when for days no sound was heard but the working of the engines, the noise of table preparations, and the infernal dinner bell.[1] Well might that be, for the cargo of this craft was the personnel and equipment of the expedition assigned by Congress to survey a railroad route to the Pacific Ocean along the desolate thirty-fifth parallel.

Their leader Lieutenant Amiel Weeks Whipple gazed over the ornate railing at the churning white water the paddles left in their wake. It was the middle of a century. The constant deep chugging of the boat's steam cylinders working at close quarters and the threshing of her propulsion system were evidence that it had been a century of great technological accomplishment; the quiet banks of the river were evidence that there was still mystery in that nineteenth-century world.

In the decade of this voyage of the *Norma*, much of that mystery lay in the country west of her river home. The war with Mexico in the late forties had made the American West a larger place than before, opening visions of the Pacific to men whose outlook the Rockies had previously limited. The trade of the Orient, it was said, waited in San Francisco for those who would take it—the riches of Cathay at the beck of America, and of steam.

Consequently, the area between the river and the ocean to the west had undergone a transformation in the minds of American businessmen. It was no longer acceptable that it remain a mystery, a reserve for the savage aborigines, a repository for half-forgotten Spanish legends, a princely domain for a few eccentric fur men. Through the medium of a short and relatively painless war, the barrier had become a bridge, a great land bridge which could carry the young United States to the world and the world to her.

Whipple booked his men in four staterooms. Number One he occupied with the secretary, his cook, and a collection of reports concerning previous expeditions. The rest of the party, numbering twelve, was housed in the other staterooms along with two German cooks.[2] North and South were represented as well as two foreign countries and a number of the sciences, an excellent composition for the accomplishment of a national work which it was hoped would quell the sectional bickering that was drawing the nation toward civil war. Only two were professional railway engineers. There was also a botanist, a geologist, a naturalist, an artist, three astronomers, two meteorologists, and a surveyor. Since two similar expeditions had departed before them on more northerly routes and Commodore Oliver Perry only recently had left for Japan, it was all the secretary of war could do to outfit this varied group with instruments proper to the disciplines represented.[3]

As they steamed south, most members took advantage of the placid time between meals to take stock of their situation. The lower Mississippi no doubt seemed aboriginal to some, yet they were to think of a frontier much more forbidding. Their orders were to proceed west from Fort Smith along the Canadian river valley to Albuquerque, thence through the mountains, locating suitable railroad passes, and on to the Colorado River and the Pacific. The provision made by the War Department for military escort in the most western regions confirmed what many must have suspected, that penetrating a little-known region would be dangerous as well as exhilarating.[4]

Nor did Whipple's group enjoy the full support of Congress. Its appropriation passed as a rider to the general bill for the army engineers, but not without an argument which reflected the tenuous link by which the Union in the fifties was bound. Senator William Gwin of California led those in favor of the surveys, and it was known that he personally was partial to a thirty-fifth parallel route.[5] Yet not all were willing to lay sectarian principles aside. Southern men headed the opposition, fearing that national surveys would lead to federal, and therefore northern, control of any railroad eventually built. Said one: "What is that survey to be made for at Government expense, if not to be followed up by other action? Cui bono? As a matter of curiosity?"[6] The question was resolved by an appeal to patriotism. The proponents argued that "the Pacific ocean is to be the great place of contest for power and supremacy between the nations of the earth by colonization on its shores." Upon the further suggestion that Great Britain was vying for control of the commerce of the Indies, and the promise that the surveys would in no way violate state sovereignty, the measure was passed.[7] Still Senator Thomas Hart Benton maintained that the Southwest was "so utterly desolate, deserted, and God forsaken that Kit Carson says a wolf could not make his living on it."[8]

In addition to the general uncertainty which the orders and this congressional ambiguity promoted in all expedition members, Lieutenant Whipple had the specific responsibilities of the journey's logistics to worry him. His evenings for a time had been spent reading the narratives of southwestern explorers, from the old manuscripts of Francisco Vásquez de Coronado to the recent reports of Randolph Marcy and Lorenzo Sitgreaves.[9] Whipple was a scientist. His New England boyhood and his West Point education combined to make him skeptical of the stories of the Spaniards concerning the seven golden cities of Cibola they had sought along the thirty-fifth parallel, and of the tales the Indians told of ancient curses and lost civilizations.[10] The Whipple party was departing loaded not with dreams but with sextants and transits for themselves, and for the superstitious Indians five-cent mirrors, four-cent artificial flowers and twelve-and-one-half-cent pipes; this was the nineteenth century.[11] Yet even so, it was not without foreboding that the lieutenant sat in his cabin poring over his maps. The area to be traversed was poorly known. All he really had to rely upon were some tracings by Sitgreaves which turned out to be inaccurate, interviews with certain reticent fur men, and the fantastic jottings of the ancient mail-clad conquistadores.[12] In guessing at Whipple's thoughts, it must be remembered that New England was the site of the superstitious witchcraft trials as well as the home of that great logician Daniel Webster.

But none of the Americans viewed the journey in quite the same light as did Baldwin Mollhausen, whose drawings of the trip are a chronicle of German romanticism. Mollhausen was the son of a Prussian artillery officer but fled the polish of the European military in favor of the vague pleasures of the American wilderness. At twenty-four, he accompanied Duke Paul William of Wurtemberg to the Rocky Mountains, became lost, and lived with the Omaha and Otoe Indians for some months. Only a year had passed between that adventure and this.[13] For Whipple the West was a source of new data, for Mollhausen of new sensations. It disgusted him that Americans were so boorishly concrete in their approach to their own wilderness.

It is fortunate that Whipple and Mollhausen were the diarists of the expedition, for their accounts complement each other, and it requires both to yield a full picture of the West they experienced.[14] When Mollhausen compared the rolling prairie to the sea, Whipple, in typical American fashion, decided the angle of the railroad cuts that would be required to pierce the hills; while the German drew exaggerated pictures of weird sandstone formations, Whipple wrote: "Here are good materials for masonry."[15]

It seemed to Mollhausen that even the steamboat reflected the American attitude of cold-blooded calculation:

> One feels almost provoked with the craft, for the indifference she manifests toward the loveliest bits of scenery, even seeming sometimes to keep perversely to one or the other bank on purpose to avoid them. Just as little does she trouble herself about the floating drift-wood that is moving slowly down the stream before her, driving the slothful swimmers to the right and left, or running them down and rushing foaming and snorting over them, as if she had been taught the shrewd doctrine, that the best and shortest way to fortune is over the shoulders of others. It is a doctrine pretty often reduced to practice in American commercial life: all things revolve round the common axis of money making, and the true man of business, whatever he does, never loses sight of the question, what profit he can make by it. . . . This want of sense of the beautiful in nature in the generality of Americans, is to a

European as remarkable as the enthusiasm of the Europeans is
to them absurd.

After a short journey up the Arkansas River, the little group landed
at Fort Smith on June 12 and quickly exchanged the philosophic musings
of a lonely river voyage for the simplistic but vibrant enthusiasm of a
town which hoped to be railhead of a transcontinental line. The village
residents were so enthralled with the thought that this small surveying
party was the precursor of the vast wealth a transportation system would
bring that it appeared to Mollhausen that they could actually envision
clearly "that the locomotives shall hereafter rush fearlessly through the
territories of the hostile Indians, establishing a connection between the
two oceans, and bring the gold mines of California within easy reach."[16]

Fort Smith for all its fervor was only one of a dozen cities along the
Mississippi valley that had been seized by desire for a railroad since
the Mexican War had opened the territory to the west. Both Memphis
and St. Louis had sponsored railroad conventions in anticipation of a
new western line that would terminate in their business districts, and
there was talk of it in Vicksburg. The river towns argued as the sections
argued: Who was to profit?—which route, which city, which cadre of
enterprising capitalists would realize the dream of Columbus, to reach
the East by moving west?

Thomas Benton at first represented most St. Louis citizens in his
desire to run a railroad straight west from that city across the Rockies
and along the thirty-eighth parallel. But two disastrous expeditions
under the command of his son-in-law, John C. Fremont, were convincing
proof to some of the impracticability of that route. Interest, therefore,
turned toward a competition with Fort Smith for the thirty-fifth parallel
franchise.[17]

This movement was encouraged by Missouri Congressman John
Phelps and others from the southwestern portion of the state. There the
price of corn was double that in St. Louis. Isolated communities had to
haul wheat 250 miles to the nearest mill; there would be universal appreciation of a railroad striking out from St. Louis toward the thirty-fifth
parallel.[18] The final change of mind among Missourians as to their
chosen route came with the news that John Gunnison, commanding an
1853 survey along Benton's thirty-eighth parallel route, had been killed
by Indians, after reporting that a railway along that path was unfeasible
because of the "enormous expense" of tunneling and bridging which
would be involved.[19] St. Louis thenceforward became the most powerful

municipal proponent of a thirty-fifth parallel route that would turn north to their city at some point in the Indian Territory west of Arkansas. This design would put Fort Smith on a branch line at best. But the wine flowed freely for the Whipple party there, the celebrants little realizing that this expedition would add its approval to the claims of Fort Smith's northern rival.

While in Arkansas the party hired the laborers it needed, broke the mules, and attended balls. Whipple was absent much of the time, scouting the area for the best terminal point, speaking with railway men about investments, visiting surrounding towns, and hearing at least one "miserable sermon."[20]

In the latter part of June the group moved into the woods to test its equipment, but not before a farewell celebration at the hotel. The proprietor sent them off with a well-designed toast:

> My boys, you have a long and dangerous journey before you, but keep a good heart and find the best line for the rails to California; and when you have found it don't forget that you are not without friends in Fort Smith, who will show themselves mindful of the trouble you have taken. You come back this way. I've got land enough hereabouts that will be worth a thousand times what it now is when we have the railroad finished, and if you like to come and settle in our town—a thriving town it will be then— I'll give every one of you a plot for building on that you may choose for yourselves.

It was an obvious bribe but they took it up with a cheer. All in the assemblage speculated in their imaginations: A New Yorker picked ground where he said he would build a hotel to catch the gold dust on its way east, a Frenchman selected a hill for a vineyard, an Irishman chose a likely distillery site. Fear of the adventure ahead was drowned in a chorus of good fellowship.

As they moved into the forest, the men took up the routine that filled their waking hours for the next several months. Wrote Mollhausen: "One sleeps well enough upon the ground when one has no choice. . . . You learn to bear the heat when it must be borne; if you get wet, the rain cannot penetrate further than the skin; and broiled meat, and black coffee sweetened with maple sugar, make a superb meal when there is nothing better to be had."[21] July 14 was spent training chainmen and rodmen and in setting the astronomic and barometric instruments on the flagstaff at Fort Smith. The next day they crossed the Poteau River and moved through a marshy canebrake toward the Pacific.

A storm broke as they crossed into the Indian Territory, miring the wagons and slowing progress, yet the third night out found them in Scullyville, a town of thirty houses which served as the seat of the Choctaw Indian Agency. The name was derived from the Choctaw word *iskuli-fehna*, which meant money. It was here that Whipple and his men first recognized a problem which would plague corporate enterprise along the route for the rest of the nineteenth century. The fact was that the Indian nations were not reacting to "civilization" in a consistent manner, and there was some reason to believe that the plans of the battling Mississippi towns for stringing track across their domain were greatly premature. The Indians had developed an agricultural economy and appreciated the money that came through the agency. They were also keenly aware that railroads were the advance agents of a foreign culture, and that political domination usually followed them. That domination would be resisted by many who remembered that they had been given this plot of scrub oak and red clay west of Arkansas and north of Texas in exchange for their rich tribal lands in the East. Some of the Indians observed by the railroad surveyors were prepared, it seemed, to become railroad contractors, and "seemed perfectly at ease in black coat, pants, vest, polished boots, and beaver hat." But, alongside them in the streets of Scullyville walked some "with naked limbs, who might well have been taken for wild savages of the prairie."[22]

Mollhausen observed that the buffalo were being sacrificed to the "uncontrollable passion for the chase," and that the Indian staff of life was disappearing along with these beasts. The German gained great respect for the cultural uniqueness of the Indian enclave in the center of an aggressive nation, sympathizing with the tribes much as he had sympathized with the driftwood plowed under by the charging steamboat. He worried about his role in bringing about their disinheritance—he and the others marking a phantom line in figures and readings across the unmarked sod. Perhaps, he thought, it would only be after the Indians had been ruined by the covetousness of the white civilized races that "Christian love will find its way to their empty wigwams, and churches and meetinghouses rise over the graves of the . . . legitimate owners of the green prairies."[23]

As they proceeded west from Scullyville, the landscape became more desolate. The Sans Bois Hills loomed up to the south, then the Shawnee villages, ruined Old Fort Arbuckle, the Chouteaus' trading post, and finally on September 6, the Antelope Hills which lay on the one hundredth meridian and the border of Texas.

They had been moving from the beginning along the valley of the Canadian River. Whipple later claimed that the Canadian was a "natural highway" formed, it seemed, by nature with their special object in view.[24] Yet in the August heat enthusiasm melted. The "roads" to which they were directed were all but nonexistent, and the river itself consisted of "some narrow shallow runnels of thick-looking water." Blackened tree trunks lay uprooted and partly covered with sand along its banks, with their "withered ghostly-looking" branches flung toward the sky. Only a lone heron was disturbed by the shots the party fired into the air. The distances became greater and greater between sources of wood and water.[25]

To Whipple the "ghostly" branches looked as though they belonged in the tender of an engine pulling a long train loaded with livestock fattened on rich prairie grass. Forgetting all the free drinks he had recently enjoyed in Arkansas, he concluded that the destination of that future train should be St. Louis rather than Fort Smith. "If the railroad proceeds from St. Louis passing Springfield, Misso. it may be readily prolonged to and unite with the Canadian . . . by this means there would be avoided the hills of carboniferous sandstone . . . west of Ft. Smith."[26]

That opinion was very encouraging to a division of the Pacific Railroad of Missouri called the South-West Branch, for its proposed route was exactly the one Whipple described. The Pacific of Missouri had been chartered in 1849 by the state of Missouri in hopes of either building straight west to the Pacific independently, by way of Kansas City, or connecting with a federally sponsored transcontinental railway. Massive state aid given to the project was further increased by a federal land grant for internal improvements given to the state in 1852. This land grant was used partly to start the South-West Branch, which was designed to run toward Indian Territory and to intercept any transcontinental running along a southern route or, failing that, to take advantage of the line skirting south of the Rockies to gain the coast on its own.[27] From the southwest corner of Missouri, which was as far as the branch had definite plans to build in 1853, it was only a few miles through the Indian Territory to the thirty-fifth parallel. Therefore, Missourians watched the Whipple party closely.

Fort Arbuckle, an abandoned army barracks used by the Delaware tribe, was reached by the Whipple party on August 20. Here they planned to meet Jesse Chisholm, and to hire him as a guide. Chisholm was there, but he was not interested; former guides quit upon news that "wild Indians" were ahead. This threw Whipple into a rage:

> I told him that I was annoyed & offended that men as intelligent as I had supposed him should show so much apathy in the operations we are engaged upon. That they should refuse—even when offered high wages—to aid in explorations for a railroad which would be vastly more beneficial to their country than a mine of gold—the largest the world ever saw—placed in their midst. I was surprised at their stupidity & offended at their indiference [sic].

Chisholm finally agreed to send his fourteen-year-old Mexican servant Vincente; so the United States Corps of Topographical Engineers hired a teenager to lead them through the uncharted regions of their own country. It literally looked like Hell, for the Indians had set a huge prairie fire to bring on new grass.[28]

They walked among ashes for days, kerchiefs pulled over the nose, hats down low on the forehead, lungs seared with a dust that made breathing a conscious experience. Out of the "eyeless sockets" of the charred skulls littering the way there appeared to flow a satanic intelligence which persecuted the sanity of the strong, and made the weak wish heartily that they had joined their companions in fleeing back to the Mississippi, to the warring towns, the handshakes of congressmen, and the blacks and whites of a developing civil conflict, back to the "joys of home and the flesh pots of Egypt."[29] To stop following this teenage boy through the land of twisted oaks fighting the sun for life's moisture was, however, quite impossible. As they wrote letters their thoughts flew to Victorian mansions on shady lands, but their eyes still watched the turning wheel of the odometer and they measured the elevations and the grade where iron would lie, firemen would curse, and people in Palace Cars would chat, transforming the wilderness.

The light of the great prairie fire made them all look strange at night, if their experience had not done enough to change their appearance. The astronomers were watching a comet between the stars Acturus and Polaris; others looked up in prayer.[30] All the while the burning made a terrible noise "like the distant hollow trembling of the earth when thousands of buffalo are tearing and trampling over it with their heavy hoofs," and none could help lying awake thinking of the mirage that had torn at the senses in the day. Once it had transformed an antelope running from the flames. He grew so large he filled half the sky, then shrank, then threw up waves in a lake that was not there, then split into two images—two phantom animals—galloping, one upside down, across the horizon. They had black coffee and maple sugar. There was no beer, no trade of the Indies, no gold dust. They had a white wolf which they had shot, the fire, the mirage, and themselves. "Do not awaken the anger of the Great Spirit," the Indians had said; "he is in possession of a terrible Medicine."[31]

In the middle of the Llano Estacado (Staked Plains) of Texas, Vincente broke. Whipple had to lead him away from a council with some Kiowa Indians after he demanded that they stop smoking at the sun. "They were bad men to do that," he said. "They were sorcerers, and were casting a spell to do us harm."[32] Mollhausen was thoughtful too and wondered where this dismal trail could lead them or American business enterprise but to disaster:

> At sea the first thing you do is to look round the horizon for a sail, and to rejoice if you discover one; you feel less forlorn then in the sublime solitude; but in the Llano you would seek in vain for such a consolation; no tree or shrub breaks the monotony of the plain; and while the ocean does but seem to sleep, and its heavings, like the breathings of a leviathan, show it to be still alive, the Llano Estacado is dead, and varied only by the deceitful mirage.

If there had been leaves to fall, they would have been falling when the party entered Albuquerque in October, bearded, sunburned, and thoroughly haunted. All hoped for refreshment in "the land of fandangos and bowie knives, of lassos and red pepper, of *Quien Sabes* and señoritas," and they got it abundantly in a month's stay which exchanged heat and the suggestion of madness for "flirting under difficulties." Mollhausen stayed with a family in Albuquerque where he caught up on his drawings and kindly catered to the curiosity of three young boys. Whipple, however, stayed at the camp, doggedly collecting the data of the journey, making lists and tables, and writing coherent letters and reports to superiors concerning a relatively incoherent experience. He was "busied with accounts, correspondence, and requisitions," as Mollhausen put it.[33] A practical cure for a practical man.

Thoughts turned again to the railroad which, after a few nights of merrymaking, again seemed possible, even probable. Railway traffic possibilities in the Indian Territory were small, at least until the roving bands of natives could be replaced with a more productive population, that is, one which shipped things on railway cars.[34] But with a subsidy sufficient to press construction through the domain of the tribes and through the Llano, there might be hope for almost immediate profit.

In common with many others of his time, Whipple had a greatly exaggerated concept of the wealth of the Orient, dating perhaps to schoolboy readings of the adventures of Marco Polo. The miles of unprofitable track to be laid over marginal or barren traffic areas could be ignored. Perhaps the cattle industry around Albuquerque or the few mining plots there would add some cars to the regular trains laden with the bullion of California and the spices of the East, but if they did or not was of secondary concern. The important thing was to gain the coast, then strike north to San Francisco, the pearl, the future "great commercial emporium" of the world, the latitudinal sister of St. Louis and the object of all her dreams.[35]

Mollhausen too was fascinated by this complex design. Whatever the Americans lacked in sensitivity, they made up for in ingenuity. Their restlessness, energy, practicality, and ability exercised a strong attraction, as did the picture they drew of power through commercial conquest. For a time, young Mollhausen was swept away by it and unhesitatingly praised the spirit

> that rolled the tide of progress far out along the Mississippi and Missouri, checked neither by the apparently impenetrable forests nor by arid plains, or savage natives. But sweeping in one mighty wave from the shores of the Atlantic, over the American continent, to meet at last, at the Rocky Mountains with another wave from the Pacific ocean; with which it united, to overflow, and shortly absorb the entire population of New Mexico.

One American, standing on top of Pyramid Rock said: "We may regard ourselves as monarchs of these regions and our empire may be considered the largest in the world, for we ourselves determine its boundaries."

November 7 saw them moving again, and again transformed from the empire builders they had been in the arms of the señoritas to puzzled searchers in the unknown. Nature was not so forbidding in New Mexico, but she was still awesome enough to awaken "feelings not easily to be expressed." And added to the enigma of nature was the mystery of the human past. At Isleta, Laguna, and again at Zuñi, Aztec dances filled the village squares while Indian faces gazed at the scientists "through the mask of chalk or the blood of cattle, with which they had seen fit to bedaub themselves."[36] For some reason Mollhausen picked up a skull from a Laguna cemetery and carried the *memento mori* with him for the rest of the trip.

The Zuñi pueblo was infested with smallpox. The wrath of the gods, the Indians explained, was at work—the same wrath that had been previously appeased only by the sacrifice of a youth and a maid. On that occasion, the victims were tossed into a great flood which had come upon the land. When it subsided the bodies had taken the form of two large stone pillars, which the residents pointed out to all tourists.[37] The laborers and muleteers in the party reacted to this last tale by drinking a large quantity of the alcohol brought along to preserve zoological specimens.[38] Whipple was seen on a high cliff, very impractical for a railroad grade, looking for the ruins of a sacrificial altar. He found them.[39]

Scarcely less amazing was El Moro Rock, for untold years a tablet for travelers' inscriptions. The Whipple group spent hours copying seventeenth-century Spanish inscriptions and Indian hieroglyphics. Wrote one Spanish Ozymandias, ". . . a so renowned and valiant soldier . . ." and there the inscription disappeared, victim of the wind and rain. Another sentence had great relevance to the railroad surveyors: "Joseph Dominquez and others came past this place in October, with much caution and some fear."[40]

Christmas eve, 1853, was like no other any of the men had ever spent. Within sight of the San Francisco Mountains, isolated pines were set afire, creating a magnificent effect, while native singers spun a web of song which charmed men far away from home. Whipple was the last to succumb, but on this Christmas in the desert he momentarily lost his grip on the Protestant Ethic and was transported to another place and time:

> The plaintive tones of the singers, and the strange simplicity of the people, leads one's fancy back to the middle ages. In this state of society, so free from ambition for wealth or power, where the realities of life are in a great measure subject to the ideal, there is a tinge of romance.

In St. Louis, the directors of the Pacific railroad also gathered around trees more artificially lighted, and spoke on and on of geographic destiny and iron rails. No doubt they wondered at Whipple's mood when a report reached them that he had named a deep gorge along his route Cañon Diablo.

The thirty-fifth parallel expedition spent a month trying to find a suitable railway grade from the mountains near present Flagstaff, Arizona, to the two-hundred-foot level of the Colorado River. As though to harry further the tired and distraught men, their maps misled them and the volcanic hills confused their magnetic instruments, once reversing entirely the poles of a compass. Mules, grazed in too tight a group, died of starvation.[41] But in the rain on February 20, 1854, they saw three sharp peaks which they called "The Needles," and beyond that the Colorado River. On March 21, they reached Los Angeles, and sailed at once for San Francisco on the steamer *Fremont,* no doubt very busy at accounts and requisitions.[42]

Their reports were avidly read in Missouri. The managers of the South-West Branch had filed a plat of their railway route as far as the western boundary of Missouri on the day Whipple was copying inscriptions at El Moro Rock.[43] On February 13, 1854, a day when the surveyors rested to repair their shoes and observe an occultation of Mars, the directors of the Missouri branch railroad had let construction contracts for their line.[44] Among the contenders for the wealth of the Indies, the thirty-fifth parallel project laid the first iron.

They would build it, they said, for $28,000 a mile, and they brought in engineers to question Whipple's estimate of $90,000 a mile.[45] The lieutenant knew their good intent and found it impossible to explain his pessimism about the bizarre contours of another world than St. Louis businessmen had ever known. He was satisfied to note that "without having been eye-witness of the uninhabited regions through which it is proposed to execute a work of such magnitude, they have failed to appreciate the extent of the difficulties which such an unprecedented condition of things would produce."[46]

Amiel Whipple would be knocked off his horse by a minieball at Chancellorsville in 1863.[47] He died knowing that the South-West Branch was then running trains to Rolla, Missouri, less than one hundred miles from its origin point.[48] When Baldwin Mollhausen died forty-two years later in 1905, there was still no trunk line along the thirty-fifth parallel. He, however, had lived to see five efficient railway corporations organized and undone in an attempt to follow with steam and steel the phantom path of the Whipple party's haunted journey.

THE SOUTH-WEST BRANCH

Missourians enthusiastically promoted the South-West Branch. They did so despite the rugged topography of the Ozark uplands to be tunneled through in a plague of mud or frozen ground, despite the twisting courses of the Meramec, the Gasconade, the Neosho rivers, and a myriad of smaller streams which would have to be bridged again and again, despite sparse population and little fluid capital for railroad purposes, and despite the probability that the enterprise would for a long time to come be dependent upon state aid. Geopoliticians spoke of the "natural destiny" of St. Louis and charted the unruffled course of imaginary lines to San Francisco Bay, while numerous alignments of speculators thought of more ready advantages: the rich mining industry of southwest Missouri crying for transportation, the agricultural traffic of a developing area, the abundant timber and coal with which to lay the roadbed and feed the locomotives, and the generosity of the state of Missouri in providing bond aid and a land grant to the incipient enterprise.

15

Speculators, according to one authority, are men who concentrate on one thing at a time. They seek immediate profit while "they discourage individual industry and frugality; weaken the moral fibre of a community; encourage trustees and agents to misuse funds and properties in their keeping; and destroy conservative judgement." The classic pattern of nineteenth-century railroad speculation was to obtain a favorable charter and large concessions of land, issue as much stock as the public would take, obtain subsidies from cities and counties, construct the road as cheaply as possible, sell the lands as high as possible, and march on to greener pastures. While the new Pacific project in Missouri lacked a solid balance sheet which would appeal to conservative investors, it made up for this in glamorous possibility and favorable grants of aid. It was the speculators' business to capitalize on the kind of public imagination and hope which was the only asset of the South-West Branch.[1] Therefore, it is not surprising that for many years the thirty-fifth parallel project was controlled by speculators.

Although the successful speculative promoter was a born enthusiast who recognized no obstacles, experts have noted that the daring mental attitude of the promoter often made him an undesirable choice for the dependable management of capital or the long-term control of a large corporation.[2] The speculator who invested in the South-West Branch cared little whether the track reached even the thirty-fifth parallel, much less the Pacific, effusive oratory to the contrary notwithstanding. To these early managers the setting for the railroad was Missouri, and the issue was not entering the China trade but reaching Rolla, Lebanon, Springfield or Vinita in order to collect lands, local subsidies, and municipal bonds.

Yet to note that the first managers of the project were speculators says more about the nature of the enterprise than about the character of the men. Use of the term "speculator" does not imply that the officers or directors were necessarily dishonest or even that they were always aware that their position was so risky as to be speculative. Though the resolution organizing the South-West Branch had carefully noted the internal improvements land grant made to Missouri by Congress in 1852, and the directors of the Pacific of Missouri admitted they were "looking to county and individual subscriptions and further loans of state credit," most connected with the enterprise believed that this aid was not a gift but a wise investment, to be paid back to the state and cities in benefits within a few years.[3] Few agreed with the St. Louis *Western Journal and Civilian* when it warned that the money for the railroad could not be generated in Missouri without damaging the whole state economy, and that the railroads would be left a monument to high hopes in an economic wasteland "like the roofless frame of an unfinished building."[4] Their ears were tuned to prophets of another sort of future, and they heard only these. "Is it not manifest now more than ever before," wrote a friendly journalist in the state capital, "that we need a railroad, if so will we not go to work and help build it, does it matter who is benefitted by it?"[5]

The dream of a St. Louis–San Francisco road that sustained all this optimism originated in 1849. The catalyst was a speech on February 7 of that year by Senator Thomas Hart Benton, who said he had developed his ideas thirty years before, when "the steam car was . . . unknown, and California was not ours." Benton claimed that Asiatic commerce had determined the seat of wealth and power in the world from Phoenician times onward, and that it was imperative that the United States immediately tap this source of strength among nations. He suggested a publicly-owned transcontinental railway, as he felt that private interest would only make such a project "a great stock-jobbing business." He also held that his friend Fremont had found the best route for transcontinental commerce along the thirty-eighth parallel. But he did not insist on these points, nor did he demand that the line be a railroad for its entire distance—sleighs and a magnetic power device were suggested as alternatives for certain sections. Benton in fact was adamant about only one thing: that the termini be set, and that these be the geographic sisters St. Louis and San Francisco—"the rest is a matter of detail."[6] On March 12, 1849, the Pacific Railroad Company of Missouri was incorporated for the purpose of building such a line west from St. Louis.

The enthusiasm in Benton's speech was contagious. Delegates to a St. Louis railroad convention that summer ignored the cholera that was rapidly reducing the city's population and the drinking water which was half Mississippi river sediment, in order seriously to consider the spot as eastern terminus of a national railway.[7] But the enthusiasm within rival factions was so great that the meeting turned out to be "not so much a deliberation as a quarrel." Benton spent one entire afternoon trying to explain why Fremont himself did not recommend the thirty-eighth parallel route, and another arguing with the pessimistic editor of the *Western Journal and Civilian*. A few memorials were composed, but in general the meeting was a failure, a casualty of an unexamined boom psychology and civic jealousy.[8]

The meeting did, however, prove something: the city of St. Louis was not prepared to back a Pacific railroad as actively as the most sanguine expected, but the young city of Chicago was. Ironically, neither of these cities became the terminus of the first completed transcontinental twenty years hence, but in 1849 it appeared that one of them surely would. The lethargy of St. Louis in promoting her interest was the result of the idea that river commerce, in which her businessmen had invested heavily, would sustain her preeminent position indefinitely with or without the railroad. In addition, long acquaintance with the Mississippi caused the city's geoeconomists to preach that the path of wealth lay along meridians, not parallels, and moved north and south, rather than east and west. Even after the Civil War nearly destroyed the city's southern market, this idea prevailed, and it deprived the thirty-fifth parallel project of a longed-for center of support.[9] A Springfield, Missouri, newspaper said it all in 1868, when the railroad had not yet reached its town square after almost twenty years of corporate existence:

> Perhaps no other city in the United States is controlled by a class of business men so utterly destitute of the enterprising go-ahead spirit of the age as those of St. Louis. . . . Chicago spreads out her railroads over the country . . . while St. Louis permits the trade which properly and naturally belongs to her to be drawn away. . . . She looks with lordly disdain on the efforts of her country neighbors to secure a connection with her markets, and thinks that her dignity and independence will not be sufficiently manifested without giving all such efforts a vigorous kick backwards. . . . No man with sufficient public spirit to invest fifty cents of ragged postal currency in fire-crackers . . . on the Fourth of July can fairly represent a St. Louis constituency. To be a representative of that locality he must be an old fogy generally, and as mean as his ability will permit. He must believe that a log wagon or a flatboat is a better vehicle for locomotion than a railroad car, and that a pair of rope lines, a poor mule, and a rickety cart, are a far more magnificent spectacle than a dozen snorting locomotives. . . . He . . . must look wise upon all occasions, assume to know all things, and prove himself to be a thorough Jackass.[10]

A disappointment then, but one that could be safely ignored by the enthusiastic, just as they had ignored the Indian Territory in following their thirty-fifth parallel projection so closely and as they ignored other obstacles. For example, any who laughed at the clumsy five-foot six-inch gauge that was planned for the Pacific of Missouri's transcontinental tracks was met quickly with a precise defensive argument to the effect that the four-foot eight-and-one-half-inch gauge in common use was accidental, that in a frontier area the wider gauge would carry more freight on fewer trains, that larger drivers would reduce piston velocity for longer wear, and that wider cars would be more stable on curves, more comfortable for passengers, and could reach the high speeds (twenty-five to thirty miles per hour) westerners would demand. The company admitted the grading would be more costly but denied vigorously that lack of ability to connect with standard-gauge eastern roads was a factor. Said Chief Engineer James Kirkwood: "The transfer of cars and engines built in another state need hardly be considered, inasmuch as all these will eventually be built in St. Louis." Were the Mississippi to be bridged, of course, transfer of cars would be essential. In 1851, however, Kirkwood discounted that as a possibility, only seventeen years before the construction of the Eads bridge proved him wrong.[11] So it was that the crowd at the river wharf on August 20, 1852, cheered the unloading of a five-foot six-inch gauge behemoth with a blunderbuss stack. It was the "Pacific," first locomotive to run on a regular schedule west of the Mississippi and a symbol of unreasoned but sincere hope that was to be tempered only very slowly.[12]

The hope in all its folly and all its attractiveness was best demonstrated in a capsule on July 19, 1853, when twelve passenger cars loaded with dignitaries followed the decorated locomotive "St. Louis" over the newly completed first division of the Pacific of Missouri to Franklin station. There they planned, with the help of the "celebrated" Sixth Infantry band, to mark the commencement of the South-West Branch.

Some were incredulous that the Pacific of Missouri, which had taken four years to build thirty-seven miles of track, was only partly ballasted, and cost $47,000 a mile (double the original estimate), should be undertaking to construct a branch at all.[13] The optimists countered that argument as neatly as they had the one concerning the gauge. The Missouri internal improvements land grant act of 1852 had provided for two routes to the Pacific. Land along the main line had been taken up to a large extent under the preemption laws by settlers and was therefore not available to aid the railroad. But a branch striking south from Franklin to Rolla, Springfield, Neosho, Seneca, and thence into the Indian Territory to strike Whipple's survey in the valley of the Canadian would be assured of a much larger amount of available Missouri land. With this in mind, the directors had petitioned the legislature for "other means for constructing the road in the direction of Kansas," arguing that 1.3 million acres were available for railroad aid on the South-West Branch while a maximum of 563,000 acres could be had on the main line. Building two lines was, naturally, more than the railroad could do without, as the directors put it, "the fostering aid of the state"; yet they consistently maintained that "experience in railroad construction has generally shown that where two-thirds of the cost of the work can be raised, the other third and sometimes the whole of the superstructure and machinery can be provided for by the credit of the road itself. . . ." The legislature believed them and gave the Pacific company $1,000,000 additional aid in state bonds for the South-West Branch; thus the occasion for a new ground-breaking.[14]

The ground-breaking for the main line toward Kansas City had been in St. Louis on July 4, 1851. It was a grand precedent not likely to be duplicated for the South-West Branch, however much some partaking of the three long tables of refreshments aboard the 1853 excursion train may have hoped so.[15] On that occasion flags had flown from the top of every public building in St. Louis, and the ceremonies were attended by cannon salutes and a vast parade. The German Emigration Society, the Switzer Benevolent Society, the Political Refugees, the Social Glee Club, the Sons of Temperance, the Hibernia Benevolent Society, the Phoenix Fire Company, and the Missouri Hose Company joined numerous other civic groups in marching from the river to the eastern terminus of the new railroad, all to the tune of massed bands playing the specially commissioned "Grand Pacific Railroad March." Once there, Thomas Allen, president of the enterprise, set the tone which remained yet strong two years later:

> It is something of a novelty that attracts us in such vast numbers to this spot to-day. It is nothing more or less than the commencement of work upon a railroad—a thing simple in itself, but in this particular time and place, an affair of great interest and importance. Missouri, with immense resources imprisoned, and giant energies long asleep, is about to make a start. . . . A railroad, fellow citizens, is a machine, and one of the most beautiful and perfect of labor-saving machines. . . . It well suits the energy of the American people. They love to go ahead fast, and to go with power. They love to annihilate the magnificent distances. . . . It is a new lever of power, more potent than any Archimedes ever dreamed of. . . .

A special poem had then been read—a hymn to Asia—and all had gone home to wait for the next festive railroad occasion, which was now at hand at Franklin station.[16]

The little trainload that stopped at Franklin really did have some cause to celebrate. Its engine was a product of the new St. Louis locomotive firm, Palm & Robertson, and seemed to justify Kirkwood's prediction. Also, the news was fresh that Congress at its recent session had appropriated $150,000 for the Pacific railway surveys and that Whipple's route could be intersected by the new South-West Branch. There is no record that even the direst pessimist had the nerve to predict anything close to what was to be actuality: the next eighteen miles of the main line would be nineteen months in building and no construction would be done on the branch until June 1855. The branch they were opening would not reach the western boundary of Missouri until 1871, and would never run along the valley of the Canadian as they and Lieutenant Whipple predicted.[17]

The oratory flowed freely as did the drinks on that ground-breaking day, dreamers dreamed dreams, and the blind led the blind in concocting "visions" of the future. The summer heat and the smooth roadbed which they pretended to see stretching west where rivers and trees now blocked the path elicited a response not unlike that created by the mirages that haunted the Whipple party as they set out from Fort Smith in those same July days. It may not have been an era of efficient rail-laying, but for speech-making it had no peer. "The Iron Horse," the celebrants claimed, "has started on his journey towards the setting sun." It would be only a matter of a few years before Asian commerce would cross the Pacific in fleets of steamers and Ericsson propellers to join with the gold of California in filling thousands of broad-gauge cars. These would then make a smooth and unmolested three-day transit to the very spot on which they now stood, there to reload with the agricultural and mineral products of Missouri's hinterland and the manufactures of St. Louis for the return journey.

Louis M. Kennett, acting president of the Pacific of Missouri, reported that President Allen was even then on Wall Street negotiating the sale of $4,000,000 of 7 per cent bonds at par, and that all were waiting for his immediate return with the good news of success, following which construction of the South-West Branch would begin. Whether the main or branch line would be the greater success, Kennett could not say, but quoted an old song: "were either dear charmer away, with the other contented I'd be." Edward Bates, who had stood on the Mississippi's banks to watch the St. Louis steamboat era begin with the arrival of the first steamer, rolled out the third wheelbarrow of earth and predicted that this ground-breaking opened an equally significant era. "Glory and honor," he said, "should be ascribed to the man who combined Fire, and Water, and Iron in the production of Steam. His labors were far more valuable than gold and pearls to the country." With that, toasts were drunk, flags were planted, and the place deserted for the considerable time it would take before the practical business of obtaining money, workers, spikes, and iron for the new section was completed.[18]

The financial problems to be solved before construction could proceed on either of the Pacific company's lines were legion. President Allen predictably failed in his attempt to sell bonds at par. Although the books of the South-West Branch were opened for a $500,000 stock subscription on February 13, 1854, on the same day the executive committee of the railroad modified the construction contract made by the president with King, Stancliff and Company of New York, so that it would read, "in case the Cos bonds cannot be negotiated within 12 months after completion of the 1st Division [Franklin to the Gasconade Valley, eighty-nine miles] at 80 cents or over, the contract to be terminated if the company so determine."[19] Aid from counties along the line was likewise less than expected. By 1855, only $369,000 of stock had been subscribed by the counties, and there was not enough private subscription to bring the total to the $500,000 in bona-fide subscriptions required by state law in order for the company to receive its land grant.[20]

Nevertheless the management pressed hard for the lands. The president submitted lists to the commissioner of the General Land Office in Washington of lands lying within a six-mile limit of the main and branch lines and also a list of settler preemption entries which appeared to have been taken up after notice had been given of the railroad grant, and which were therefore in conflict with it.[21] Senator John S. Phelps of Missouri, who had early been fascinated by the thirty-fifth parallel route, was also enlisted to petition the commissioner on behalf of the railroad, and he did so with vigor. Phelps requested that land auctions on the alternate public sections within the grant be postponed for some months. The area around Springfield, he wrote, had been drained of money by entries of land in expectation of the arrival of the South-West Branch. "The draught has cut short the crops & the people are unprepared at this time to enter the Rail Road lands.—Consequently if the sale shall take place in Dec. next the lands will be principally entered by nonresidents for speculation." Phelps and the railroad officers were no doubt acutely aware that, although the price of public lands was raised to $2.50 on the public sections within the checkerboard pattern of railroad land grants, this price still represented a considerable savings over the prices they wished to charge for the railroad sections. While public sections were available, sale of railroad lands was inhibited.

The railroad lobby was not perfectly successful in its attempt to influence the land office. Phelps had maintained that passing up the public auction for 1854 could do no damage, "as the Treasy is overflowing & the money not needed by the Govt."[22] The commissioner of the General Land Office agreed, but his superior, the secretary of the interior, did not and outlined his reasons to his own superior, President Franklin Pierce. A postponement of the sale, he wrote, would result practically in a further withdrawal of lands from market for the benefit of the railroad (exactly what the company had in mind) and would therefore conflict with the Interior Department policy regarding withdrawals for railroad purposes. As to Phelps's plea for the poor farmer, the secretary very sensibly observed that "if the inhabitants of the district are not at this time prepared to purchase and pay for the lands; it is probable that the speculators are not in a better condition, nor is it at all certain that the people will be better prepared to purchase within any reasonable time of postponement, than they now are." In addition, the treasury was not so well off as Phelps had supposed. Most of the expense attending the sale of land had already been paid, and lands bid on at public sale did not bring such a great price over the $2.50 minimum that the government would be rewarded for any extra expense caused by a postponement of the auction.[23]

The state of Missouri was far more generous than the General Land Office. Since its first constitution had been framed during the Panic of 1819, the state had assumed broad economic powers with the intent of fostering and protecting her industry, at first banking, and then railroads. Some individualists, such as William Gilpin, geopolitician par excellence, ultimately governor of Colorado Territory and director of a successor to the South-West Branch, felt that state government intervention in the economy had gone to an extreme even by 1840. The world was governed too much, he wrote, and men are being crushed "by legislatures and by corporations . . . they come forth like the locusts of Egypt."[24]

The railroad policy of the state was outlined by Governor Austin King in December 1850. The message stated that water transportation would not suffice in the new era—something that St. Louis was years in learning—and that in order to develop a thriving economy the state must undertake what modern economic historians have called "mixed enterprise," that is, a combination of public and private funds. The public funds were designed to draw private capital to a risky project and then be withdrawn when a private corporation was sufficiently strong to take over alone. Public monies were to act as a sort of pump primer the receipt of which, in the case of railroad companies, depended on a certain bona-fide subscription, the maintenance of a reasonable construction schedule, and a first mortgage on the road to be held by the state. Other than that, there was little regulation. Rates could be whatever was in the interest of the company; the legislature required only an annual report plus free access to the books of the corporation.[25]

A spate of acts on behalf of the Pacific and her branch line followed the governor's message, but unfortunately did not always include the limits and protections for the state which were recommended. In 1851, the ratio of state aid to private capital was set by the legislature at fifty-fifty on the Pacific; for every $50,000 expended by the company, $50,000 in state bonds would be issued.[26] Later this was increased to two state dollars for every one private and finally to much more. This steady increase in the original ratio in the face of slow construction and the declining price of state bonds can, according to one student, be explained only "as a phenomenon of the speculative intoxication of the times."[27] In addition to state bond aid, cities were allowed to subscribe stock using municipal bond issues.[28] More important, the lines were exempted entirely from taxation until completed or paying a dividend.[29] Yet so eager was the state to aid the lines that when, after all this and numerous loans, construction was not progressing, the first mortgage held by the state as security for its aid was temporarily released. The excuse was that the mortgage to the state seemed "an impediment to the credit of the companies in raising further large sums."[30]

The release of the mortgage was the climax of the state's naïve effort to push the lines at any cost, and when that tactic failed, revulsion and taxpayer revolt followed. The mortgage forfeiture had passed only over the veto of Governor Sterling Price, and he refused to issue the bond aid provided on the grounds that the act was unconstitutional. The case went to the State Supreme Court, which upheld the law on the grounds that "a large portion of the people feel a deep interest in the execution of a law, which they believe is not only essential to prevent a great sacrifice of capital already invested but is ultimately connected with the improvement and permanent welfare of the state."[31]

But the turning point was at hand. The Missouri House noted in 1856 that the contractors on the South-West Branch were not being paid because no South-West Branch bonds could be sold to conservative investors, or anyone else. Potential buyers recognized that the only security for the bonds was the newly released mortgage and the land grant. But the road was not being built, and failure to build meant no property for the mortgage holder to foreclose upon and might also bring forfeiture of title to the land.[32] A new law was passed in 1857 granting more aid but also including a provision that if the South-West Branch were not completed within four years, it would become the property of the state.[33] By 1859, the company had laid only sixty-one miles of track.[34]

The pressure this deteriorating situation exerted on the directors and officers was tremendous. New state restrictions forbade contractors from sitting on the board of directors, provided that members of the newly organized State Board of Public Works should be in attendance at all directors' meetings,[35] and granted increased protection to settlers on company lands.[36] These laws, combined with a tight money market coincident with the general financial Panic of 1857, slowed down the oratory about the trade of the Indies a little bit and speeded up the process of a realistic self-examination by those responsible for the thirty-fifth parallel project.

A sobering incident occurred in 1855. The legislators were then already restless, and some had openly charged in the State Senate that the contractors on the Pacific lines were enriching themselves and impoverishing the company and the state by a complex process of subletting construction. During the building to Franklin, labor costs had risen from 75¢ to $1.25 a day, cholera was taking a huge toll of work days lost, and the tariff duties on rolled bar iron greatly increased the cost of the English rail being used.[37] It was to soothe the legislators and to petition for a better bridge over the Gasconade River that an excursion was announced leaving St. Louis on November 1, 1855. The chief engineer of the Pacific, Thomas Sullivan, argued the bridge was sound. He rode the tender that day and was the first person killed when the thirteen-car train plunged through the collapsing structure and down thirty feet into the icy Gasconade. The forward engine turned completely over backwards onto the following cars, killing forty-three legislators, officers, and directors. The rear engine, following the train, could only reverse its ponderous high driving wheels and back into St. Louis, keeping up a steady, frightening shriek of its steam whistle, as though to mirror in its mechanical way the frustration its owners felt.[38]

After that, officials of the road had to keep one eye on San Francisco in order to obtain more loans and county subscriptions and the other on the perilous financial condition of a tiny and so far very local railroad line. A perfect example of the two-sided behavior which resulted is found in the person of Edward Miller, who replaced the ill-fated Sullivan as chief engineer. Miller was the picture of confidence when writing his portion of the annual report or when speaking at town meetings in search of aid, but he was a bundle of nerves in his private correspondence with his fellow railroaders.

The confident Ed Miller attended the railroad meeting at Boonville, Missouri, in April 1858 and painted a rosy picture. The railroad would make of Boonville an Athens or a Rome, would introduce grape culture until "the demon of intemperance is exorcised from Missouri by substituting the mild and wholesome juice of the grape for the fiery and poisonous product of the still," would astronomically increase the value of real estate, and would prove a healthy influence on all the baser passions. Yet to bring the "resonant steam eagles" required local capital, since the East was chastened by the Panic and looked upon "the officers of finished roads . . . as necessary evils, and the projectors of new ones as public nuisances." The age of magic carpets, and magical flying horses was over, as Whipple's party had observed some years before, but in Ed Miller's speeches citizens saw the new magic of science outlined by a scientific man, and it was scarcely less bizarre. "Instead of building fortifications," he told them, "we build factories; instead of hiring thousands of men to butcher each other, we hire them to make our railroads; instead of constructing war gallies and war chariots, we construct commercial steamboats and locomotives, the great civilizers of modern times."[39]

If the impending Civil War could be ignored, so could the musings of oversensitive poets. Ed Miller quoted Nathaniel Lee, a not-too-famous poet, whose not-too-famous lines—"Ye Gods! annihilate but time and space / And make two lovers happy"—Miller felt epitomized the railroad quest. The unfavorable comments of Washington Irving when the railroad had penetrated his beloved Sleepy Hollow were, on the other hand, viewed by the engineer as "the very embodiment and essense of 'Old Fogyism.'" What was needed was hardheaded enterprise of the kind Whipple had when he started his journey, the kind Fort Smith had when it lost its battle. "Whether you shall feel the influence of the mighty iron steed, with his heart of flame, and steel sinews, and trumpet voice, and lightning breath, resembling, as he rushes irresistibly over your prairies, one of the fabled Dragons of old, harnessed and utilized by modern science, depends on yourselves." One wonders if the age of myth was really over.[40]

The other Ed Miller was a man more meek. He was the man who knew that among the few who had subscribed to Pacific stock were those who sued to escape their obligation when the South-West Branch was authorized.[41] He was the man who knew that the president's trips to Europe were to buy rail not to sell stock as advertised,[42] and that the donations of right-of-way for the branch by farmers were valid only if the road were built on that route and that these donations were given on threat of exercising eminent domain.[43] To the vice president of the Phoenix Iron Company, from which the South-West Branch had borrowed heavily on the promise, no doubt, of providing cheap transportation someday, Miller wrote several notes at the height of the 1857 Panic which do not reveal overconfidence. He wrote the following in October as an excuse for default on a note owed by the railroad:

> The state of the currency here is in such a frightfully disorganized condition (all the ordinary circulating medium being the notes of adjoining states, now entirely discredited) that it is difficult to perform the ordinary operations of trade. Our company whose receipts last month exceeded $74,000, have been obliged to take a very large portion of it in this depreciated paper, which will not now pay our laborers, nor can it be sold at any price. . . . Yesterday is said to have been the darkest day financially that St. Louis ever knew. . . . I have hardly the heart to write and am almost afraid to look into a newspaper lest the news of some new misfortune to my friends . . . shall stare me in the face.—I fear there will soon be no use for engineers.[44]

There was hope that new taxation would raise the price of state bonds and that the publication of a survey of the company's route would create excitement, but the outlook in 1860 was dim.[45] Yet not dead. Ed Miller wrote in the 1858 annual report that

> if it is not unreasonable to assume that the appropriate termini of a national road from the Mississippi to the Pacific are St. Louis and San Francisco . . . then it is certain that the South-West Branch, pointing direct towards Albuquerque must inevitably form a part of what has well been called 'THE HIGHWAY OF NATIONS'! . . . This scheme is indeed gigantic, and the difficulties formidable, but the surveys show nothing which may not be overcome by skill, science, perseverance and money.[46]

On the note of this more realistic vision, the company faced the Civil War.

3

DISUNION AND DISRUPTION

The imagination strains to discover reasons for the appearance of Anthony Trollope, noted British traveler and essayist, in Rolla, Missouri, in the middle of the American Civil War. The South-West Branch railroad, which terminated there, was probably not as well known as some of the visitor's random comments, and guerrilla bands operating in the area were a real threat to the casual wanderer. It could be that novelty drew Trollope—the novelty of following his description of the Egyptian pyramids with one of a town but a few years removed from a patch of prairie sod, or the novelty of comparing the dirty, taciturn western type with the Bedouin tribesmen who peopled his former works. His public excuse was that he was examining the holdings, near Rolla, of the Missouri Land Company of Edinburgh, Scotland. Whatever his motive, the winter of 1862 found Trollope and his elaborate accompaniment of the luggage proper to a British gentleman bouncing uncomfortably in a smoking car on the South-West Branch railroad, bound for end-of-track.[1]

Rolla was an archetypal American railroad town. In January of 1860, the site of the town had been an unimproved prairie ridge; by July, it boasted of seventy-five houses and six hundred people.[2] The transformation had been due entirely to the railroad crews, who called the town first "White House" because of the color of the residence built for the engineers, then "Hardscrabble" for a while, and finally Raleigh. Raleigh became Rolla because that was easier to spell, though one of the educated objected that "Sir Walter, the discoverer of Virginia and the destroyer of the Spanish Armada, has his name thus transformed to that of the Peruvian hidalgo." Strangers were thrown together, found a common interest, were joined soon by troops involved in the Southwest campaign, and formed a city. It was not elegant. When Trollope was there most of the buildings were barracks, and the center of the town was covered with dense chaparral and brush broken only by bridle paths.[3] But it had a railroad, and that seemed to make all the difference to the citizens. Yet the local newspaper that brought the report of the "shrill whistle of the steam horse" in Rolla streets in December 1860 also reported the secession of South Carolina from the Union.[4]

Trollope's trip to Rolla was a shock to him. Expecting European decorum and military bearing, he found John C. Fremont's ragged Missouri troops commuting between Rolla and St. Louis by wagon and an occasional farmer riding the train toward a perusal of damaged property and burned-out lands. The porter would not carry his bags; the car, which was populated by soldiers and teamsters, was filled with "tobacco smoke, apple peel, and foul air"; and the atmosphere of the closed conveyance was stifled by a stove "that might cook all the dinners for a French hotel." One man struck Trollope particularly. He sat silently picking his teeth with a bowie knife and staring at the rather foppish gentleman of literature. Strangely, however, he had read the books of Anthony's mother, Frances, and engaged him in an intelligent conversation.[5]

The facilities for the English gentleman at Rolla were no better than aboard the South-West Branch cars. Trollope, again finding no porter, had to load his goods on his back, climb a hill, jump a stream, and negotiate slippery ice, only to find a hotel in which there was a single large common meeting room and the same free mixture of classes the Englishman had found unusual on the train. Teamsters greased their boots, soldiers snored, and women bantered with the best. "Burdened with a dozen shirts," wrote Trollope, "and a suit of dress clothes, and three pairs of boots, and four or five thick volumes, and a set of maps, and a box of cigars, and a washing tub, I confessed to myself that I was a fool."[6]

The slovenly behavior observed about the town was not, however, for want of strict laws: willfully disturbing a church service with profane language brought a $5.00 fine, driving a horse "faster than a trot or pace" in the city limits was a $1.00 fine, and public singing of an obscene song brought quick conviction of a misdemeanor.[7] The Southern Hotel and the Phelps House enforced discipline among their clientele of railway men, soldiers, and the drivers of the ox-wagons and mule-teams which backed up to Rolla merchants' porches to load materials for the grading crews to the West. The Board of Trade worried that unless good schools and churches were provided, these transients would never become permanent or good citizens. Donations for churches were asked and received from the railroad and subdividers who bought railroad lands, so that the age-old fight against sin could run its course unsuccessfully in one more new western village.[8] With the arrival of the railroad, land prices went up,[9] commodity prices, especially on luxuries, went down,[10] the ague carried away residents who had hastily bought in the lowlands, newspapers joked at each other concerning the virtues of mile-square utopias, guest lecturers bored students at second-rate commercial colleges with analyses of Rolla's markets, and the railroad itself met with "unavoidable" delays in its construction schedule.[11] It was a familiar pattern —the familiar pattern of a boom on a shifting foundation which had come west with the pioneers.

Indeed, the building to the west of Rolla was difficult for the South-West Branch. One passenger train a day, which on alternate days consisted of nothing but a single car hitched to a freight train, came down the line from Franklin loaded with passengers who then rode stages from Rolla to their new lands. Many unscheduled trains rumbled over the same line with construction materials which it was difficult to use.[12] One editor, touring the grade, reported that he believed he had seen the hill on which Noah laid his ark as well as lesser peaks, which constituted together "some of the ungodliest hills ever a Railroad was thought of being built over."[13]

But the topographical obstacles were small when compared with the difficulties involved in constructing a railroad through a war zone. It was thought necessary to build railroads to move troops, but an officer guarding workers on the line noted that the two major obstacles to its completion were guerrilla raids and the scarcity of labor, both situations occasioned by the war.[14] The Union sent troops down the South-West

Branch with the basic strategy of occupying territory before the other side could organize. One major engagement, Wilson's Creek, was supplied by the establishment at Rolla, but that resulted in more glory for the South-West Branch railroad than for the Union troops.[15] The latter were beaten badly and thereby gave the former the dubious distinction of carrying the body of General Nathaniel Lyon back to St. Louis in a black-draped car. The retreating soldiers walked, and the supplies went in wagons; rail carriage on the new road was too expensive for general use.[16]

All the while, the likes of "Bloody Bill" Anderson, William Quantrill, and George Todd kept construction crews busy rebuilding bridges and relaying track which were destroyed in irregular raids.[17] The formation of a Pacific Railroad Regiment with the sole duty of protecting the line did not lessen the danger throughout the war from those who would "take Missouri out of the Union, or take her to hell."[18] Late in August of 1861, a hand-made mine exploded under a South-West Branch engine near Dillon, Missouri, doing small damage but lifting the passengers far enough out of their seats to lead a general hue and cry for more government aid.[19]

The company solicited Washington for financial reasons as well as those of security. Large forces were already engaged in repairing bridges, leaving few to extend the road, to guard it from raiders, or to increase its supply of rolling stock and motive power as old equipment gave way under the heavy strain of war traffic. In August 1861 the Pacific directors reported that they had transportation for four thousand men at a moment's notice, and capacity for three thousand more if fifty platform cars could be altered. However, four engines which needed only minor repairs remained idle in the machine shop for lack of sufficient funds to fix them. Also, employees were on the verge of revolt. In his request to General Fremont for an advance of $10,000, Pacific railroad President George Taylor claimed that the only reason any workmen at all remained was on the gamble that the company's earnings, all of which were pledged to them, would be sufficient to pay an unusually high wage in the end.[20] Daniel Garrison, the superintendent of construction, could only suggest that regular army barracks maintained at fixed intervals along the line might ease the labor crisis somewhat.[21]

The War Department, in considering the railroad's requests for aid, had to evaluate a political situation which was at best confusing. Martial law was in effect in numerous portions of Missouri, and only orders countermanding many of the citizens' civil rights bound these sections to the Union. Especially active in the move to secede from Missouri and the Union was the southwest section of the state, which the South-West Branch served. Here numerous secret organizations conspired against what was later to be revealed as corrupt administration by Union officers and spat at those from whom the railroad was requesting aid. In return the officers in charge sapped the area's little remaining economic strength through a series of extortion rings which were revealed in 1865 by General Clinton B. Fisk, later an important figure in the history of the thirty-fifth parallel project.[22]

The tension was there. To aid the railroad was, in the long run, to aid the area where the bushwhackers lived, and to benefit their descendents. On the other hand, not to aid the railroad denied the Union a vital supply link in operations against these very guerrillas. Economics, morality, and honor collided in the heads of Washington bureaucrats regarding future policy toward the South-West Branch.

The question reached the White House in 1864 in the form of an offer by the Pacific company to furnish free transportation to the government on the new section of South-West Branch line from Rolla to Lebanon, fifty-six miles, provided the United States would furnish the iron for the same section. Abraham Lincoln liked the idea and wrote to General William Rosecrans in the field instructing him to make a contract to that effect with the company, subject to Lincoln's approval.[23] This broke the deadlock and freed the War Department to proceed in its plans to aid the road for military reasons. Lincoln could look with favor on a line into the slavers' domain; so could those with less principle at stake.

Then, too, there were signs that Missouri citizens were yielding to the inevitable, and the statements issuing from that section were less vehement and much more aware of the importance of emerging on the winning side. A correspondent of a St. Louis daily saw this early in the secession process:

> I am aware that our Missouri delegation in Congress attach much more importance to this everlasting nigger question than any other; but are we to sacrifice a permanent material advantage to a political abstraction? Suppose the North concedes all that is claimed? What then? We have made no material or moral advancement. We have got nothing but the settlement of a doubtful theory. . . . And by this very course we drive the Pacific RR away from us. . . . The States that are loyal to the Union will reap the *benefits* of the Union. . . . Tie Missouri to the tail

> of secession, and the geographical advantage of St. Louis is sacri-
> ficed and the trade of the boundless West . . . is thrown into the
> lap of Chicago.

The commerce of the Pacific railroad, he added, as a gesture to Southern-
ism, was worth more to Missouri "than all the niggers in the state."[24]

To this attitude was added the very real fatigue with the war and
the manner in which it upset normal affairs. Rolla, for example, had
other ambitions than to tend the two thirty-two pounders that sat on her
ridge or to serve as the butt of Anthony Trollope's joking. She had great
hopes of building a local dairy industry which would be pushed to success by cheap lands and new railroad connections, and would allow the
town to "keep a little of the money at home that we are now constantly
sending to St. Louis to pay into the pockets of Suckers, Yankees, and
Yorkers." The trains, however, brought only soldiers and British observers, and carried them back again.[25] "It would seem," wrote the
editor of the little *Rolla Express*, "that Rolla is a God-forgotten and
dangerous place. . . . The 'necessary evils' attending a war (for evils are
deemed necessary by a majority of warriors) like that in which we are
involved seem to overshadow the land with immorality and lay waste all
that is good. . . . O, that a flaming two-edged sword might sever the
devil and his emissaries from a would-be righteous people!"[26]

It was this war-weariness, combined with a new understanding of
economic necessity and a distaste for being tied to a lost cause, which was
responsible for the enthusiasm with which southwest Missouri greeted
the announcement, in June 1862, that the War Department had entirely
taken over the construction of the South-West Branch from Rolla to
Lebanon. All machinery and equipment as well as the surveys and pro-
files of the railway's engineering department were turned over to the
federal government, and work proceeded for a time at a rapid pace.[27]

The takeover was really a great relief. The government had refused
at first to pay for transportation of troops over the line, since free transportation of troops was one of the things the line had agreed to in ac-
cepting the land grant of 1852. Though Pacific railroad lobbyists, after a
trying time in Washington, had obtained a joint resolution of Congress
ameliorating the effects of this somewhat, the line still could not charge
the United States its regular rates, and often operated troop trains at a
loss.[28] The influence of the government engineers no doubt also speeded
legislation to change the gauge of Missouri's railroads to four feet, eight

and one-half inches. This was authorized in 1866[29] and done on the South-West Branch in twenty-four hours, but not until 1869.[30]

Speed was a relative thing on the thirty-fifth parallel project. Throughout its history it was to be subject to mistakes in timing, usually of the "too late" variety. Sometimes fate was responsible; more often, as in the case of the change of gauge, it was failure by the management to grasp a trend and act upon it. They risked large amounts of capital, but only a small fund of ideas.

These ideas circulated only among the managers, and much of the record of what their plans might have been at this juncture has been destroyed, mostly on purpose. Astute observers of the time noted that a new type of man emerged during and after the Civil War. Trained in command by the campaigns of the civil struggle, numerous generals found it natural to assume administration of railroads, the next largest unit to an army. Names of officers of all western railroads after the 1860s are studded with military titles, and the South-West Branch and its successors were no exception.

It may be argued that out of the cool efficiency which proved so much more successful in war than the earlier Napoleonic flamboyance of George McClellan, there arose the type which history recognizes as the late nineteenth-century businessman. His ideals were simple:

> He is so absorbed in business that he has little time for culture and less for social converse. . . . Conversation as a means of persuasion, or as a prelude to some enterprise is well enough, but indulged in merely as a pastime, or for the discussion of abstractions, or to gain philosophical knowledge, or to entertain friends is intolerable to the practical man. He regards it as a bore, and an unwarrantable trespass on his time. . . . The experienced businessman appreciates silence for itself alone. In silence is safety, circumspection, dignity. No babbling of important business secrets—no indiscreet revelations of one's intentions, no careless bit of gossip. . . . 'Few words and plenty of money' is a fair motto for this utilitarian generation.[31]

As the war drew toward a close, it was this type of man that the investors in the South-West Branch wished to attract to its management —taciturn, dignified, and with a reputation of national scope, preferably derived from the late war. The debts the railroad owed to the state had been held in moratorium during the war, but could not be avoided after its close and these would throw the road into the control of the state unless a suitable buyer could be found. Therefore in 1865 the search for new blood began in earnest.

One of the men most interested in new management for the South-West Branch was Henry T. Blow. He came from a wealthy Missouri family, and had, as a boy, played with Dred Scott, then a slave of the family and later famous as the subject of the Supreme Court decision that did much to make compromise between the sections impossible in the years preceding the war.[32] Blow served in the Missouri State Senate, was appointed minister to Venezuela by Lincoln in 1862, and upon his return after the war was elected to Congress from Missouri's Second District.[33]

Blow's interest in the South-West Branch came primarily from his presidency of the Granby Mining and Smelting Company, an extensive lead and zinc processing plant which was located on a part of the South-West Branch's land grant in western Missouri and operated under a lease from the company. Relations between the branch line and its largest customer were not uniformly good. As early as 1858, the Granby Company had refused to pay the railroad the agreed percentage of the mining profits, and this had resulted in bitter litigation.[34] Also, there was a controversy about the rates charged. Blow expected that as a large shipper he might expect sufficient rebates from the South-West Branch to make railroad transport competitive with the wagon teams. These he had to employ anyway to get his products to the railhead at Rolla. On the other hand, the Granby Company, before the war, reportedly made one-half million dollars' clear profit from one section of land after deducting the cost of a one-hundred-sixty-mile wagon haul. Thus the rail managers felt it could well afford the rates which their frontier railroad found it necessary to charge. Mr. Blow, they claimed, rejected lead ore that yielded less than 85 per cent pure metal. The slag heaps on his property, going to waste, were 20 per cent lead and valued at seventy-five thousand dollars.[35]

The settlers in the area wished a plague on both houses, the railroad and the Granby Company. Southwest Missourians had complained about Blow's lack of interest in the section from which he had drawn so many dollars. It was whispered that Governor Thomas Fletcher was associated with the Granby Company and that this was the reason the state had not taken over the railroad. In short, many believed that "the profuse professions of interest in the building of our railroad are meaningless phrases, 'mere sound and fury,' soft corn, on which the poor Southwesterners and their poorer, more confiding, unsophisticated and uninfluential Representatives and Senators have for some time past been kindly fed."

Locomotive Atlantic of the A&P at Baldwin Locomotive Works
Photo courtesy Harvard University
Railway and Locomotive Historical Society Collection

Frisco Engine 98, built at the Manchester Locomotive Works, 1880
Photo courtesy Harvard University
Railway and Locomotive Historical Society Collection

Locomotive Seligman hauling a Frisco passenger train on the line from
Seligman, Mo., to Eureka Springs, Ark., 1882

Photo obtained from Association of American Railroads
by J. & W. Seligman & Co.

Frisco train at "the Narrows," White River, Ark. From the booklet
There Is Something to See Along the Frisco System published by the
company in 1903

Photo courtesy State Historical Society of Missouri, Columbia

Mass meetings were held to protest the supposed union of the monied classes to the detriment of the farmer who still awaited a rail connection.[36]

One of these settlers' meetings in Phelps County, where Rolla was located, was brought to the attention of Blow in a letter delivered to him in January 1866 from the South-West Branch directors. This letter was also highly critical of a circular the mining magnate had issued to his workers in Illinois and Wisconsin suggesting a shift in interest away from Southwest Missouri and its tiny Pacific railroad. Blow replied immediately to the charges, claiming that he had every desire to deal exclusively with the South-West Branch to send merchandise and materials out and return pig lead. The only thing preventing this was "that transportation is now so high as almost to be ruinous." The Granby Company was forced to ship by wagon to Sedalia, and thence by the main line to St. Louis.

Blow's letter also contained a hint of the solution he was pondering. After reminding the present management of the constant efforts he had made in St. Louis, New York, and elsewhere to extend the South-West Branch, he suggested that they might do well to look to the East for the support they so badly needed. "I do not think that the directors of this great road in St. Louis, our Government officials, or the Capitalists of New York, will fail to satisfy you when applied to," he wrote. He reported that a bill was being drawn up in the Missouri legislature to sell the railroad to the highest bidder and thereby to secure its debt to the state (and incidentally to insure the value of its securities, of which Blow was a large holder). Blow expressed the hope that he might be "honorably connected" with the new management, and bid the directors in office "to take a high stand on the matter" so as to "merit the approval of every intelligent & honest man in the state." How much easier for one privy to the new dispensation to be generous than those manacled to the old.[37]

Henry Blow was involved in legislative lobbying and negotiations on the highest level regarding the scheme to draw new management and new capital to the war-damaged South-West Branch. But the movement was not confined to the wealthy or the politically influential. Rolla citizens were tired of deadwood. Dead men, they said, were fit only to inhabit cemeteries. If the managers of the railroad, dead to enterprise, persisted in "moving their dry bones and calloused hearts where real business is want [sic] to throb and push with vigor, they are only like the drone bees, in the way until they are stung to death and dragged outside the hive of legitimate industry."[38]

Springfield was no less demanding. All produce to and from Springfield markets had to be hauled a hundred and fifteen miles by wagon, and hopes that the railroad would soon be extended to that western Missouri town had been so often blasted that its newspapers editorialized with an impatience characteristic of the oft-denied. Now that the war was over, Springfield boosters reasoned, there was a large amount of capital in the country in the form of treasury notes and government bonds ripe for investment. Yet it had become evident to these people that the Pacific Railroad Company did not intend to build the South-West Branch, were opposed to anyone else building it, and were therefore bringing investment in it to a standstill.[39] "Let the railroad be sold," was splashed in fillers and advertising columns.

> If the purchasers will bind themselves to furnish a given number of settlers to each square mile within a given limit, so much the better. We want more men—more mind and muscle—more farm houses and workshops and manufactories. Our forests are waiting for the saw mill; our prairies lying waste when they should be covered by herds of cattle and sheep; our splendid water power is running to waste as it did a thousand years ago. We are to-day selling our hides to New England, to be tanned and made into boots and shoes, and buy them back at enormous increases—paying freight both ways. While we have forests of all kinds at our very doors, we send to St. Louis for our furniture, which we should make here and export.[40]

Only one thing was missing from the Springfield prospectus. Under the column headed "Inducements to Capitalists" they wanted in the worst way to list "Thirty-Fifth Parallel Transcontinental Railway."

But there were practical considerations, and in assessing these the newspapers sometimes showed more skill than the railroad managers. The winter of 1865–66 which saw the burst of enthusiasm for sale also witnessed some hesitation lest overenthusiasm decrease the probability of leaving the thirty-fifth parallel project in good hands.

First, it was obvious to most that the South-West Branch had interests fundamentally different from those of the main line and should be operated by a separate corporation. Even counting the danger in the dependence on the Pacific Railroad Company for the connection from Franklin to St. Louis should that corporation ever fall into unfriendly hands, it was generally felt that one of the prerequisites of any sale was that the management of the branch should be independent. The people of southwest Missouri had too many times seen the Pacific railroad launch new enterprises or lease new far-flung lines "while the work in which they were chiefly interested was treated as a step child in the family."[41]

Secondly, some, especially in conservative St. Louis, saw that impatience should not be carried to the point of unreason. Although the growth of the area and the value of the road was certain, it was in the future. Therefore, sage advice warned against being too quickly attracted by men promising easy miracles and quick profits from an enterprise that the most intelligent realized was developmental in nature—of more value to the general public than to early sets of investors. "Men who expend money upon the road," wrote a St. Louis reporter,

> must be content to wait for the returns. These returns cannot be realized in a day. . . . Any one can see how detrimental it would be for the road to pass into weak hands or dishonest hands; we mean into the hands of mere speculators and schemers who would like to get hold of it merely to "trade with."

The proceeds of the sale, the article continued, would not much more than reimburse the state for the losses and deteriorations on the railroad caused by the war.[42]

This last skepticism, however, was farther than southwest Missourians wished to go. Springfield papers insisted that while care should be exercised in selecting a buyer, the inducement of immediate profit could be honestly used, as, by their somewhat optimistic calculation, the South-West Branch was profitable even at that moment. Perhaps many realized that what St. Louis said about big profits being far in the future was true, but, unlike St. Louis, the very existence of some cities in the southwest depended on the railroad. Rumors were afloat that the Pacific directors might tear up the South-West Branch within three years, simply because there was a "sickly prejudice against letting Northern Capitalists . . . have any interest in our roads." The only way to combat this was to crowd the South-West Branch with business, ignoring the higher rates via Rolla which had been set to convince farmers to ship on the main line. This business would, they hoped, result in profits for the branch which would attract investors.[43]

A propaganda campaign was initiated to draw new settlement, activity, and traffic to the road. Read one Rolla lyric:

Come forth from your cities, come out to the West
Ye have hearts, ye have hands—leave to nature the rest;
The prairie, the forest, the stream at command
'The world is too crowded,'—psaw! come and take land.[44]

Since the state of Missouri, which could take over the road due to the debts it owed her, did not relish operating the line as a state enterprise, she was therefore quickly convinced that a sale would be best. A year before the directors voted formally in March 1866 to turn over the South-West Branch to the state, word had leaked out that the governor would soon advertise for bids.[45]

A prospective buyer was found late in the year of 1865. He was John C. Fremont of New York—pathfinder, first Republican presidential candidate, player of important roles in the Mexican and Civil Wars, speculator in risky business schemes, and confidant of important figures in the political and financial world. Whether Fremont was moved most by his conversations with Blow or with Governor Thomas Fletcher or by town boosting is not known. What is certain is that the influence of all these factors faded in comparison with a product of Fremont's own imagination, the Atlantic and Pacific Railroad Company.

Incorporated in July 1866, this new company could produce one of the most impressive gatherings of national figures ever to grace a list of incorporators, and was also blessed, partly through their influence, with a congressional land grant along the thirty-fifth parallel route from Springfield to the Pacific which, if entirely earned, would approach fifty million acres.[46] Congress obviously intended that the thirty-fifth parallel route should be given aid enough to establish a genuine competition with the Union Pacific, which had received a great amount of federal aid in 1862 and 1864 for the first transcontinental trunk line. Fremont presumably would press construction of the South-West Branch to Springfield, where it would be merged with the Atlantic and Pacific and extended to San Francisco.

True, Fremont did not present the perfect image, but he had elements of what the enthusiasts wanted for their little railroad. He was a national figure, he was using his influence to get congressional aid for the project, and he could be addressed as "General." Also, he had a distinguished look about him, was married to Senator Benton's daughter, and had commanded troops in the Missouri district. Best, he was willing to take over the fortunes of the struggling South-West Branch and reinject into it some of the transcontinental imagery that was responsible for its inception.

The questionable aspects of this man's character were laid aside in an initial acceptance of him as a sort of deliverer for southwest Missouri. He paid a disconcerting amount of attention to the possibilities for land and townsite speculation when talking to townspeople before a speech on the trade of the Indies; he had been court-martialed in the Mexican War and relieved of command in the Civil War due to his behavior in office; his only previous venture into big business, the Mariposa mining scheme, was an abysmal failure in which he had been duped by clever operators and stolen blind. Yet when he toured Missouri early in 1866 to solicit support for his purchase of the branch railroad, and to explain his plans for the Atlantic and Pacific, he was universally applauded.[47] The South-West Branch, in passing out of existence under that name, seemed to be vindicating at last the hopes placed in it. It was to be separate, independent, and hopefully stronger than its parent corporation, the Pacific of Missouri.

4

JOHN C. FREMONT AND THE ATLANTIC AND PACIFIC RAILROAD COMPANY

When the South-West Branch, re-named the Southwest Pacific Railroad, was offered for sale, numerous investors joined the competition. Newspapers of the period mention at least five: Fremont, Daniel S. Dickonson of New York, a firm called simply the "English Company," D. C. Freeman, and Jay Cooke and Company. The last party, by riding in spring wagons from Rolla into the Indian Territory to examine the grade all the way to the thirty-fifth parallel, attracted by far the most attention. Cooke's investment house had largely financed the Civil War and so had a capital pool second to none. The engineer for Cooke told reporters that the country "was well deserving a 'good road,'" expressed interest in townsite speculation at the village of Nine Oaks, and said he would give his superior a favorable report.[1] Apparently the Philadelphia capitalist was not impressed.

The "English Company" faded quickly, but Dickonson made a determined if misguided effort to acquire the road for just the sort of reasons the St. Louis papers abhorred. In May 1865 Governor Thomas

Fletcher had said in a newspaper interview that if he were not governor he could make a half million dollars by taking over the South-West Branch lands including the Granby Mines. He was immediately contacted by Samuel Coleman, an agent for Dickonson. In a letter to Coleman on May 20, Fletcher authorized him to negotiate for the road. The governor hoped to take over the road and then turn it over to a company to be organized by Dickonson. In return, Fletcher was to receive bonds of the company, which was also to deposit bonds amounting to $5,580,000 with the state. The security for these would be the lands of the South-West Branch and Granby Lead Mines stock. Apparently this plan was too transparent a speculation to survive, even with the probable support of Henry Blow. By March 1866 it was obvious that only Freeman and Fremont would actually make bids.[2]

Fremont's life as a businessman is not well known, perhaps because of sympathetic biographers and because his extensive memoirs concentrate on explorations in the company of Kit Carson, obviously a higher point in his career than his experience with the Southwest Pacific, the Union Pacific Eastern Division, or the Memphis, El Paso and Pacific. The U.P.E.D. was unsuccessful, but the Missouri road was a disaster, and the Memphis, El Paso and Pacific was a national scandal in which the Pathfinder was heavily implicated. When the Civil War began, Fremont had been a multimillionaire; a dozen years later he was so nearly penniless that he had to dictate his memoirs to provide a living for his family. Fremont's life is the story of that most frustrating of historical figures, the almost-great man.[3]

General Fremont captivated Missourians in 1866, just as he had captured their imaginations during the Civil War. They had defended him against charges by his superiors, and it was said there were tears in the eyes of hardened soldiers when he said farewell to his troops at Springfield. He was under five feet nine inches in height and rather thin, but, according to his campaign biographer, was "eminently prepossessing in his personal appearance." He had very large, blue eyes, an aquiline nose, curly and long hair parted at the center, and a full beard. In addition, his life had a romance about it. His parents were wanderers, and John inherited a nomadic nature which seemed to lead him always into new adventures that were exciting and attractive to many of his contemporaries. He was loyal to a fault to his friends.[4]

Fremont created excitement when he announced plans to purchase the Southwest Pacific in order to assure St. Louis connection with his Atlantic and Pacific road. In November 1865, when called out on the balcony of the Ferguson House to speak to a crowd in Jefferson City, the general, referring to the South-West Branch as one of the roads engaged in a race to the Pacific Ocean, said that he would like to be in the race and ride one of the horses.[5] He made sure that local editors were informed of the progress of the new A. & P. company, usually reporting that he was "successful beyond his most sanguine expectations in his negotiations with capitalists."[6]

Fremont's speeches set Missouri aflame. A new railroad age was predicted in which "adventurous bands of engineers will thread the valleys" and the spirit of American enterprise will "gird her loins" for the struggle.[7] By February 1866 schemes were afoot to build new railroads from Kansas City to Cameron, Leavenworth, Danville, and Fort Scott; from Pleasant Hill to Lawrence; from Boonville to Fort Scott; and from Chillicothe to Brunswick to mention only a few, and to extend all the existing lines in the state. Noted one editor: "The phenomenon would amount to a railroad mania if we only had the money to expend on the new schemes."[8]

Fremont had been advised of the availability of the Missouri branch line as early as July 1865, two months after the Dickonson negotiations began, but still long before any official action had been taken regarding the sale. Again the railroad's agent was Governor Fletcher. In correspondence with Fremont, Fletcher stated the road would not be sold until appropriate legislation was passed by the Missouri General Assembly. He must have given some encouragement, however, because Fremont's associates immediately induced Senator B. Gratz Brown of Missouri to expedite the Atlantic and Pacific bill in Congress.[9]

Charges of collusion between Fremont and Fletcher were numerous and, though perfect proof is unavailable, there is some reason to suspect that Freeman and others were justified in their assumption that the deck was stacked against them. Fletcher stumped the state advocating the sale,[10] and in a series of public letters printed in a Springfield paper, he by implication recommended Fremont's project.

> Don't despair of your railroad, and don't forsake the old Kikapoo country—its "day of redemption draweth nigh." . . . You observe the bill introduced in the U.S. Senate by Hon. B. Gratz Brown. . . . The passage of that bill will make the most valuable franchise in America, from which, comparatively, no benefits can be derived until the road is built to the western line of Missouri, and that road cannot be built until the road is extended from Rolla to Springfield. Millions of capital eagerly awaits the passage

of Senator Brown's bill. . . . You and I know that the country
west of the Missouri line, in the Cherokee Country and up the
valley of the Arkansas and the Canadian fork, all the way to
Santa Fe, is . . . rich beyond comparison. . . . All the world will
know as soon as Senator Brown's bill becomes a law. . . . Capital
will find it out, and a railroad will penetrate it from the eastward
as certainly as the sun's rays do from the same direction.[11]

In February, the governor wrote: "The Atlantic & Pacific railroad, or
the Southern road to California, has been my dream and occupied my
waking thoughts for ten years past. . . . It is the greatest enterprise of
the age."[12]

More damning was the fact that Fletcher's name appeared with
Fremont's on the list of Atlantic and Pacific incorporators submitted to
Congress before the sale of the Missouri road.[13] The question also arose
as to how Fletcher, on a governor's salary of $5,000, had acquired a for-
tune estimated at $100,000, in addition to a $40,000 house, "if he didn't
steal it, nor have it bequeathed to him."[14] In 1867, he was investigated
by a committee of the Missouri legislature for fraud in connection with
the sale of Missouri railroads. They, however, found no information
more legally binding then innuendo and rumor.[15] Fletcher defended
himself against the "howlings" of the St. Louis dailies and their "small
barkers and snappers" in the hinterland.[16] If he was involved in any
shady deals in 1866, it is certain that the events of the next year changed
his mind about the desirability of a business association with the Pathfinder.

D. C. Freeman and Company, on the assumption there was collusion between Fremont and the governor, resorted to questionable tactics.
Freeman's representatives asked Senator Brown to take Fremont's name
out of the Atlantic and Pacific bill, arguing that the Pathfinder's friends
intended to make him senator (instead of Brown) if the Radicals succeeded that November. When this failed, the Freeman lobby sought to
delay passage of the A. & P. bill by the House, at least until after ad-
journment in December. In that they succeeded. When the bill came up
again in the Senate in January 1866, they pressed for amendments which
were distasteful to Fremont.[17]

There had been an earlier Atlantic and Pacific Railroad, organized
in New York in 1853 and managed by Robert J. Walker, secretary of the
treasury in the Polk administration. Walker and his associates had
given the name a bad reputation for, though their corporation was the

largest ever formed to that date (capitalization, $100,000,000), they built only a few miles of track along the thirty-second parallel in Texas.[18] It was charged that Walker fostered a slavocracy in Texas, that he speculated with company funds for purchase of one of the northern states of Mexico, and that his impressive list of incorporators had exchanged almost no hard cash for their massive paper subscriptions.[19] While the new A. & P. had no formal connection with the old company, the capitalization was the same, the plans were similar albeit on a parallel farther north, and the list of incorporators was similarly overloaded with politicians. The Texas road had changed its name during the Civil War to Southern Pacific Railroad Company, and it was under this name that Senator Brown had first introduced Senate bill number twenty in 1865.

It was not, however, on this coincidence that the congressional debates turned. No questions were asked concerning the financial responsibility of the group to whom the United States was preparing to make an enormous grant of its public domain. For the same period the pages of the *Congressional Globe* were filled with details of an investigation of Fremont's behavior during the war, which should have aroused some suspicions of his ability as a businessman. Instead discussions about Senate bill number twenty centered almost entirely on clerical detail: The change of name to Atlantic and Pacific in the various sections of the act, misspellings of the names of incorporators, errors in the placement of commas.

Only once was a significant issue raised. The longest of the debates took place in the Senate on March 1, 1866. Present in the lobby of the chambers that day were delegations from several of the tribes in the Indian Territory, and it was at their urging that Samuel Pomeroy of Kansas asked some relevant questions concerning Indians' rights along the route. How, he asked, was it possible to grant land to the A. & P. along the Canadian River through the center of Indian Territory when this land was not in the public domain but had been given to the tribes residing there? His argument failed to elicit the answer the Indians wanted. There was no real response at all, just an unexcited acceptance of the axiom that the interest of the United States and the railroads it aided was superior to any so-called rights claimed by pockets of alien people standing in the way of commerce. After the March 1 debate, the success of the bill was assured, though its passage was not completed until July 27.[20]

On February 19, the Missouri legislature authorized the sale of the Southwest Pacific.[21] Fremont made two bids on May 9 for $350,000, one on the 11th, and one on the 12th for $1,000,000. This last one was submitted on the condition that it be acted upon within two days, causing the commissioners for the sale to work on Saturday afternoon. They agreed to accept the general's offer if he would raise it to $1,300,000.[22] He did, the road was turned over to him, and he transferred it to the new Southwest Pacific Railroad Company in exchange for a good majority of that company's stocks and bonds.[23]

Controversy arose immediately. A. W. Maupin claimed that the commission had accepted Fremont's bid only on condition that no higher proposal was received before May 21. Maupin refused to sign the bill of sale for a time, holding that D. C. Freeman's offer of $1,350,000, submitted May 17, should have been accepted. Maupin claimed that Freeman and Company were determined to give $2,000,000 for the road before losing it, and he threatened to introduce impeachment proceedings against Governor Fletcher for collusion in the matter.[24]

The other two commissioners defended their decision on the ground that the conditional sale to Fremont was final as of May 12 and that bidding was closed. R. J. Mc Elhany, of Springfield, denied that Freeman and Company had the capital to buy the road and suggested that their bid was part of a scheme to blackmail Fremont. According to Mc Elhany, "the milk in the cocoanut" was this: Freeman's representatives had approached Fremont's agents on or after May 17 and offered to withdraw their proposal if Fremont would withdraw his. Then the companies were to write and bid $300,000 for the road, thus saving a million dollars. This the Fremont men rejected as a fraud.[25]

In assessing the likelihood of this story, it must be noted that Mc Elhany's name appeared on the list of incorporators of the Atlantic and Pacific railroad, which guaranteed all the securities of the new Southwest Pacific and by December had merged with it in all but name. It was Mc Elhany to whom Fletcher had written many letters favoring Fremont.

Late in May, the down payment of $350,000 was made to the state. Mc Elhany kept up a regular correspondence with the *Missouri Weekly Patriot* in Springfield, reporting the arrival of the money and bonds from New York with great glee. "I apprehend no danger or delay," he wrote, "nor never did after I was put into possession of certain facts as to who was to compose the company of Fremont.—There are whole families who want to get into it now."[26] Commissioner Maupin, on the other hand, was bitter, and was characterized by one editor favorable to Fremont as "the wild man of Iowa notoriety, more recently known as the ten thousand dollar Swamp Land Commissioner and voluntary blower and wet nurse for parties in the purchase of the South West Pacific Railroad."[27]

Other railroads were the targets of questionable purchase procedures. Lobbyists for the Pacific Railroad Company only by "observing with ceaseless vigilance the motions and operations of those representing foreign capital, with the hope and design of purchasing the road from the State and cutting out and depriving the stockholders of all interest in the company" prevented Fremont from purchasing that line. They saw the Southwest Pacific sale as a *"Sell Out* transferring the whole concern, State, Counties, towns and individual's interest to Genl. J. C. Fremont."[28]

The *San Francisco Bulletin* was openly critical. Fremont, they reported, bought the Southwest Pacific purely as a land and townsite speculation. He had calculated that the Franchise Charter could be purchased for $1,300,000 and built for $5,000,000, but that it was worth $12,000,000, leaving him $6,000,000 profit. Land grants and bonds often filled private pockets rather than completed great enterprises, and Fremont, especially to Californians, who knew the odd role he played in their war for independence, was not to be trusted to press the road to San Francisco. The *Bulletin* observed:

> It is rare that a national fame ever rested on such an unsubstantial foundation, or was ever acquired by the exercise of so little ability. . . . He has certainly been successful in planning and getting hold of great enterprises, and has always had sagacity enough to perceive the direction which public opinion was likely to take. And by his identification with bold pioneer ventures he has commanded sympathy and influence in certain quarters where he could not command success.[29]

This uncomplimentary article was one of the first items pasted in a scrapbook kept by the new Southwest Pacific management.

Late in July, the Atlantic and Pacific was formally chartered. Its list of incorporators seemed to promise success even if its subscription list did not. The incorporators included John Edgar Thomson and Thomas A. Scott, both officers of the Pennsylvania Railroad, men who commanded the loyalties of a significant group of investors; Levi Parsons, who later became the corporate head of the Missouri, Kansas, and Texas, an A. & P. competitor; Charles Dupont of Delaware, a wealthy manufacturer; Nathaniel Brooks, who had an early success with the Michigan Central Railroad; James G. Blunt of Kansas, a well-known Civil War general; William Gilpin, former governor of Colorado; Edward F. Beale, who had become convinced of the merits of the route while making a government wagon-road survey; and Frederick Billings, later president of the Northern Pacific. States represented were Maine, Massachusetts, New York, Pennsylvania, New Jersey, Maryland, Delaware, Indiana, Illinois, Michigan, Wisconsin, Minnesota, Iowa, Missouri, Kentucky, Kansas, West Virginia, Texas, Colorado, California, Oregon, New Mexico, Nevada, Arizona, and the District of Columbia. Fremont had done his initial work well.[30]

The list of Missourians among the incorporators indicated how carefully these men had been selected. It was headed by Governor Fletcher and included James B. Eads, builder of the great St. Louis railroad bridge and vice-president of the Granby Mining Company; B. R. Bonner, a St. Louis businessman who had been in the U.S. House of Representatives; John M. Richardson, former Missouri secretary of state and a large landowner in Springfield; Emil Pretorius, editor of the largest St. Louis German-language newspaper; E. W. Fox, a leading member of the legislature and partner in Pratt and Fox, one of the largest hardware dealers in the West; R. J. Mc Elhany, a wealthy Springfield merchant and commissioner for the sale of the Southwest Pacific; Charles Howland, state senator and president of a large St. Louis corporation; Madison Miller, a state senator experienced in railroad investment; George W. Fishback, one of the owners of the *Daily Missouri Democrat*; George Knapp, owner of the *Missouri Republican*; and "Commodore" Daniel R. Garrison, later president of the Missouri Pacific and one of the men who had profited most from the St. Louis steamboat era.[31] Southwest Missouri was impressed: "Ere long we will write ourselves Empire State in wealth and population. . . . St. Louis will rival New York, for it will be the receptacle of the wealth of the Asias."[32]

The Atlantic and Pacific received no bond aid from Congress as had the Union Pacific, but was granted ten alternate sections of land on each side of the railroad actually constructed in the states and twenty in the territories from Springfield to the Pacific shore. Land for forty miles in width on both sides of the entire proposed line was to be surveyed by the United States and withdrawn from private entry for the benefit of the railroad. These "indemnity lands" were available to the company, provided land within the regular limits had already been taken up by settlers.

The route was defined by the act of incorporation in general terms. It was to commence at or near Springfield and proceed to the western boundary of Missouri, then "by the most eligible railroad route" to a point on the Canadian River, then to Albuquerque, then by a "suitable pass" to the headwaters of the Colorado Chiquito and along the thirty-fifth parallel to the Colorado River, "thence by the most practicable and eligible route to the Pacific." A branch was authorized from the point at which the road struck the Canadian River, eastwardly to Van Buren or Fort Smith, Arkansas. Fremont thought the charter could be bent to authorize a connection from the Colorado River to Guaymas or some other trade center which tapped the Mexican silver mines.

Three clauses were potential sources of trouble. Section Two of the act stated: "The United States shall extinguish as rapidly as may be consistent with public policy and the welfare of the Indians, and only by their voluntary cession, the Indian title to all lands falling under the operation of this act. . . ." That was ambiguous and easier to promise than to deliver. Section Eighteen provided that the Southern Pacific Railroad of California was authorized to connect with the Atlantic and Pacific at the Colorado River. Could the new road then afford to build a parallel line into California? Finally, Section Eight specified that work on the line had to begin within two years; at least fifty miles had to be completed each year thereafter to earn the land grant; and the entire road had to be finished by July 4, 1878.[33] Twelve years to reach the coast! It had taken that long to reach Rolla.

On October 2, Turner's Hall in St. Louis was the site of the first directors' meeting of the Atlantic and Pacific. There, as at other public meetings of the enterprise, the oratory was uniformly optimistic. Fremont was elected president and conducted ceremoniously to the chair. After thanking Senator Brown for Senate bill number twenty, Fremont acknowledged his intent to push the Southwest Pacific rapidly to Springfield and launched into the re-creation of the old thirty-fifth parallel mirage, now titled Atlantic and Pacific Railroad Company.

The route, he said, was direct and easy of construction, lying mostly along the valleys of streams and crossing no major mountain chains. Valuable way traffic could be solicited in New Mexico and Arizona, where large sheep flocks already grazed, and there was the possibility of creating a major city at the crossing of the Colorado. The winters on the route were so mild that a large passenger traffic should be built on the only transcontinental free from snow.

The General saved Asia for the latter part of his talk, and drove the point hard:

The . . . Asiatic shore is the great reservoir of trade and wealth which has fertilized and enriched wherever it flowed. It is teeming with ideas and processes in the arts and manufactures which are in greater part totally unknown to us. . . . The people of the Asiatic shore had the problem of fitting crowded population to insufficient soil. Ours has been the reverse. In the unrestricted intercourse . . . we shall . . . [be given] great advantages by applying to our immense unused resources the finish of detail and the perfection of economy which they have been compelled to practice. In return we shall confer great benefits on them, and we shall undoubtedly do a grand missionary work by carrying them the advanced ideas of our social and political conditions.

All present, he said, should be excited, as he was, at the prospect of giving "some useful point" to their lives through participation in this enterprise:

For ourselves, we have enough to stimulate our best exertions in the fact that we shall be among the projectors and sharers in this large prosperity; this creating of new industry; this opening out of new channels of commerce; this peopling of millions of acres of waste lands; this great part in the building up out of all the nations a new one and giving its people homes under a government which secures to every individual of them the fruits of his industry, and an open field for the fullest use of his powers, limited only by his own capacity.[34]

It was magnificent. Tears must have formed in the eyes of some of the politicians, who had come from their faraway homes for this first meeting. They heard the oratory and the promises, and then never returned to Missouri to supervise the business of building a railroad across the continent. The Springfield *Weekly Patriot* was ecstatic, for local citizens saw their town blossoming with commerce, emerging as a great division point on a continental trunk line. "It has ceased to be a myth, and become a reality; and we will one day be able to step aboard the cars at Springfield, and keep our seats until we step off at . . . San Francisco."[35]

To insiders the picture was more bleak. One St. Louis editor noted in passing that in response to the requirement that work begin within thirty days, "Fremont has complied by putting a force of one wagon and six men at work on the road at Rolla. How long it will take this force to build the road to the southwest corner of the state practical men can

Uriel Crocker
Photo courtesy Harvard University

Joseph Seligman
Photo courtesy J. & W. Seligman & Co.

Captain C. W. Rogers
Photo courtesy St. Louis-San Francisco Railway Co.

Jay Gould
Photo courtesy J. & W. Seligman & Co.

estimate." It was rumored that a quarrel between Fremont and the man in New York from whom he had borrowed bonds to make the down payment had prevented the organization of the new company.[36] Also, though it was expressly stated in the instrument transferring the road from Fremont to the Southwest Pacific Company that the latter would assume the remaining installments on the purchase price, that amount, $975,000, was never entered as a liability on the books of the corporation.[37] These two facts led informed people to wonder whether the company ever intended to pay the second installment or even the down payment. Perhaps the plan was to play upon the good will of the state and of the New York men who had loaned the original $350,000, and on Fremont's reputation in order to speculate in land as long as possible before finally allowing foreclosure.

The Pathfinder had made extravagant promises. In his purchase agreement, Fremont had stated he would pay for the road in four equal annual installments, and that it would touch the western line of the state within three years, six months. He had promised in addition to expend at least $500,000 a year on construction throughout that period. Failure to perform in any of these cases would result in forfeiture of the road to the state.[38]

His resources were smaller than his confidence. The directorate of the Southwest Pacific Railroad consisted of thirteen men, selected from the subscribers to the Atlantic and Pacific. Eight resided in New York, one in Pennsylvania, one in Massachusetts, and only three in Missouri. The stockholders were also the directors. Fremont held 2500 shares (his reward for raising the down payment), but the most anyone else had been willing to subscribe was 200, for friendship's sake.[39] The commissioners for the sale had petitioned the Pacific railroad to surrender the line to St. Louis, but were unsuccessful.[40] The outstanding debt was $4,500,000 on which a discount of $561,853 had been given, and many state bonds held by the South-West Branch had been given to contractors at a loss of almost a half million dollars.[41] To offset this liability, the assets of the thirty-fifth parallel transcontinental included seventy-six miles of track, twenty miles of grading, two partially cut tunnels west of Rolla, six engines and tenders, forty-six freight cars, and two passenger cars.[42]

Land was the one asset that amounted to something. Advertisements and circulars tried to capitalize on the land by offering $2,000,000 in first mortgage bonds of the Southwest Pacific. The principal and interest were to be paid in 1886 through a special fund accumulated from land sales. The bonds were available at the "low rate" of 80 at Ward and Company, 54 Wall Street, New York.[43]

Intelligent investors, noting that the bonds were based on an inflated estimate of the value of the property, refused to buy. The mortgage divided the lands of the road in Missouri into seven classes, the lowest of which was described as "above average agricultural and timber" and represented as worth $5.00 an acre. Class number six was "good" at $8.00, class five "on line" at $15.00, class four "near towns and stations" at $20.00, class three "mineral" at $50.00, class two "undeveloped lead" at $300.00, class one "developed lead mines" at $500.00 per acre. A total holding of 688,000 acres was thus valued at $8,335,260, a highly unrealistic figure, and the company obligated itself by the mortgage to sell lands of each class at not less than the figures indicated until the debt was paid off.[44] So few were the sales under this arrangement that Fremont himself soon sold much of his holdings at a large discount.[45] He could afford to do this because he had received $2,000,000 worth of stocks and bonds in return for his $350,000 investment.[46]

When the bond issue failed, it was decided to assign the business of land sales to an independent agency, which, it was hoped, would colonize the country with settlers from Europe. Accordingly, a contract was entered into on September 8, 1866, with the American Emigrant Aid and Homestead Company, authorizing that corporation to contract for the sale of Southwest Pacific lands, mineral land not included. The commission to the railroad would be 12½ per cent, and it would provide transportation to homeseekers at half the usual rate. The directors, who had failed to reach a quorum for the first two board meetings, and had managed only the business of adopting a pretty green corporate seal at the third, were more than happy to place the bothersome details of land sales in other hands.[47]

The new scheme was very nearly the salvation of the railroad. The American Aid Company owned a steamship line which made semimonthly runs to Denmark and Sweden, returning with emigrants willing to form agricultural colonies in Missouri. In September 1866 the first ship, the *Ottawa*, arrived at New York with four hundred passengers, who embarked by a special train of the Pennsylvania Railroad for new homes in Rolla township.[48] The Homestead Company's method was highly organized, much in contrast to the way in which Southwest Pacific's affairs were conducted. The enterprise aroused such a lively interest within the Danish Court that the King of Denmark appointed two men to conduct the emigrants to their new homes in the American West.

The Scandinavians divided into companies of fifty, each with an elected foreman who was responsible for the maintenance of strict order during the trip.[49] These groups were urged to stay together as a colonizing unit.

> Not for many rubies, sapphires or emeralds should a man, single-handed and alone, take an intelligent family to this country, nor even close to a station, for, though it may look large on the map, it is likely to have nothing more than a platform and a few wild-looking houses. . . . The little colony is indispensible, for it will be a nucleus around which others will gather.[50]

On arrival in Missouri, the foreigners were met by Anselm Albert, the Southwest Pacific's land agent. He had been appointed to that position because of his facility with Scandinavian languages.[51] He conducted the newcomers over the lands, allowing them to make selections, while the two agents of the Danish government saw that nothing was misrepresented. Once plots had been selected, the ship's muster rolls were sent back to the old country, plus such information as the portion of land chosen by each new resident, occupation adopted, and post-office address —this, to attract friends and relatives.[52] Immigrants employed by the company were allowed to repay their transportation through a regular plan of withholding from their wages.[53] Agents for the railroad, in Europe to attract settlers, doubled as salesmen for Southwest Pacific bonds, which found a good German market.[54]

Administering the land grant by proxy, although an accident in the first place, drew for the railroad company high praise. From all reports it appeared that Albert was a competent agent, full of "genuine courtesy and sympathy with the immigrant." Whatever complaints there were, even St. Louis admitted that the Scandinavian colonization was "prosecuted in a thoroughly humane and liberal spirit."[55] To make it unquestionable, the railroad donated a tract of land for an orphan asylum at Rolla.[56]

Unfortunately even the colonization scheme had grievous flaws. Although the American Emigrant Aid and Homestead Company did relatively well in Missouri, it failed in other sections of the country and soon went bankrupt. The immigrant workers on the Southwest Pacific went on a strike soon after they arrived, charging bad faith on the part of both the Emigrant Company and the railroad. In the end, the Southwest Pacific directors had to describe the venture as a "wretched failure, and a dead loss of some forty thousand dollars."[57]

Jerome City, the new terminal town on the west bank of the Gasconade River, was a company town, created from bare prairie. It was
named in honor of Leonard Jerome, a director of the Atlantic and Pacific.
While work progressed on an eight-hundred-foot bridge across the river,
a company-owned ferry linked the town with the main track.[58] Benjamin Holladay opened a stage line from Jerome City to Springfield and
Neosho,[59] the Atlantic and Pacific put in a branch office at Jerome,[60] and
Rolla merchants were subjected to none-too-subtle pressures to move
their establishments to the railhead, where fine lots could be had on
reasonable terms.[61] By April 1867, seven hundred men were selling lots
at Jerome, while only fifteen hundred worked on the railroad line.[62]

The lots in Jerome were owned by a group of the Atlantic and
Pacific's directors. After the Southwest Pacific executive committee had
voted in December 1866 to merge with the Atlantic and Pacific, stock
adjustment increased the officers' holdings and juggled the road's debt
from one set of corporate accounts to another.[63] At the directors' meeting
following this action, it was agreed to pass out concessions at the future
terminus, and to pay a Mr. Stephens half the money he had invested in
the purchase of a town site at the crossing of the Gasconade.[64] Both
actions appeared to be a part of a desperate scheme to salvage something
from the franchise following the realization that building and operating
the railroad was not going to be profitable of itself. At the stockholders'
meeting the next month, the holders of preferred stock passed a resolution to protect themselves to the exclusion of all other stockholders "in
case of judgement, decree of foreclosure or sale." By this time two-thirds
of the stock and all of the bonds had been delivered to the Atlantic and
Pacific.[65] The maneuvers of the security holders were of course unknown
to the local population. They believed that Fremont would take the road
to the Pacific, despite the fact that in one year he only laid iron on
twelve miles of road that had been graded before he took over.

Jerome City, however, affected everyone. The company, as late as
May 1867, bought out for $487.50 a man who held a half interest in the
town site. Yet town lots had long sold for $20 to $40 an acre, since they
were class four lands according to the mortgage.[66] Businessmen claimed
that the railroad charged them $200 for a building lot, that the "land
sharks and shysters" did not intend to push the road beyond that point
as long as sales were lucrative, that side switches and cattle pens at other
points had been torn up by the railroad so as to direct traffic to Jerome,
that contractors hired to build the railroad were diverted to employment

at laying out streets in Jerome, and in short that "men connected with the road are simply using the name of the company to sell corner lots."[67]

The *Rolla Express* said that in early 1867 a drove of cattle arrived in that city for shipment to St. Louis. The owners, however, found that shipment was impossible on the sole railroad serving the area unless they drove their cattle ten miles to the west and loaded them at Jerome City. Since the Southwest Pacific had a monopoly on railway freightage, these men had to go to Jerome City and "pay the ferry company, hotel company, transfer company, Jerome company, mutual admiration company, &c." The *Rolla Express* printed thirteen hundred copies of its exposé; these sold so quickly that the article was reprinted and distributed again.

Fremont became desperate. His workers began to strike for back pay, once becoming so violent that some were locked in a freight car and hauled to St. Louis, lest they destroy too much company property. Their pay was reduced in June 1867 from $1.75 to $1.60 a day.[68]

Even when rail was laid, it did little good. The company made a deal with George T. M. Davis to furnish English rail at $50 a ton, for which he was paid upon delivery in New Orleans with the Southwest Pacific's disastrous issue of first mortgage bonds at 50¢ on the dollar. The company thus got rid of some of its depreciated bonds and Davis disposed of four thousand tons of very bad rail.[69] Even the rails previously provided had been little better than potmetal. Employees complained that they were so brittle that some had been broken getting them into position, and many more broken daily in running over the track.[70] Davis claimed that the bad rails were provided by one of his suppliers without his knowledge, and the question was submitted to arbitration.[71] Meanwhile, repairs to the road cost $2,400 a month, and for an extended period were the most substantial item of expense recorded in the treasurer's hasty entries in the account book.

Next to repairs for bad rail, the largest item on the Southwest Pacific list of expenses was "Agents and Clerks," partly of the corner-lot type. Third was payments to the Pacific Railroad, for rent of engines and use of the St. Louis line. One entry for the rent of four Pacific Railroad locomotives at $10 a day each contained an addendum in the margin: "one not in use 7 days."[72] A survey for an independent line into St. Louis was made in May 1867,[73] but that was as much an exercise in wishful thinking as was Fremont's plan at the same time to connect the Southwest Pacific with his Union Pacific, Eastern Division,[74] or the coordinate attempt by the Atlantic and Pacific to buy eight hundred thousand acres of a former Cherokee reserve in southeast Kansas.[75] The company was reduced to dreaming, its practical effort entirely beyond redemption. Even the secretary was too busy with something else to keep proper minutes. The company's minute book for late 1866 and early 1867, a snarl of hastily written notations, cramped, small, slanted, filled with addenda and marginal notations, reflected the capitalistic spirit gone sour.

The end came on June 27, 1867, when Governor Fletcher seized the road for nonpayment of the first installment on the purchase price. Clinton Fisk, who had eliminated administrative corruption in Missouri during the Civil War, was put in charge of the road and asked to clean out an even stickier morass.[76] Property belonging to officers of the company at Jerome City was attached to pay workers; the furniture and fixtures of the Atlantic and Pacific offices on Fourth Street in St. Louis were seized by the sheriff.[77] It was learned to the surprise of some that Dinsmore and Company, one of Fremont's contractors, had a total capital of $266.67 in cash, four gold watches, a piano, and a set of spoons, and that the Southwest Pacific company had "quite as much ability to build a railroad to the moon as to Springfield."[78] Universal satisfaction was expressed concerning the seizure. Rolla had a mass celebration to commemorate the demise of Jerome (now a village of two hundred with probably no idea of its origin), and the first train under state control was followed by "a broad smile . . . all the way from Franklin to the Gasconade."[79]

Emil Pretorius, one of the Atlantic and Pacific's directors, wrote the obituary of the Southwest Pacific, after the parent company had canceled all stock in it and purged Fremont from both directorates: "The defect in Fremont was that he was a dreamer. Impractical, visionary things went a long way with him. He was a poor judge of men and formed strange associations."[80] Historian Cardinal Goodwin, writing in 1930, came to much the same conclusion.[81] Fremont's son claimed that there was a division in his father's character—the questing side and the human—never perfectly reconciled, and that his tragic flaw was that, in his confidence that he was right, he ignored appearances and public opinion, which were often more important than fact. But perhaps best is John Greenleaf Whittier's simple line:

> Thy error, Fremont, simply was to act
> A brave man's part without a statesman's tact.[82]

For all his shortcomings as a businessman, it must be admitted that John Fremont was a magnificent dreamer. In the organizing of the Atlantic and Pacific, he lit a fire not to be extinguished until the beginning of the next century. The road survived despite obstacles inherent in the route along the thirty-fifth parallel.

Fremont's spirit remained. The Missourians who were glad to see him go had only a few months before being delighted in the replacement of the mixed trains with a first-class train of passenger cars to Jerome City. They rode the construction trains by the hundreds, often endangering themselves in the process, just to watch what few rails were laid be spiked down to form one more link with California. The arrival of each train drew admiring crowds to watch in operation "the greatest enterprise of the 19th century." Newspapers appealed for support for it:

> Away with all politics as applicable to the railway. Let ALL PARTIES unite in hurrying on to completion of the railway that is to traverse the 35th parallel. Radicals! Democrats! Constructed and re-constructed, lend your influence and money to the railway, talk about it, and pray of it, and preach about it, for it is a consummation devoutly to be wished for.[83]

That enthusiasm and the corporate device in which it continued to rest were the legacy of John C. Fremont.

5

THE SOUTH PACIFIC RAILROAD COMPANY

Clinton Fisk held the line very well as manager for the state-operated Southwest Pacific. Expenses were pared, there was no talk of extending the line, Fremont's bills were slowly paid, and disgruntled purchasers of Jerome City lots and on-line agricultural tracts were allowed to air their considerable grievances.

When Fremont's accounts were revealed, the state learned just how inefficient the private operation had been: A total of $2,561,821 had been invested in the road and equipment by the Southwest Pacific; $2,000,000 of this was the book entry for purchase of the line and was never paid. Iron rails were the major expense, amounting to $290,969, but there were also numerous irregular items included in the investment in road and equipment, such as $30,000 in bonds issued to four individuals and itemized only as for "services rendered." For the year of Fremont management (June 1866 to June 1867), the road had a net operating income of $27,546. Even the state could attract more traffic than that; the net operating income for the next year was $75,798.[1]

The people of southwest Missouri, however, were not satisfied that the company should remain solvent but stagnant under state control. The call went out for a new company, preferably controlled by local people rather than outside speculators. The "Home Company" movement was led by James Baker of Springfield, a leading lawyer of the region. On July 4, 1867, Baker took the first step in a long association with the thirty-fifth parallel project, when he wrote a letter describing his plan to the *Missouri Weekly Patriot*.

Baker believed that by ruling that stockholders in the new organization be citizens of Missouri, "mere adventurers" would be excluded. A home company could secure more liberal terms in the purchase of the road from the state and could build quickly to the local lead mines, thereby guaranteeing subscribers a profit whatever the fate of the transcontinental extension.

The line had a reputation that frightened investors. Baker therefore proposed that before the new company was organized, a committee should be appointed to make certain that any new investor would be able to control his shares without being harassed by Fremont, and to determine the condition of the company. If this report was favorable, the new company should promise that no money, or at most 5 per cent, need be paid on stock subscriptions until the road was completed, the money for construction to be raised entirely by a mortgage on the physical plant and land sales. The mortgage would be so drawn that it could not be changed without the individual consent of each bondholder. This last guarantee assured that a combination of a few eastern capitalists holding the majority of the stock could not mortgage the road to themselves for the purpose of purchasing it and cheating local stockholders.[2]

These complicated guarantees indicated the extent of the previous abuse. Baker was not a novice. He was educated at Indiana University, trained in his father's Jacksonian democracy. After graduation he had been appointed register of an Iowa land office by President Pierce, had served as attorney general of Indiana, and had done battle in the late war at Shiloh, Iuka, and Corinth. He was a strict Baptist and a temperance man, and his steel-hard eyes and grizzled beard and mustache gave him the look of Jehovah, come to save Missouri from the corruption of eastern men and eastern money. Many felt that Baker could put Fremont's dream into operation. The completion of that project required a solid legal mind such as his rather than a crowd of "broken-down speculators." In 1868, Governor Fletcher appointed him to the Supreme

Court bench in Missouri, and he thus acquired the dignified title "Judge" to add to his imposing appearance.[3]

Baker called a mass meeting at the Springfield Courthouse on the afternoon of July 17, 1867. The courtroom would not contain the crowd, so the affair was removed outside. Governor Fletcher spoke. He said that a new law must be passed providing for a new sale, and that it must be a more liberal law than the one which had placed strict limitations on the Southwest Pacific company. The bill proposed by the legislature included strict protection for the state, but this conservatism would, according to the governor, only drive away investors. A newspaper report of Fletcher's Springfield speech interpreted it to mean that the state should leave the new company free of all obligations to the government except that the company build at a specified rate. The governor's proposal was that the state mortgage be released, as it had been, briefly, in the 1850s.[4] An extra legislative session met to consider these suggestions.[5]

The possibility that a liberal bill would pass with the support of the governor sent capitalists scrambling for a share of the boom that was freely predicted. Montgomery Blair, a Missouri politician, felt he should use his family's political power to increase the chances that his own investment in the Atlantic and Pacific would eventually pay him something. In August, he wrote to James Eads, one of the incorporators of the transcontinental venture:

> As a money making enterprize [sic] I am certain it [the A. & P.] will be successful. . . . Successful management of this Road is an undertaking worthy of any man's ambition. It will be *the* Pacific R. Road & the successful making of it will revolutionize the commerce of the world—I hope you will therefore let go the smaller irons you have in the fire & take hold of this really great enterprize [sic] in which you can build up not only a colossal fortune probably, but a national reputation.[6]

Eads had some trouble letting go one of his "irons in the fire," an illegal speculation with the aid of Governor Fletcher in the sale of shares held by the State of Missouri for the school fund. He later went before a grand jury on a charge of "wholesale robbery."

Yet in a way Eads was typical of the kind of man who was attracted by the prospect of investing in a western railroad with large plans but no immediate prospects. He had begun his business life in Tucher & Salisbury's shoe store in St. Louis, then had become a steamboat clerk and salvager of sunken steamboats, and finally had been appointed chief

engineer for the great Mississippi bridge at St. Louis. There was no lack
of talent in Eads or in many of the others who made up the Atlantic and
Pacific organization. The problem was a certain affinity for short-term
speculative gain which they seemed to have in common as they looked at
the 1867 opportunity and many opportunities after that. Eads was to sell
out the stockholders in his bridge to the London bondholders who then
would own the bridge at one-fifth its cost. Yet the scoundrel was also a
dreamer who planned all the while a magnificent structure to span the
Bosphorus. Eads, the "small, pale, sick-looking man," was a low thief
and a great engineering genius—both despicable and magnificent, like
the Atlantic and Pacific company itself.[7]

Such were the types with whom the straight-laced Baker and his
companion Eli Paris were forced to deal on their journey to the East in
the fall of 1867. They spent three months in New York trying to drum
up support for a new company only to find that the line's reputation as
a profitable undertaking was at a low ebb. The investors, even the bold
ones, were taken aback by the information that the road in fourteen years
had not built one-third of its Missouri line and could not pay its running
expenses, much less fight the court battles instigated by Fremont. Many
did not wish to talk about it, much less invest in it. Still, Baker managed to put together a list of investors with the help of Fisk and Fletcher
and with some compromise in the Judge's preferences as to their character and place of residence.[8]

Opinion in Missouri was divided. A railroad convention at Mount
Vernon, Missouri, where Paris lived, strongly endorsed Baker's plan and
asked that some temporary expedient be employed to hasten settlement
of the railroad lands while negotiations were proceeding.[9] At Neosho,
however, Baker and Paris were accused of shady dealings in league with
a Springfield ring. Springfield in turn condemned this criticism, and
blamed "a class of small minds who have no other capacity than to
oppose whatever is proposed" for delaying progress on the railroad. The
Springfield paper strongly contended that civic jealousy should be laid
aside: "The [Neosho] 'Tribune' cannot understand that the road must
be built to Springfield *first*, and that the citizens of Springfield are not
responsible for the fact that Neosho lies west of them." The editor offered to support any plan Neosho could offer to build the road to Neosho
first, "for the sake of establishing harmony among the people *once* on
this question."[10]

The Atlantic and Pacific, meanwhile, published a pamphlet entitled
Route to the Pacific Ocean on the 35th Parallel. It contained extracts

from reports of Whipple and Beale, outlined two branches to St. Louis and to Fort Smith, and claimed Indians along the route would be "easily and economically controlled."[11] Southern papers reported that due to "improper treatment" by the Missouri authorities, the Atlantic and Pacific would commence at Fort Smith rather than Springfield, thus insuring water communication and allowing the road to begin construction without waiting for a new company to complete the link from St. Louis to Springfield.[12]

While this last was only a rumor, it increased the effort by those in Missouri favoring a quick sale of the old Southwest Pacific on liberal terms. Governor Fletcher urged that the state should make a liberal adjustment with the Atlantic and Pacific for the $450,000 in liabilities which that company had floated on behalf of the Southwest Pacific, and for the $50,000 owed to contractors. He added pressure by implying that he was privy to a plan to divert the Union Pacific, Eastern Division south from Pond Creek to meet the thirty-fifth parallel at Albuquerque. This would make the Atlantic and Pacific its most important feeder. The governor also reminded the legislature that the thirty-fifth parallel land grant was "unnaturally great in quantity per mile," and that the whole cost of extending the Southwest Pacific was actually less than its floating debt.[13]

In the first months of 1868, several bills were introduced in the state legislature. One, a bill requiring any new company to make a strict accounting to the state, was defeated, partly because of unfavorable editorials in the St. Louis *Missouri Daily Democrat,* which Henry Blow controlled. Another, known as the Price-Richardson bill, was as obvious a swindle as the Dickonson bill of 1866. It proposed that the road should be turned over to a new company immediately on the promise of a deposit ninety days thereafter; that would let the incorporators run the road three months and then sell it without paying a cent. A third bill was a resolution to ask Congress to divert the Union Pacific, Eastern Division, to the thirty-fifth parallel. St. Louis supported this last measure, and was roundly criticized for failing to see that the Union Pacific, Eastern Division would primarily benefit Chicago, while the A. & P. was exclusively a St. Louis road.[14] St. Louis, wrote one of her dailies, "is still wrapped up in her life-long conservatism and fogyism."[15]

A fourth bill before the legislators that winter was on behalf of the Southwest Missouri Company, the group headed by Baker. Baker said that some of the other bills were put forward by rival railroad companies simply to ward off the competition a Missouri-based transcontinental would provide. A good deal of paper was employed in making up citizen resolutions in support of the home company.

Baker, however, did not encounter the same public naïveté which had carried Fremont to leadership. His company was nicknamed by cynics the "Incorporated Springfield Bar," and some reports of its activities were scathing:

> They passed their resolutions which, considering the terrible labor by which they were brought forth, were the smallest and most ridiculous of mice. If the Home Company is not already vanquished, another such victory would prove its utter overthrow. They resolved two or three pages of *whereases,* that "everything else being equal,"—that is, ability, security against failure, swindling, &c.,—that they preferred the road to be built by our own citizens, a proposition to which we presume not a man, woman or child in the State of Missouri would object.[16]

Generalities of the Fremontian genre were not sufficient in 1868 and would not be tolerated from the lips of Judge Baker, whose reputation was based on the sharpness of his logic. When Baker lapsed into "whereases" and empty rhetoric, hearts sank. The agent at Larimore Station expressed the feeling best in an elaborate parody of Poe's *The Raven*:

> Much they talked and loud they listened; but the audience
> never swallowed
> Half the railroads that their fancy builded, and their
> brilliant language bore.
> All their words, so aptly spoken, left us not a single token,
> that the mighty locomotive would soon whistle at our
> door. What need we for locomotives, while such
> eloquence doth roar—roars, then slumbers—nothing
> more.[17]

Late in February a break came from an unexpected quarter: Boston. Francis B. Hayes and his associate, Andrew Peirce, Jr., arrived in Missouri and quickly combined with the principal contenders for the road.[18] Others, hearing of the visitors' money and their policy of buying out all competition, quickly formed groups, made propositions, and allowed themselves to be bought out, causing some delay and difficulty.[19] The result was that when the road was sold by the state in March 1868 the list of incorporators of the new South Pacific Railroad Company included not only Peirce and Hayes, but Clinton Fisk; G. V. Fox, a principal contending bidder; Eli Paris of the home company; James Harrison and C. P. Choteau, who had made a late bid in order to be bribed; and Benjamin Holladay, the former Jerome stage operator.[20]

Hayes was elected president and Fisk vice-president.[21] Arrangements were made to satisfy the Fremont bondholders by assuming the liabilities of the Southwest Pacific company[22] and the directors contracted for $180,000 worth of rolling stock and three thousand tons of rail. By April the company had already spent $450,000 on construction, and $105,000 paying Fremont's old debts in order to insure harmony.[23] At the first board meeting of the South Pacific company, it was resolved to confer with the directors of the Atlantic and Pacific with regard to a merger.[24] These directors were much the same as those of the South Pacific, and both boards met in new Boston offices. Eastern men moved into all the key positions. Peirce was induced by a $25,000 salary to leave his home in Boston and to take the position of superintendent of construction and managing director in Missouri.[25] Hayes located in Washington to lobby for further congressional aid.[26] The company made a $1.5 million deposit with the state to guarantee its good intent.[27]

Peirce and Hayes took too much power to please Clinton Fisk. He had run the railroad successfully for the state and had been instrumental in acquiring the franchise for the new purchasers. Then to be shuffled into the mostly honorary position of vice-president and denied the chance at the really large salaries paid to other managers upset Fisk greatly. He carried on a running feud with Peirce which became so violent that the latter threatened to resign unless Fisk were withdrawn from all authority.[28] When Fisk was not in Missouri, he used trips to Washington on assignments to aid Hayes to do just the opposite by telling tall tales about the president to powerful directors, while inflating his own qualifications as a replacement.[29] He withheld the account books of the old Southwest Pacific from inspection by the South Pacific directors and used company funds for such questionable purposes that by 1870 the directors launched a full-scale investigation of his activities.[30]

Something, however, may be said for Fisk's side of the argument. There seemed to be a salary discrimination against residents of Missouri. Fisk received $10,000 a year as vice-president.[31] That was within $2,000 of President Hayes's salary, but less than half Peirce's. Fisk did as much work as Peirce, and it was later revealed that Peirce was not more seraphic than Fisk in his scruples about use of company funds. Governor Fletcher and Judge Baker, other Missouri residents in company employ, were paid only $3,000 as attorneys.[32] Baker lobbied at Jefferson City and advised Hayes on legal matters,[33] while Fletcher also used his good legislative connections and was often employed when prestige was needed for an important speech or with an official in Washington.[34] It may, of course, be argued that all salaries, including Fisk's, were much higher than a frontier railroad could afford to pay.

Fisk, for all his complaints, was valuable. He was in correspondence with all parts of the organization and was its most spellbinding orator. He advised Hayes on detailed matters such as construction of the laws relating to registers and receivers fees for the selection of lands,[35] and was an unflinching negotiator in dealings with such difficult men as Henry Blow of the Granby Company.[36] He aided more intangibly through his reputation: he was a former officer of the Freedmen's Bureau, founder of Fisk University, had been baptised in the river, and remembered only two occasions when oaths had escaped his lips. His shortcomings were known to a few, his virtues to many.[37]

Fisk gave the speech at the Atlantic and Pacific groundbreaking July 4, 1868; this was to satisfy the congressional requirement that construction begin within two years of the land-grant act. Springfield had a crowd of ten thousand that day. At 7:00 A.M. they rode in carriages to a spot on the survey four miles west of town. Judge Baker introduced Peirce, who made a brief speech. Then Miss Mary Fisk, the vice-president's daughter, took hold of a shovel draped with red, white, and blue ribbon sent from Boston expressly for the occasion. She broke the first ground for the Atlantic and Pacific, received three hearty cheers, and proceeded with her father back to the grove, where the Declaration of Independence was read. John Phelps spoke in praise of Thomas Benton's "genius and foresight," Henry Blow spoke on the economic impact of the project, and Andrew Peirce promised to bring soon a speechmaker better than all these, the steam locomotive.[38]

Fisk's speech was the highlight, and he was interrupted constantly by cheers and laughter at his stories of Fremont's excesses and of Peirce's discomfort at riding the stage to Springfield. The pudgy, balding man on the platform praised Peirce with such sincerity that no one would guess at the feud between them. Loud cheers were elicited by his reading of a telegram from Hayes: "Be sure and commence the work at Springfield on the 4th of July, and keep at the work until the road is finished."[39]

But it was as a Christian orator that Fisk was at his best. It was this that would make him Prohibition party candidate for president of the United States in 1888,[40] and this that most impressed the listeners at Springfield:

Railways promote Christian civilization—Every locomotive, with its sinews of brass, and steel and breathing of flame that comes thundering across the continent, with its shrill whistle on the mountains, is a messenger of peace. [Cheers] . . . Whatever promotes the assimilation of mankind, whatever brings sections and people into communion, thus supplementing each other in the completeness of humanity, is a step in the advancing kingdom of God.

Fisk had a marvelous ability to equate technological and Christian progress—a comforting felicity of relieving the guilt feelings of a rural people entering an industrial age. He invoked Andrew Jackson, "the iron man who sleeps at the Hermitage," and he called for "a new covenant to live for God, for progress"—the covenant of the Gilded Age.[41] Indicative of his influence in the management was a gift by the South Pacific directors of a silver communion service to the Colored Methodist Episcopal Church at Springfield. The card read: "These vessels may serve to remind you from time to time of the friendly interest of strangers."[42]

Fisk's New Year's cards to the directors in 1869 were on South Pacific stationery and showed the Atlantic and Pacific complete to the coast.[43] That no doubt amused Hayes in Washington. In addition to fielding Fisk's continued complaints that he was being reduced to a "first or second class clerk," Hayes attended conferences as far away as Portland, Maine, to defend the road's interest, and he was forced to face the large Washington lobbies of more affluent companies quite alone.[44]

The most important matter that Hayes tried to get before the Congress was a bill to provide a bond subsidy for the Atlantic and Pacific similar to that granted to the Union Pacific. In December 1868 A. & P. Director William Coffin wrote to Director Uriel Crocker that no effort was being made to sell the bonds of the road and that Hayes had been forced to borrow from his own directors in order to meet interest on them. In Missouri an attempt to pay contractors with land grant bonds at seventy failed due to the workers' demand for certain guarantees; Hayes argued that there was already a thirty- to fifty-thousand-dollar premium in their contract.[45] These were good arguments for a bond subsidy, but the president found it difficult to work in Congress alone. He wrote to Boston:

I have to prepare bills for Congress, negotiate with members, attend to preparation of reports, make large bargains, and with no one to consult. . . . I try to do the best I can, and have made no mistake, I believe, yet, but it is not a safe policy to trust to my judgment and efforts alone.

Hayes feared that President Ulysses Grant and Vice-President Schuyler Colfax were against the granting of subsidies, and he suggested that influential directors write letters to members of Congress and take turns helping him lobby in person.[46] He was, however, left in Washington alone. The subsidy bill failed.

As a result of his close contact with affairs in the Capitol, Hayes, from his small room at 222 F Street, was in a much better position to assess the chances of the new company than were any of his associates. Though the subsidy failed and though his optimism was not of the Fisk variety, he wrote in February 1869 that he was satisfied with the investment and thought the new managers were beginning to get matters in order. "We have I believe a safe investment and a very promising prospect for realizing large profits from it, always provided we manage it with good business sense, with principles we have laid down."[47] Newspaper accounts, he said, should be disregarded, for "they are paid for abusing us generally."[48]

The strength of the road, according to Hayes, was not so much that it had done anything positive, but that it seemed to have made the reforms necessary to counteract the negative image previous management had built. For one thing, the directors had throttled Fisk who, while a likable gentleman, was too garrulous and noticeable to make a good railway manager: "The General has many genial social qualities that I am not unmindful of—," wrote William Coffin, "he is kind-hearted to a fault, very much wanting in firmness and decision of character. Promises everybody pleasant things & feels badly to think he cannot give a place to every man he promises."[49] Second, the road was "entirely clean" financially with no elaborate promises to plague it later. "We stand well here—," Hayes wrote, "our enemies have not caught us."[50]

In Missouri also the prospects were encouraging. The six months ending December 31, 1868, showed net earnings of $24,589 which Fisk concluded was "not so bad a showing for a poor short line."[51] Hayes led an excursion to the Indian Territory late in September 1868, which included a number of prominent directors and several wives. The Springfield stage overturned and threw Governor Fletcher out, injuring him seriously, but that only demonstrated the need for a railroad, as did the horrible weather and the necessity for the ladies to sleep in open wagons due to lack of accommodations in the Indian domain. Springfield passed a resolution to help the Atlantic and Pacific secure a subsidy, since it was "the true route to the Pacific Ocean, and the only one that will be unobstructed by snow and ice."[52]

Construction proceeded more rapidly than ever it had in the history of the line. Engraved invitations were sent to five hundred people for the celebration at Lebanon on October 5, 1869,[53] and four passenger cars which had lately run on an Eastern railroad were brought to Missouri and relettered "South Pacific Railroad" for the occasion. So enthusiastic was Hayes about traffic prospects that he wrote to Boston requesting more cars, preferably to be obtained used at bargain prices. He wrote also that Fisk had departed mysteriously for New York and that there was no truth to Fisk's charge that Governor Fletcher had stolen some of Peirce's letters. It was "sheer fabrication," he claimed, that Fletcher had ever written the general manager's name as "Purse."

By September 28, the company had sold all seventy of its house lots at Lebanon and forty-six houses and stores were in the process of construction on the site. Hayes estimated $100,000 profit from these lots, all of which were located on the prairie west of the old town of Lebanon. Buildings were being rapidly removed from the old town to the "railroad addition," much to the chagrin of some residents no doubt;[54] the scheme had the marks of another Jerome City. Hayes, however, stated that "People are entirely satisfied—more than that—are delighted with what has been done."[55]

A large baggage car was attached to the Lebanon excursion train with "a full supply of wines and edibles, cigars &c," and when the first engine chugged into the new Lebanon town square Mrs. M. S. Beckwith was there representing the ladies of the town. She presented the engineer with an American flag, with the wish that "success attend you and the noble Lebanon until you have borne this Star-Spangled Banner to the coast."[56] The road between the Gasconade and Lebanon had been built for $16,000 a mile. However, one mile cost $41,000, and the engineers hoped for easier going to the west.[57]

The grade was smoother around Springfield, but public relations were rougher. The arrival of the first train in Springfield on May 5, 1870, was greeted by cheers and the firing of cannon, even though the day was marred for lack of proper arrangement for carriages to meet the ladies. Nine speeches were well received.[58]

The company, however, had made enemies in its push to Springfield. In building from Arlington, where Fremont left off, to Springfield, the

South Pacific had created thirteen new towns and kept twelve thousand men at work. At Springfield the new railroad town where the company erected a hotel and depot was over a mile to the north of the old one.[59] The South Pacific had been induced to build to the North Springfield tract of land by a group of speculators who promised forty acres for shops and a half interest in the town site for the railroad company. Peirce told a group of Springfield citizens that he would bring the railroad through their town for $25,000. They in turn argued that the charter called for the railroad to run through Springfield, not north of it, and that no bonus was necessary. Peirce at that jumped up and said, "I'll show you very soon where I'll build." Shortly thereafter the Ozark Land Company was formed with Peirce as president to sell lots in North Springfield. The new town and the old town feuded until 1887 when they were finally consolidated.[60] Up and down the line, it was the same. Peirce City citizens became so disgusted with the Peirce City Real Estate Company that the town eventually changed its spelling to Pierce City to avoid association with the founder.[61]

On October 28, 1870, all the town companies came under the control of the Atlantic and Pacific company. The South Pacific, having built to Springfield, insured its continued wealth by a simple stock exchange with the A. & P. This agreement carried out a plan made and put in writing in June 1868, when the merger had been planned. Peirce, Fisk, and Hayes had been issued A. & P. stock for the amount of their deposit with the state, and during its entire existence the South Pacific Railroad Company elected also the directors of the A. & P. In a way the name which some Missourians had learned to respect and some to hate, South Pacific, was a legal fiction.[62]

The settlers, in viewing the A. & P.–South Pacific merger, perhaps needed some of the understanding of the maneuvers of western railroads possessed by their fellow Missourian Samuel Clemens. In *The Gilded Age*, published in 1873, Mark Twain and his coauthor imagined a Missouri railroad which they called the Salt Lick Branch of the Pacific Railroad. This fictitious railroad laid its track from Slouchburg via Poodleville and Hallelujah to Corruptionville, creating artificial markets for town lots on prairie ridges all the way while established towns were ruined.[63] Perhaps the South-West Branch and its successors served as a model for Twain, perhaps not; he was certainly familiar with the project. What is sure is that he understood the way it worked. In an 1867 letter he wrote:

A railroad is like a lie—you have to keep building to it to make it stand. A railroad is a ravenous destroyer of towns, unless these towns are put at the end of it and a sea beyond, so that you can't go further and find another terminus.[64]

PLAYED OUT

West of Springfield, the vexation of the settlers at the high price of company-owned agricultural lands was at least as great as that over the town lot difficulty. The South Pacific was heir to the state land grant originally made to the South-West Branch in 1852, a twenty-mile-wide band of all the even-numbered sections from Franklin to the western border of the state. The Atlantic and Pacific was able to secure these sections through merger with the South Pacific, while at the same time claiming possession of all the odd-numbered sections in the same area by authority of its federal charter. The fiction of separate companies was maintained after the merger in order to secure these overlapping grants.

To the settler, it looked as though the railroad literally owned western Missouri. East of Springfield there had been government sections available within the checkerboard pattern of the South Pacific grant. The price of these was raised by the government from the usual $1.25 to $2.50 an acre, but this was a bargain for lands with easy access to the railroad, as the South Pacific charged a minimum of $5 an acre for the very worst lands of the same class. West of Springfield, however, land ownership was solidly in the hands of the railroad, and the settler had no choice but to deal with what naturally enough came to be known by many as the "soulless corporation."

Nor was the situation better when dealing with the United States. The federal land office at Springfield often appealed to Washington to clarify the situation regarding land titles. Due to a confused state administration of sales, people who had settled on the public lands prior to the grant to the railroad had to resort to hiring attorneys who charged them $1 an acre to make good their title. Many who could not afford this fee lost the fruits of years of hard labor and saw their farms deeded to the railroad or sold to speculators who had no claim whatever to them. The General Land Office was urged to reform this system else the federal government become as unpopular in the area as was the Atlantic and Pacific.[1]

President Grant and the Interior Department received a number of letters from farmers protesting the overlapping grants west of Springfield. One of these complained that the A. & P. "are treating the Preemptors & all the Settlers on the even sections most inhumanly" and inquired if there were any relief from "a soulless Co Robing [sic] the actual settlers of all they have on earth." If not, they would be compelled to try to protect themselves.[2] The Atlantic and Pacific land commissioner responded to these complaints by stating that the company was canceling abandoned homestead claims or those with imperfect title in order to make up for deficiencies within its grant due to bonafide prior settlement. The intent of the 1866 act, he said, was clearly that lands should be taken within the ten-mile limit of the primary grant when possible, rather than from the indemnity lands which were farther from the line and therefore less valuable.[3]

If land monopoly had not been a sufficient item of contention between farmer and railroad, the question of rates would have set tempers boiling. In 1871, 463,363 bushels of wheat and 39,000 head of cattle were hauled by rail from southwest Missouri.[4] Rates for these commodities were set high, as were passenger rates. A ticket from Springfield to St. Louis cost over $3 more than from a point one hundred miles west where there was competition among railroads for fares.[5] In the summer of 1871, rates on wheat were raised from $50 to $70 a car, even though more traffic was passing over the line than ever before. The Springfield *Weekly Leader* did not at first comment on this change. Later, however, when the editor's pass was taken away by the company for loaning it out to his friends, he joined the others, and "his eyes were suddenly opened to the fact that Mr. Pierce [*sic*] and other railroad officials were a set of thieving rascals."[6] By 1872, the only paper in southwest Missouri consistently favorable to the railroad was the *Southwest,* a company sheet "whose inside is edited by the Atl. & Pac.R.R. at North Springfield and printed the Lord knows where."[7]

A third issue was taxation. James Baker was arrested in 1872 by the sheriff of Phelps County for refusal to authorize payment of county taxes by the South Pacific company. Baker and the company claimed that under the 1852 state land grant act, their corporation was exempt from taxation.[8] Counties and municipalities, to which the railroad property presented a large potential source of revenue, argued that the line was exempt only until completed, and that the original line was completed early in 1871 when rail was laid through Seneca and over the state line into the Indian Territory. County authorities noted that construction was delayed for some time just short of the state line. This delay presumably demonstrated that the officers of the company realized the limits of their tax exemption and wished by the delay to avoid taxation until arrangements could be made for the land grant in Indian Territory.[9]

The taxation question resulted in a great amount of litigation, especially in 1873 when the State Board of Equalization trebled the assessed valuation of the Atlantic and Pacific over that of a year previous, even though there had been no further construction.[10] Judge Baker was in court on tax issues from 1870 forward and in jurisdictions all the way to the Supreme Court of the United States. The final decisions were ambiguous but generally favorable to the railroad. The valuation was reduced to a more reasonable level,[11] and it was determined that since the line had paid no dividend, it was entitled to two years' exemption from taxation following completion to the state line.[12]

Fighting the railroad on the issues of lands, rates, and taxation led some settlers to the conclusion that glee at the completion of the road to Springfield and its rapid extension into Indian Territory "was as misplaced as the untimely sport of lambs, while the keen blade of the butcher is preparing." A more sinister influence than Fremont was at work, they said, for the new railroad company was efficient: "Here it asks for a land grant from the 'poor Indian'; there, through some obscure medium, it dickers for an eighty acre tract dangerously convenient to some doomed little town."

There were still bright colors in the bubbles blown on imaginary roads yet to be built, and people still dreamed of the prosperity the railroad would bring, but many hopes were drowned:

> We have seen this company a thing, nebulous and intangible, quietly but persistently taking life of us. We see it to-day, bland, insatiable, and immense, taking in our towns as nutriment, before starting on its march to the Pacific.[13]

The fly, wrote a Springfield editor, fanned himself to sleep as the toils were woven around him:

> The spider had high intelligence, lofty aims, noble schemes and purposes, and he knew how to carry them out. He lived on flies. He was in the fly trade. He was shipping flies.[14]

The railroad had a much more conservative image of its own power than did area newspapers. Clinton Fisk had departed for Europe with a good deal of the company's funds and some of its records,[15] and the Atchison, Topeka and Santa Fe railroad was obstructing government approval of A. & P. construction in fear of competition.[16] Peirce City citizens had stated that they would rather have the town named Sodom, Gomorrah, or Hell's Half-Acre than Hayes City after the president of the South Pacific/Atlantic and Pacific combination.[17] There were rumors of a national financial panic, and construction was stalled in the Indian Territory.

Trouble in Indian Territory dated from September 1870, when Frederick Hodges, a surveyor for the Atlantic and Pacific, was expelled from the region by order of the commissioner of Indian affairs. Hodges had to cut short the collection of data for a railroad bridge across the Arkansas and return to Boston to ask the directors whether they had overlooked something in planning the thirty-fifth parallel transcontinental.[18]

What they had overlooked was that, although Congress had made a large grant to the railroad in Indian Territory, it also had treaties with the tribes which were inconsistent with such a grant. For example, the Cherokee treaty of 1866 provided *right of way only* for one north and south road and one east and west. Cherokee Principal Chief Lewis Downing accepted the Atlantic and Pacific as the east-west road,[19] but sharply refused the company's application to him for validation of its land grant.[20]

Early in 1871 rail was laid into the Indian Territory from the east. The Grand River was alive with activity. Six flat boats carried fish plates, rail, bolts, and work engines to the grading and laying crews on the west bank until a bridge could be built. To provide ballast quarries were opened at the bridge site, and the sparse timber was swiftly cut for telegraph poles and ties. Chief Engineer Lawrence Kellitt's crews cut 21,236 ties and 722 telegraph poles from the Cherokee timber and gave the tribe in return five cents apiece for the ties, and a cent and a half per telegraph pole.[21]

The grading crews first erected tent cities along the right of way.[22] Then came the railroad towns. The station at Prairie City was provided with large stockyards to catch traffic from the Texas Trail. By October 1871, ten thousand head of cattle a month were shipped from there; seven trains were loaded one brisk day.[23] Then came Vinita, laid out in September and named after the young sculptress Vinnie Ream. Lots there sold for up to $800, and there Atlantic and Pacific rails crossed those of the Missouri, Kansas, and Texas railroad.[24]

Many of the Indians felt they were being invaded. The railroad ran excursions to Seneca in the spring of 1871 and made about $550 apiece on them. St. Louis citizens, provided with a picnic lunch, could view the red man first hand. One perceptive journalist described the scene in an article entitled "Ten Car Loads of Christians Turned loose on Seneca":

> The wars of the Pic-nics are becoming as interesting as the history of the Crusaders. . . . The attacks on Seneca have opened with ice cream and strawberries, root beer and lemonade, ginger snaps, cold ham, and dead chicken. . . . If it has been the intention to vanquish Seneca with gingerbread and coffee, that attempt has failed. If it was meant to show the redman how ravenous and hungry the white man or woman may be: how voracious a Church Pic-nic may be, Lesson No. one will satisfy "Lo" and his whole posterity for all time.

The population, whiskey, and morals of Seneca while it was the terminus of the road were all described by the same phrase, "active but mixed."[25] It was jokingly said that the only inhabitants of Vinita were United States marshals, there to regulate the houses of ill-repute.[26]

John Jones, an Indian agent, wrote to the secretary of the interior that all this would have been fine had the Indians wanted to sell their lands or to speculate in town lots. Since they did not, the coming of the two railroads was a disaster. Railroad timber policy was unpopular, exaggerated advertising by the roads created a desire on the part of white speculators for Indian lands, and the railroad lobby's support of bills in

Congress to organize the Indian lands as a United States Territory gave the Indians a "deep feeling of insecurity."[27] Lands taken for right of way gave the tribes demonstration enough of what would happen if the land grant were ratified. One Cherokee farmer valued his one and a quarter acres of corn at $400; the A. & P. was willing to give him $2.50.[28]

The philosophy of the Atlantic and Pacific concerning the Indians and their lands was outlined in a pamphlet written by a company attorney, C. J. Hillyer, and published in 1871. In it was a defense of the "Manifest Destiny" of white industrial civilization. The pamphlet claimed that the Indian practice of holding their lands in common and pursuing subsistence agriculture was wasteful and indolent. Such an economy would not create the sort of traffic on which a railroad must depend. "A railroad and a wilderness," Hillyer wrote, "are incompatible things and cannot long co-exist. Either the wilderness will be subdued or the railroad will die of starvation."

The position of the company was that there was no great sacredness in an old treaty stipulation made years ago with an Indian tribe. The law of American development should be allowed to operate in the Indian Territory, just as it had to the east of there, especially since white civilization was intrinsically superior to that of the savages. The A. & P. asked the Congress to validate the land grant by force "whether one Indian or ten thousand be killed in the operation" and to allow the Atlantic and Pacific company to pursue its town, land, rate, and taxation policy in the Indian domain just as it had in Missouri.[29]

Very few people questioned the company's position. An exception was James Harlan, chairman of the Senate Committee on Indian Affairs, who in 1872 called attention to the "demoralizing effect" on the Indians of the introduction of thousands of railroad laborers into a country outside the usual restraints of civilized society. Harlan spoke with Francis Hayes on this subject, and the railroad president agreed to halt construction on the road for a year, provided Congress extended the time allowed for its completion.[30] The request was a clever ploy by Hayes, who knew well enough that he could not press construction anyway so long as he could not use a land grant for revenue. Nothing came of it.

Meanwhile trouble brewed at Vinita. Blood was shed in battles between crews in the employ of the two railroads joining there over which was to have the privilege of selling corner lots in a town that was sure to grow.[31] There was no cooperation between the two. Passengers transferring from one line to the other had to brave a mile-and-a-half journey through the mud or else jump from the train at a point where the roads came closer together than were the depots; the A. & P. sent firearms to Vinita to protect its crews. Missouri, Kansas and Texas trains went straight past the Atlantic and Pacific depot without stopping, arguing that this was to punish the Missouri company for erecting its depot without consulting the connecting road. Andrew Peirce said this was a "childish excuse," that the Missouri, Kansas and Texas had not consulted him about its depot either, and that officers of that company had conspired to keep the Atlantic and Pacific from crossing into the Indian Territory.

On August 25, 1871, a meeting was held at the office of J. & W. Seligman and Company in New York. The Atlantic and Pacific offered to give its competitor a half interest in the depot and to divide equally proceeds from all the lands acquired by both companies.[32] In December the M. K. & T. countered by making a determined attempt to buy a majority of the A. & P. securities.[33] Neither plan worked, and until an agreement was reached in March 1872[34] passengers boarding the Atlantic and Pacific at Vinita added their complaints to those of Missouri farmers and Cherokee chiefs.

But while the railroad found the new decade full of new problems, it also had competent minds to deal with them. One of the most creative of these was Joseph Seligman, a wealthy Jewish banker who sat on the board of directors and whose firm, J. & W. Seligman and Company, had been selling South Pacific bonds in Europe since 1869.[35]

Seligman had come to the United States from Bavaria in 1837, made a fortune in the dry goods business, and become prominent as one of the reformers that ousted the Tweed ring in New York.[36] He had large investments in the Pacific of Missouri and the Missouri, Kansas and Texas, as well as the South Pacific and Atlantic and Pacific, and he thought of his whole portfolio as a "consortium" which should ideally be operated as a unit.[37] His first action upon being elected to the Atlantic and Pacific board of directors on March 8, 1870, was to arrange the merger with the South Pacific, and it was he who was behind-the-scenes manager in the 1871 negotiations to merge the A. & P. and the M. K. & T.[38] His New York office, where cablegrams were sent and received concerning the European sale of the South Pacific bonds (code-named "Southerly"), became the unofficial headquarters of the Atlantic and Pacific.[39] Seligman had demanded a place on the board of directors of the A. & P. as a condition of his bank's handling of that company's securities.[40] He felt that the best guarantee for his firm's investment was his own personal direction of the affairs of the corporations involved. This attitude made him one of the first practitioners of finance capitalism, a method which, according to most historians, had its origin with J. P. Morgan in the 1890s.

Seligman had three creative ideas about how best to free the thirty-fifth parallel project from the financial ruin facing it as a result of the Indian Territory difficulty and the consequent inability of the company to build its Central Division or to sell its Central Division Land Grant Bonds. First, an appeal for financial aid should be made to San Francisco, where citizens were complaining about the Central Pacific–Southern Pacific monopoly as loudly as Missourians complained about the South Pacific–Atlantic and Pacific cartel. Second, the road should extend its rate monopoly in Southwest Missouri by leasing the Pacific of Missouri. Third, these stratagems should be used to attract one of the large capital pools of the East to invest in the line, possibly with the hope of an exclusive traffic exchange for an eastern trunk line. The years between 1872 and 1875 were spent experimenting with Seligman's suggestions.

An editorial in a January 1872 issue of the *San Francisco Chronicle* was encouraging. It was idle, wrote the editor, for San Francisco to think about controlling the trade of China if the goods were subject to the extraordinary delay caused by the snow blockades on the Central and Union Pacific transcontinental. St. Louis and San Francisco were interested alike, though for different reasons, in the completion of a road on the thirty-fifth parallel. The mayors and councils of the two cities should get together and discuss the matter.[41]

The A. & P. had already been at work in St. Louis. Joseph Brown, the mayor of that city, was also president of the Pacific of Missouri thanks to Seligman, who saw the value of keeping him in that position, despite the mayor's constant complaints of too much railroad work and too little salary. The New York banker realized, as some others interested in the "consortium" did not, that Brown's political influence in St. Louis was worth enough to the railroads to pay for frequent raises in his salary. In February 1872 Seligman sweetened his relationship with the city fathers by offering to take a sizable issue of St. Louis municipal water bonds.[42] The same month, the St. Louis Board of Trade, in response to pressure from Brown, petitioned Congress to ratify the A. & P. land grant in Indian Territory, and made speeches in the Mercantile Library rooms more favorable to the project than any heard in St. Louis before.[43] Brown told the gathering that he had been a friend of the Negro and the Indian, but was a better friend of the white man.[44]

In response to Brown's contention that his salary should be brought in line with Boston officers Peirce and Hayes, Seligman wrote that he felt satisfied the directors would grant him a "reasonable increase" provided he could influence the people of St. Louis to join with San Francisco citizens in providing a subsidy adequate to market an A. & P. bond "at fair prices" in the Seligman's European branches.[45] Brown's salary was raised several times from the original sum of $5,000, and Hayes gave him a $25,000 interest in the Atlantic and Pacific.[46] In a private letter to Peirce, Seligman admitted that Brown "is probably no expert R.R. man," but held that his political influence in St. Louis was vital, especially if the San Francisco scheme worked and if the A. & P. lobby could press a bill through Congress extending the time for completion of the thirty-fifth parallel line. Peirce was advised to do twenty-five miles of cheap grading in Indian Territory "to keep the charter alive" in the hope that either the time extension bill or a bill making the Indian domain a United States territory would be passed:

> The grading could be done for a small sum, although we have not even the small sum to spare but the Iron will be the great trouble. The road still owes me a deal of money, nothing can be done at present with the A. & P. Land Grant Bonds, and a good deal of money will have to be raised on the 1st of May & 1st of July to pay interest.[47]

Seligman did not let temporary financial setbacks throw his plans awry. South Pacific bonds were quoted in 1872 at six and a quarter cents on the dollar, but Seligman thought that was due to problems in his English house over the diplomatic crisis of the Alabama claims; he would not sell them at less than eighty-seven.[48] When the road hardly had money for a few miles of construction or to pay interest, Seligman made loans to it regularly, and he recommended that Brown's salary be upped to $10,000 even though Peirce and Hayes were against it.[49]

There was great hope that the prospects of the behind-the-scenes "consortium" under the control of the Seligman Brothers in New York, Paris, Frankfort, and London, would be far better than the public outlook for the Atlantic and Pacific Railroad Company, Francis B. Hayes, president. Peirce, then general manager of both the Pacific of Missouri and the A. & P., reported that earnings were increasing, and the New York firm of J. & W. Seligman wrote to its German branch in March that "we shall probably join both of these together before long to save the expense of a double management."[50] Joseph Seligman requested from Fisk some sketches which he promised to include in a pamphlet printed by the banking firm; also in the pamphlet were "some good letters from Governors and Mayors &c which would help the sale of the Bond."[51] Seligman was offered all the A. & P. preferred stock he wanted at fifteen cents. But his offer to the seller to pay a good bonus to be allowed to call at twenty even if certain bills passed Congress was declined.[52]

In April, the New York bank got the word from its San Francisco branch that the California city was ready to grant a subsidy to the Atlantic and Pacific. Joseph Seligman wrote to Hayes and Peirce as well as to several other Boston investors asking them, possibly accompanied by Mayor Brown and Clinton Fisk, to travel to the coast and close the deal. "A subsidy of four or five millions of City Bonds would enable us to prosecute our road to Albuquerque or near there; would enable us to market an Atlantic & Pacific Bond; and in time the valuable tracts of land in the Indian Territory would be sure to fall into our lap."[53]

Hayes wrote to the Interior Department to check on the right of the company to construct its line as filed to San Francisco, this in order to protect the proposed large outlay of capital in California "which its stock holders would not wish to jeopardize."[54] He also asked for a liberal interpretation of sections eight and nine of the 1866 land grant act, regarding speed of completion.[55]

C. J. Hillyer, more optimistic yet about prospects in San Francisco, asked the secretary of the interior to authorize and withdraw lands for a branch from the Canadian River to Van Buren, Arkansas. This route had been specifically mentioned in Hillyer's pamphlet and in the land grant act, but was specifically prohibited by the Cherokee treaty.[56] The Cherokee delegation inquired where the "public lands" to be withdrawn were located.[57] Yet the acting secretary of the interior approved in principle the requests of both Hayes and Hillyer and wrote a letter to the Indians stating that land for the branch line would be withdrawn entirely in Arkansas.[58] It appeared that the railroad's transcontinental dreams were being revived.

On April 26, 1872, the A. & P. delegation arrived in San Francisco. Joseph Brown was among them as well as Fisk, Peirce, Hayes, and Secretary of the Interior Columbus Delano. After some argument as to whether an independent road should be encouraged or the A. & P. should buy the Southern Pacific, the St. Louis and San Francisco delegations agreed that San Francisco should subscribe fifteen million dollars of A. & P. stock and place several directors on the board, provided that a California inspection team approved of the company's progress.[59] The

A. & P. directors already had examined the route in California and driven survey stakes up the rich inland valleys from the thirty-fifth parallel to the great western port.[60] Seligman wrote to his London office: "We shall shortly have a Bond to propose to you which will equal the Central Pacific, only at a lower price."[61]

Collis Huntington, president of the Southern Pacific, worked against completion of the California deal. He was thought to be behind the San Francisco and Colorado railroad which built east with the purpose of preempting the A. & P. route. Yet opinion in Missouri was that victory on the California front was won and that San Francisco and St. Louis would build the thirty-fifth parallel road when the "plausible sophistry" of Huntington's "ring of monopolists" was exposed.[62]

Seligman therefore launched phase two of his plan. Two weeks before the delegation arrived on the coast, he made final arrangements with Andrew Peirce concerning the proper amount the Atlantic and Pacific should pay for a lease of the Pacific of Missouri, in order to "do justice to every body, both members of the pool & outsiders."[63] The lease, drawn June 19, 1872, was a mistake from the beginning. The Atlantic and Pacific stockholders had controlled the securities of the Pacific, and for all practical purposes its management, since February 1871.[64] By leasing the road, they acquired also its financial and physical liabilities.

Most of the Pacific of Missouri line had been cheaply built during the Civil War in order to reach Kansas City as soon as possible. In 1872, the physical plant was in deplorable condition: new ties were needed throughout; of sixty-nine bridges, twenty-three had to be replaced immediately; old iron cut in odd lengths had been used over much of the route; and of ninety-seven locomotives, twenty-nine were in "fair" shape, fifty needed general overhaul, four had never been converted from wide gauge, and fourteen were worthless.[65] Yet the lease agreement stipulated that the Atlantic and Pacific guaranteed dividends on the Pacific's share capital of 5 per cent the first three years, 6 per cent for two more years, and 7 per cent for the remaining 994 years of the lease.[66]

Two subscription circulars were quickly published by the A. & P. The first, October 14, 1871, sold bonds with a par value of $4,046,000 for $1,400,000 cash, an average price of thirty-four; the second, June 18, 1873, yielded $1,055,000 cash for $3,192,500 par value in securities. This debt was added to the increase of $10,028,519 in A. & P. outstanding securities issued only two years earlier as the result of the assumption of the liabilities of the South Pacific (which included those of Fremont's old Southwest Pacific).[67] "It will be observed," Peirce reported in 1873, "that the floating debt of the Company is inconveniently large."[68]

The lease arrangement, which allowed the A. & P., by means of discriminatory rates at the Pacific railroad station at Sedalia, to cut off the access of the Missouri, Kansas and Texas to St. Louis, made the opposition of that road more bitter. General Manager Robert Stevens was convinced that it would be easier to "checkmate" the Pacific–Atlantic and Pacific monopoly by throwing suspicion on its financial structure in Wall Street circles than for his railroad to build an independent line to St. Louis.[69] A month before the formal lease had been drawn up, Seligman warned Brown to pay no attention to offers of consolidation with the M. K. & T., "who will not give up the control of their road to any one altho they would probably not object to control the entire network of lines to Kansas as well as to the Pacific."

Seligman felt "sanguine" that the lease would sell fifty million dollars in A. & P. securities on the European market at ninety cents, could put an army of men on various parts of the line, and "start the ball, before Tom Scott working on the thirty-second parallel and others take the wind out of our sails."[70] It did not work. The committee from San Francisco was against the lease and asked that it be delayed. When this was refused the committee withdrew the promise of aid on which the new combination had depended.[71] Also, Seligman's ideal of "peace & harmony" within the directorate was upset when a number of influential Boston directors refused to support the lease on the ground that it was illegal without specific legislation, and that it increased the liabilities of the line to an unacceptable extent.[72] The New York papers notified Wall Street investors that the lease was far beyond the authority of the thirty-fifth parallel company.[73] To complete the misfire, the Southern Pacific made a serious effort to force the Interior Department to disallow the A. & P. California Survey altogether.[74]

The winter of 1872–73 was a dark time. Seligman's third idea, that of attracting a large eastern investor, was tried by bringing in Alden Stockwell, president of the Pacific Mail Steamship Company, and known Wall Street gambler, as president of the A. & P.[75] That raised the quotation on the securities temporarily from twenty-five to thirty-five cents.[76] But Stockwell was a lightweight, not the man at all Seligman had wanted. He was made president partly because he agreed to take thirty thousand shares of Pacific stock at twenty-five cents and an option on a new Atlantic and Pacific bond issue.[77] Construction came to an absolute halt that winter.[78] A horse disease often caused the line to stop receiving freight orders,[79] passengers were forced to take a cattle train west out of Vinita because the A. & P. missed connections with the M. K. & T. passenger train by over an hour,[80] crews complained that brakemen nearly froze due to a senseless order that they ride on top of the cars, and conductors often came in battered from their attempts to collect fares in the hard times of 1873.[81]

Only a few years earlier Stockwell had been the proprietor of a livery stable in Cleveland. He had married the daughter of Elias Howe, inventor of the sewing machine. He had gained control of the Pacific Mail Steamship Company and the A. & P. railroad, using sewing-machine funds recklessly on Wall Street.[82] He was, however, no Daniel Drew or Jay Gould, nor was the A. & P. the Union Pacific. The treasurer of the Atlantic and Pacific reported in March 1873 that Stockwell had lost about $4,000,000 of his own money and that A. & P. stock was selling as low as twenty cents. Though the treasurer claimed that Stockwell "has not lost all his money or any of his pluck," Seligman began desperately to look elsewhere for salvation.[83]

In August 1873 Thomas Scott, one of the original incorporators, took the presidency of the company.[84] Scott was the darling of the investment group backing the Pennsylvania railroad, held a large interest in the Texas and Pacific, and had recently sold a large stake in the Union Pacific to Jay Gould.[85] He was in 1871 president of five roads, vice-president of twelve, director of thirty-three, and "general consolidator of the balance." He kept four secretaries busy looking after his varied transportation and manufacturing interests. One western paper claimed that he "finds relaxation in running the Pennsylvania and Virginia legislatures, and finds entire repose in directing Congress, the president, and the supreme bench."[86] Eastern papers referred to him as the "Pennsylvania Napoleon" and feared that the "boa constrictor" of Pennsylvania Railroad Company interests was "ambitious to take possession of the Republic on a nine hundred and ninety nine years' lease."[87]

It was not long, however, before Scott became thoroughly tired of leases, particularly that of the Pacific of Missouri. The Pacific was tediously overcapitalized,[88] and the Atlantic and Pacific, which was supposed to guarantee its securities, was itself involved in a court battle over its default on the last six years' interest due to the Fremont group holding Southwest Pacific bonds.[89] Bonds of the combined system did not sell better due to the lease. So many were dumped on the relatively naïve German market that the *New York Times* commented that if the tide of empire should shift to St. Louis, the ideas of government found there would not be American.[90] About five German families a day were located on A. & P. lands. Meanwhile, a San Francisco company, organized to connect with the A. & P. and backed by city bonds, collapsed because of investor doubts about the future of the A. & P.[91]

Jay Cooke and Company closed its doors in the fall of 1873, setting off a national financial panic. Pennsylvania capitalists thereafter took a conservative turn[92] and withdrew their agent, Scott, from the management of the thirty-fifth parallel route in August 1874. Peirce became president.[93] The third section of Seligman's plan, attraction of new outside capital, had failed. Even Scott, who had always been "as cheerful as a robin in May,"[94] must have changed his expression as railroad corporations were blamed for the panic. "There is no reason in the world," noted a Springfield paper, "why the entire industrial and commercial prosperity of a great portion of our country should for a day be jeopardized to enable these railroad cormorants to fatten their bloated corporations and innundate the purlieus of Wall Street with their dirty waterings."[95] As though to highlight the confusion, an Atlantic and Pacific and a Pacific passenger train collided: the engines telescoped, children screamed, men turned pale, and a woman with a bottle of brandy moved through the cars, tearing up undergarments for bandages, and presiding, as it were, over the ruin of an idea.[96]

The reaction of Fisk and Peirce to the continuing crises was to supply the road with a constant stream of pipe dreams. A New York reporter was treated to a trip to end-of-track in May 1873. He was told that the A. & P. was contemplating a branch from Independence to Memphis called the Memphis, Carthage and Northwestern.[97] In truth, only twenty-seven miles of it had been finished, and that only because Joseph Seligman had adopted the short line as a personal hobby. He advanced the branch money[98] and even bought it an engine named the "Seligman."[99] Yet Seligman could not convince his Paris office that the M. C. & N. W. was not a "gigantic wild scheme," nor did others believe him when he told them that the certificate resting in his safe for sixty thousand shares of an A. & P. branch line would "probably have a value in a few years."[100] By October 1874 Judge Baker, installed as Memphis, Carthage and Northwestern president, had to announce that the line had gone to the receivers, even though all its officers served without pay, and a room was kindly provided by the A. & P. for board meetings.[101] Yet to the eastern reporter, the picture was painted in rosy colors. Fisk, Seligman, and the reporter rode down the twenty-seven-mile line on the cowcatcher of an A. & P. engine at sixty miles per hour; horses bolted, farmers cursed, and a duck landed in an excursionist's lap. When it was over, Fisk had to be "soothed with cocktails."[102] It was a great lark, this railroad business.

Seligman, however, wore a forced smile. He did not have the comfort of believing, like Fisk, that the locomotive was bringing Christian civilization despite its inglorious balance sheet, and he was on the paying rather than the receiving end of Peirce's enormous salary and the huge advances necessary to build branch lines when the main line was insolvent. Peirce predicted in 1873 that the road would be making profits by 1874, and projected a $3.6 million a year profit by 1880.[103] In 1874, he maintained that the A. & P. exhibit compared favorably with those of the early years of the Illinois Central.[104] Seligman felt otherwise. He had a $150,000 investment in A. & P. bonds and the road owed him $300,000 in advances, secured by South Pacific and Atlantic and Pacific bonds "which our wiseacres cannot sell." Granted that his house had made a fortune in new railroads, Seligman promised his European branches in 1872 to get out of his western railroad projects as soon as possible and to "be satisfied hereafter with a balance sheet of one third the size as last years."[105]

> Experience has taught me that Am.R.R.s . . . extend and expand too fast, taking every dollar of earnings & proceeds of loans to branch out into new lines & new schemes, and while ultimately the great majority of RRs will pay dividends . . . the Banker issuing a loan is morally drawn in by degrees to lend large sums ostensibly to protect the coupons, but actually to extend the line. . . . I presume that in the end we shall make a profit on every investment thus made, but I see that the prospective & uncertain profit does not compensate for the risk, the anxiety, the inconvenience, the loss of time & temper, and I am determined to quit it.[106]

Although Seligman believed the A. & P. securities were "intrinsically good," he complained that his railroads were continuously wanting money and "managers are envious and do not work in accord." One of the greatest troubles with new roads was "that once you go in at all it is almost impossible to refrain from going in deeper." Joseph deeply believed that there would be a "turn in the tide ere long" but that conviction, which kept a member of his family on the board of the thirty-fifth parallel project until the 1890s, did not dampen the effect of his wavering at the critical moment in the seventies.[107] In August 1872 his nephew, Ignatz Steinhart, accepted a position as treasurer of the A. & P. without consulting his uncle. Joseph wrote him that in so doing he had compromised the house:

> You are playing with edged tools you know. . . . I don't intend
> to let it cost us one Dollar. . . . Whatever the Prest. or Secrty
> may swear to is nothing improper or incorrect. . . . I will not
> have it. . . . I was offered the Vice Prescy or the Treasurership
> of the A. & P. . . . but declined all . . . office as they are only a
> trouble . . . without proportionate pay.[108]

In October 1872 Jesse Seligman, Joseph's brother, went to Missouri with a number of eastern men "trying to get them interested with us in the MoPac and the A. & P., so as to enable us to withdraw . . . $800,000 of . . . capital locked up in these 2 concerns."[109] In Missouri, this and similar events in years following were known as the "Millionaire Excursions." One of the members of the 1875 group was Edward Winslow, who in less than ten years would be president of a new thirty-fifth parallel company, still taking orders from Joseph Seligman.[110] In 1874, however, all of Seligman's cards had been played and had failed to take a trick. His temporary withdrawal of active support, the continued complaints of farmers through their new Grange organization about taxes, rates, and towns, the intransigence of the Indian tribes, the failure of the San Francisco scheme, the failure of the lease, and the effects of a financial panic, placed the Atlantic and Pacific in deep difficulty, from which it could not emerge intact.

THE ST. LOUIS AND SAN FRANCISCO RAILWAY COMPANY

On November 3, 1875, receivers were appointed for the Atlantic and Pacific Railroad Company.[1] The defaults on interest payments which led to this situation were inevitable when in 1875 the final news arrived of the complete failure of all the road's schemes to revitalize itself as an aspirant transcontinental trunk line. There was in 1875 a St. Louis convention and a memorial by Peirce and Thomas Scott to the Congress. Both tried to convince the United States to give bond aid to a Texas and Pacific–Atlantic and Pacific combine; both failed.[2]

Also, an Interior Department official threw even graver doubts than existed on the right of the road to its California land grant, even if it could reach the coast to claim it. The A. & P., he wrote, was granted no land by Congress for building through California to San Francisco, and any interpretation of the 1866 act by railroad officials to the contrary was incorrect: "It could as well be extended to Portland Oregon, or to Puget Sound."[3] Congress was pressing the General Land Office to go even further, and to force the A. & P. to forfeit *all* its unpatented lands along the thirty-fifth parallel.[4] This and the financial difficulty of the road benefited the Southern Pacific and pleased its president, C. P. Huntington, immensely. "I could get control of the Atlantic and P. R.R. at a very small cost," Huntington wrote in December 1875, "but do we want it as a gift?"[5]

The perennial local problems of the A. & P. pursued it with a special vengeance when the beast was helpless, frustrated in its broader aims. Farmers were advised to pay no more than the three cents a mile passenger rate lately set by the new Missouri Board of Railway Commissioners. If the conductor demanded more, they were to refuse and accuse him of assault if they were put off the train. The fines for freight and passenger rate violations would go to the school fund, to which it was expected the A. & P. would contribute significantly. Although the state board was weak and could prosecute cases only through county attorneys, to the farmers it was a symbol of reform.[6]

Indian problems also remained. The *New York Times* editorialized late in 1874 that the A. & P. was more interested in securing a land subsidy in the Indian Territory than extending its line beyond that country.[7] Perhaps, given the circumstances to which the road was reduced, that observation was correct. The Cherokee delegation in Washington successfully vetoed bills which would have allowed the railroad to change its east-west route in order to divert south and join Scott on the thirty-second parallel, and at the same time argued that the A. & P. land grant was void due to an expired time allowance for construction.[8] The territorial bills introduced for the Indian Territory, were, according to the Chickasaw lobby, promoted by "a few misled or deluded individuals . . . subsidized and corrupted by the Atlantic and Pacific . . . , against which we have been compelled from year to year to fight for our property right in our lands and for our very national existence."

Clinton Fisk, an A. & P. officer and head of the Board of Indian Commissioners, especially galled the tribes. The board had been appointed by the Quaker Indian administration favored by Grant. These men found in Fisk the perfect combination of piety on the one hand, and on the other unrelenting zeal for the promotion of industrial civilization. When Fisk proclaimed, as a member of the board, that territorial government for the Indian domain was an "immediate necessity,"[9] it raised the Indians to a fever pitch of vexation. They advised congressmen to look in the U.S. statutes under railroad land grants, and there would be found "a key by which you may unlock the motives and con-

sciences . . . of those who are pleading humanity in order to destroy us."
One delegation compared Fisk and the railroad, with their promises of
prosperity, to Satan tempting Jesus in the wilderness: "All these things
will I give thee if thou wilt fall down and worship me" (Matthew 4:9).[10]

The immediate cause of bankruptcy, however, was the lease of the
Pacific; this had been Seligman's least wise decision. While the A. & P.
directors authorized a new branch for the Pacific to connect St. Louis
with a suburb via scenic Creve Coeur Lake, debts on the main line
mounted.[11] Stock of the Pacific fell from a quotation of 55 in April
1875, to 7½ in October; by September 1876, it sold for 1½. The third
mortgage bondholders charged the A. & P. with extravagance and fraud
in the operation of the leased line. The Pacific, they claimed, was being
run by men with no financial interest in it, and was being robbed
mechanically and financially in favor of the A. & P.[12]

In the fall of 1875, the Pacific stockholders met in New York several
times with the directors of the A. & P.[13] Peirce could and did argue
accurately that the A. & P. had advanced the Pacific over $3,500,000 since
1872 for construction and improvements, of which only $2,900,000 had
been repaid.[14] The Pacific stockholders countered that Peirce held
$1,800,000 in Pacific bonds as security for this debt and was using these to
raise money for the A. & P.[15] At one meeting Fisk unsuccessfully defended the railroad against charges that it had made no attempt to pay
back taxes.[16]

Early in November came demands for the resignation of the board
of directors and an audit of the accounts; Peirce and Fisk began at this
point to decline invitations to stockholders' meetings.[17] To Peirce's argument that the shaky finances were due to the effect of grasshoppers on
grain traffic, the aroused stockholders replied that it was "not at all likely
that these pests had eaten up the road by taking breakfast on sleeping
coaches and dining off locomotives."[18] For this they blamed Peirce, Fisk,
and the rest of the A. & P. crowd. The Pacific investors demanded and
got a termination of the lease and the appointment of separate receivers
for their line, shortly to emerge as the Missouri Pacific.[19]

The Atlantic and Pacific directorate, after the lapse into receivership
in November 1875, moved to create a new corporate structure which
could claim the old A. & P. franchise and land grant while at the same
time freeing itself from that corporation's liabilities. In May 1876 Boston
capitalist Oliver Ames, the A. & P.'s largest stockholder, aided finances by
purchasing 96,697 acres of the road's Missouri lands.[20] That same month,
the second largest stockholder, Joseph Seligman, wrote letters to the

directors in Boston and New York advising them that an informal committee which he headed wished to lay before the bondholders a plan for "reconstruction" of the A. & P. railroad, and were awaiting only the receivers' accounts from St. Louis regarding the road's debts.[21] In June the circuit court at St. Louis issued a decree of foreclosure and ordered the Missouri Division of the A. & P. sold. Peirce, Seligman, Coffin, James Fish, and James P. Robinson were appointed by the Seligman committee to buy the road for the bondholders and to organize a new corporation.[22] Coffin wrote hurriedly to Uriel Crocker in Boston asking him to come to New York right away "to help *us make figures*."[23]

Crocker was hesitant. He suggested reduction of capital stock. But Robinson was unyielding in his belief that all the managers should yield their convictions about what would be best for them as bondholders in order to support Peirce's plan for further expansion. Peirce, Robinson wrote, deserved the confidence of the more conservative investors in the matter of reorganization because he had been "captain" of the group since he came to Missouri to reorganize Fremont's venture and make the South Pacific a success, all the while "sustained and activated by the utmost integrity of purpose." Peirce had sold large amounts of stock to those who believed his optimistic stories about reorganization. He told the stockholders: "Carry out our programme as now determined upon and it will be the first time in a *wrecked* Railroad, where its officers showed no partiality in endeavoring to save those who were on board."[24] Ames, Seligman, and Crocker, the three largest stockholders, must have quivered at that, but Peirce, the fourth largest, was also risking his own fortune in deciding to continue pursuit of the thirty-fifth parallel dream.[25] Robinson, who had no investment, could only note, "A good deal to say ain't it?"[26]

In August, Crocker gave to Fisk his qualified acceptance of the new scheme, thus risking a little more of the capital he had made over the years as a publisher. He asked only that the new corporation could sustain itself, and warned that as long as stock was issued so rapidly that it sold for only a few cents a share, no bank or monied institution would want to give the company a loan. "I have my fears—my doubts. . . . Twenty millions of stock selling at twenty five cents on a Dollar per share, will injure the credit of any corporation."[27] Yet on September 1, 1876, the reorganization committee voted on a plan. The *Railroad Gazette* reported with tongue in cheek that "the new company is to be called the St. Louis & San Francisco Railway Company—because, perhaps, it has no terminus in either city."[28]

September 8, 1876, was a hot day, especially so at the east front of the courthouse in St. Louis—where the foreclosure sale of the Atlantic and Pacific was held. The square block bounded by Chestnut, Market, Fourth, and Fifth Streets was filled with spectators, most attracted by idle curiosity to see the eastern railway magnates bid in one of the largest auctions ever held in Missouri. Present were Peirce, Seligman, Coffin, Fisk, Robinson, and other A. & P. directors, all looking calm "indicating that the programme had been satisfactorily arranged and that the track was clear of obstruction." While the lengthy, dull court foreclosure decree was read (which took forty minutes by the town clock), Fisk cracked jokes. A woman on other business pushed up to the auctioneer, listened for fifteen minutes, then loudly proclaimed: "Arrah, I've heard enough of that story anyway." But the auctioneer when he had finished the decree launched into a speech of his own which contained the comment that the line when completed to San Francisco would be "the most magnificent property on the globe—the Suez Canal not excepted." The temperature meanwhile had risen into the nineties; all were glad to see the bidding begin.[29]

The A. & P. group was calm. Two days before at a similar auction Peirce had outbid local investors and bought the Pacific of Missouri, renamed Missouri Pacific, for $3,000,000. His performance then was described by one reporter as possessing "the coolness and sang-froid of a jockey at a race course pool auction." With the chance to buy the A. & P. also and thus to reestablish the complete consortium empire as it existed in 1872, he was not about to make a false move this day.[30] "With a protracted smile," he spoke: "I'll give you 25,000. . . ." The auctioneer scowled. Peirce pulled on his cigar to indicate $35,000. Then William Buckley, another A. & P. director bid $50,000, after which he and Fisk proceeded to play the game by bidding against each other up to $450,000. The auctioneer indicated that he thought that was "a mighty small bid." They all waited, sweating in the sun, for a raise, but silence reigned. The gavel came down.

In a negotiation the night before with St. Louis capitalist Commodore C. K. Garrison, the A. & P. group had prearranged the lack of competition at the September 8 auction. Garrison was promised that he would be allowed to form a separate directorate for the Missouri Pacific provided he promise to operate it for "the mutual benefit" of its own and A. & P. investors, and provided he make no attempt to outbid Peirce at the upcoming sale.[31] This move was to satisfy the aggressive Pacific bondholders who raised cries of "monopoly" at first news of the Missouri

Pacific sale to Peirce. Garrison was able to tell those who charged that the sales simply recreated the old lease situation under a new corporate guise that he had "saved them from . . . a great wrong" by repurchasing the line from the A. & P. group. Garrison was serenaded at the Lindell Hotel in St. Louis and splashed with champagne by commuters who rode the Missouri Pacific while the Arsenal band played.[32]

A few Pacific bondholders, however, were poor sports and instituted a suit to resist these arrangements. One of these, doubting Garrison's statement that the Missouri Pacific was free of A. & P. influence, sent a hot telegram to the commodore: "We will insist that you keep your agreement with us. It looks very much like collusion between you and Peirce."[33] Garrison and Peirce were properly indignant at this, but the fact remained that 97 per cent of the bonds of the two roads were held by a common group of capitalists.[34] While the lines later grew apart, it is probable that the situation in late 1876 was exactly as the Missouri Pacific bondholders assessed it: a recreation of the lease of 1872 without that document's promises of dividends for the 3 per cent of the securities outside the "consortium" pool.

The night excursions on the road that autumn, when men hung on the engines and tenders carrying torches, were ostensibly to rally support for presidential candidate Rutherford Hayes, or to celebrate the hundredth anniversary of the nation.[35] These torchlight parades, however, must also have celebrated the birth of a new enterprise and the revitalization of the thirty-fifth parallel hope which Fremont ignited. Men still filled the centers of their wool sacks with feathers to avoid the higher rates for shipping the feathers,[36] but the St. Louis and San Francisco (or Frisco, as it was soon nicknamed) enjoyed from the start a better reputation than its predecessor. This was partly due to the popularity of the new superintendent, Charles Rogers, the man who represented the company in the minds of most along the line.[37] Local newspapers directed their editorials against the company attorneys rather than the operating managers. The attorneys, wrote the editors, sought trouble in order to keep their jobs and "represent a raw-head and bloody bones when there is in reality nothing to disturb the equanimity of anybody."[38] John O'Day, a pugnacious Irishman appointed to help Judge Baker with the legal business of the road, was as unpopular as Rogers was popular.[39]

Fisk, always the optimist, was positive of success this time. Late in September, he assured Crocker that "there is not the slightest ripple on the waters." He dismissed the suit of the Missouri Pacific bondholders lightly, and called those opposing the gentlemen's agreement with the

Missouri Pacific "wreckers." Any allegation that "the Commodore and Andrew were in collusion playing some sort of a *Heathen Chinee* game" might be bothersome, but not dangerous. All that remained was court confirmation of the sale of the A. & P. to the Frisco, after which "the new *volumes* of stationery will be issued in place of the dead past."[40]

William Coffin was more cautious in his report to Crocker in October. He reported that the Missouri Pacific stockholders might appeal to the U.S. Supreme Court (they did), and that assessments of 5 per cent on the "blue Back" bonds were necessary to get the road out of debt. But Coffin's promises of a new financial scheme probably did not appeal to Crocker.[41] Peirce still sat in the president's office at Number 3 Broad Street, New York, still drew his large salary, and still clung to his grandiose plans to tap the Indies trade. That dream was more powerful than the proposals of the large investors, and they always yielded to it in the end.

The first Frisco board meeting on September 11 authorized the president to buy the road from William Buckley, who had won the bidding contest with Fisk.[42] At the second meeting, held the next morning, it was resolved that since the Frisco had purchased only the Missouri Division of the A. & P. and since it was desirable to maintain that road's franchise and land grant, the president should be empowered to purchase a controlling interest in the Central Division of the A. & P. (Seneca to Vinita, thirty-seven miles) through a stock exchange.[43] Thus there would exist thirty-seven miles of road with the corporate name Atlantic and Pacific which technically could claim the entire land grant made to it in 1866 even though it was the puppet of a new corporation. This matter was accomplished with dispatch, for it had all been prearranged. Early in October, a special committee of directors was appointed to renew the old task of opening the Indian Territory to railroads and settlement. Heading the committee was Joseph Seligman, who had convinced his European houses to give the thirty-fifth parallel project another chance.[44]

Through the winter of 1876–77 an honest effort was made at reform. The president's salary was set at a relatively modest $12,000, Frisco stocks and bonds were placed on the New York Stock Exchange in the hope of creating an American market for them,[45] a traffic contract was negotiated with the Missouri, Kansas and Texas line, and the company put up new and substantial hotels at Vinita[46] and North Springfield, the latter by then a town of fifteen hundred. People flocked to North Springfield to take jobs in the large machine shops built there to function as the mechanical and operating center of the railroad. A car shop went up, then a paint shop, an oil house, a brass foundry, an ice house, a coal chute, and pleasant dormitories for the employees. It was said that by Christmas of its first year, the Frisco could build an engine or car complete except for heavy castings at its North Springfield shops. Said a Springfield paper: "Ever since the management of the road passed into the hands of Capt. C. B [sic] Rogers . . . familiarly known all along the line as Charley Rogers, a feeling of friendship toward it has been gradually but surely supplanting the enmity which existed under the former management. . . ."[47]

Charles Rogers, unlike other officers of the line, was a resident of Missouri and had gained practical railroading experience by working his way up through the ranks of the organization he now managed. At fifteen he had run away to sea and at thirty was the owner of a merchant vessel sailing from Boston,[48] and he served in the Union Navy during the war as master of the *Hydrangea,* an ironclad. But when he came west in 1871 the "Captain" started at the bottom, as tie agent for the Atlantic and Pacific.[49] His experience as tie agent, then purchasing agent, gave Rogers a kind of tact at public relations which his predecessors as general superintendent had not possessed, and his full sideburns added a look of distinction.

This combination of years of practical railroad experience and a natural felicity with words was especially useful to the Frisco in handling Indian claims against the A. & P. One of Rogers's 1877 letters to a Quapaw Indian agent survives, outlining the road's determination not to pay for hogs killed by its engines which in most cases was "entirely unavoidable," and called for "mutual forbearance on the part of Indians and railroad officials."[50] In 1879, he wrote concerning a dead horse:

> As prices on all kinds of stock are now very low (I have myself a horse of good stock, broken in for driving in *the City* for which I paid $90.00 only within a few months) I fail to understand on what ground a horse out in the territory should be valued as high as $125.00. We are willing to do what is right, but object to paying any fancy values. We have offered Mr. Harris $50.00 in full settlement and can do no better unless fully and reliably informed of reasons and circumstances why it should be done.[51]

A class of managers on a par with Rogers appeared from top Frisco officials on down—busy, efficient, friendly. The chief ticket agent, Dempster Wishart, had attended business college in his Canadian homeland, had been in railway service since 1867, and had been with the line since he signed on with the South Pacific as telegraph operator at Rolla in 1869.[52] John O'Day of Limerick, Ireland, had a reputation as one of the outstanding trial lawyers in the Southwest, and had practiced in Springfield since 1865. He was for years chairman of the Missouri state Democratic central committee, and his political power was so great that it led to charges of conflict of interest and demands that he resign from his job as Frisco attorney.[53] A visitor to the Frisco general offices in St. Louis in 1878 was impressed. "This proposed trans-continental high way for commerce in many respects is the most important road St. Louis has," he wrote. The officers he met (Baker, Rogers, Wishart, and Coffin) were men with whom it was "an absolute pleasure to come in contact," and who freely predicted "the near dawn of a new empire."[54]

The company was generous to its customers. In 1877 it furnished rails for a fence around the company stock pond at Rolla and opened it for public use,[55] employing in part profits from 2,855 head of cattle, 4,372 head of sheep, and 3,475 hogs shipped from that village alone in 1876.[56] For the employees, however, there was some belt-tightening. In the first two years of the new company's existence, land department salaries and expenses were cut drastically,[57] John O'Day's urgent request for a salary hike was denied,[58] wages for general employees were cut across the board,[59] and the rent for the Frisco offices in rooms 85, 86, 87 of the Drexel Building in New York was reduced by subletting one room to the Atwood Car Wheel Company for nearly half the cost of three.[60]

This general salary cut combined with the institution of a strict voucher system[61] reformed the directorate quickly. Fisk resigned quietly as director in December 1876.[62] Then Peirce, who had earlier exposed Fisk, was himself exposed. In September 1877 an audit of the books by Judge Baker revealed that the president had been raking off amounts of A. & P. and Frisco profits for his personal use that made him at least the equal of Fisk in chicanery.[63] When Peirce returned $114,000 of his winnings at the corporate game and after "a long matured deliberation" tendered his resignation, Baker, promising to "do his duty," was elected vice-president,[64] and very shortly (December 1877) president.[65] Peirce retained $76,500 in bonds which, despite resolutions by the board, he never returned.[66] "While this Board exonerates Mr. Peirce from any dishonest intentions," read the minutes, "it does not approve of the settlement of Mr. Peirce's account in the manner he has done."[67] It is significant that by this time Peirce's salary as president had been reduced to $10,000, a far cry from his $25,000 stipend in the speculative days of the South Pacific.[68] Perhaps he could no longer afford honesty.

The purge was healthy. When railroads across the nation cut wages in 1877, it resulted in one of the most destructive strikes in labor history. In St. Louis that summer Baker and Rogers could look from the windows of the Frisco ticket office and watch marching railroad employees singing the *Marseillaise,* waving coupling pins and red signal flags, and chanting Communist slogans. Two Gatling guns were set up at St. Louis Union Station and six carloads of troops were necessary to control the strikers there.[69] Frisco employees, however, stayed on the job, and the company benefited from the inactivity of the competition. This was in no small part due to the recent purge of management. Workers could not fail to note that while salaries of general employees of the Frisco had been reduced a total of $51,991, officers' salaries were reduced by $23,700, a greater proportionate loss for management than for employees.[70] This evidence of good faith on the part of the company in facing the hard times allowed the new, more tactful officers to avert the strike.

Workingmen's meetings were attended by men hand-picked by management who spoke on the theme of the need of labor for capital, and leadership in workingmen's organizations along the Frisco was infiltrated by those sympathetic to the railroad's interest to such a degree that on the streets of North Springfield it was called "a shame and an outrage."[71] Yet the only violence that occurred was the wrecking of the Frisco's crack passenger train, the Texas Express, at a lonely station in the Missouri Ozarks. The track had been tampered with and the engine plunged over a forty-foot embankment, killing the engineer and a train buff who had hitched a ride contrary to company regulations. Several shots were fired through the dark and rain, but no further action was taken by the wreckers. This happened in June, before the climax of the strike, and there is no evidence that it was connected with labor trouble. If it was, it backfired. The mangled and scalded engineer lived two hours, long enough to show himself unflinchingly loyal to the company. "I could have jumped and saved myself," he said, "but the train would have gone down."[72]

How much of the good labor relations was planned and how much resulted accidentally from more efficient management and better feeling toward the officers is impossible to say. But Rogers could truthfully tell a reporter at the height of labor violence in St. Louis that "the men are all working harmoniously with the management." The superintendent claimed this was because engineer's pay on the Frisco had been reduced 6 to 8 per cent rather than the 10 per cent of other roads, and that the pay reduction for switchmen and brakemen had been made eight months before the strike atmosphere became national. "The only way out of this difficulty," Rogers added, "is to build the Texas Pacific and then you'll see lively business times."[73] The old plan to join the A. & P. with the thirty-second parallel died hard. So did the plan of expansion along the original thirty-fifth parallel route and in other directions. The directorate was determined that the new company should not repeat the failures of its predecessors.

8

EXPANSION

When the strikes died down, the Frisco pursued an expansionist policy. William Coffin, who had been appointed president of the A. & P., wrote directly to President Rutherford Hayes about that overriding difficulty, the Indian Territory. The land office had been remiss in surveying lands within railroad land grants, and there was therefore a delay in patenting these lands to the companies involved.[1] The Frisco (A. & P.) grant in Indian Territory was subject to the further complication that it was not certain whether the Indian title could be extinguished. Addressing the president as "Your Excellency," Coffin attacked the problem boldly. He cited the clauses in the 1866 act requiring the U.S. to extinguish Indian titles, and concluded that failure to do this could not be used as an excuse for not surveying and patenting the lands: "The Government cannot claim that because it has neglected to perform one of its obligations it cannot be called upon to perform the others."[2] J. P. Robinson, A. & P. vice-president, wrote the secretary of the interior at the same time and to the same point. The "apparent informality" of directors who had visited Washington with former President Peirce was explained by the fact that Peirce had sold all his Central Division (Indian Territory section) securities and therefore had no personal interest in expansion in that direction.[3]

President Baker of the Frisco, meanwhile, was testifying before the Committee on Territories and pressing for territorial government for the Indians. In March 1878 he met a stone wall in the form of William Adair, chairman of the Cherokee congressional lobby:

> Baker: It [the territorial bill proposed] proposes to give them more than they have got or ever had before—a better government.
>
> Adair: Have you ever read the constitution and laws of the Cherokee Nation?
>
> Baker: I have read part, but not all, a long time ago.
>
> Adair: Do you know how long the Cherokees have had a written form of government?
>
> Baker: I believe over thirty years or more—you know.
>
> Adair: Have you seen the code?
>
> Baker: Yes, I have seen the code of your laws.
>
> Adair: Have you not read it?
>
> Baker: Not a great deal.
>
> Adair: How do you happen to know they have no government if you have not read it and do not know anything about it?
>
> Baker: I do not believe I put it in that light—a good government in place of a bad one. I think, however, your government is a mockery, an absolute mockery.[4]

Further trouble for the Indian Territory extension plan came on October 13, 1877. On that day, James Williamson, commissioner of the General Land Office, replied to Coffin's letters in no uncertain terms. Neither the A. & P. nor the Frisco, which controlled it, had any claim to lands in the Indian Territory except if the tribes pleased to grant it. It was obvious, Williamson wrote, that the company understood this from the first; why else should it have applied to the Cherokees for a grant of land in 1869? Only when the Cherokees had refused did Hillyer's pamphlet appear introducing the concept that the company had a right to the land, enforceable by the United States. Williamson laid that contention finally to rest.[5]

The General Land Office and the Interior Department as a whole did not want the California situation repeated in Indian Territory. There the department had for a long time only vaguely defined the rights of the

A. & P. and as a result set off a flurry of speculation. One California senator had written to Secretary of the Interior Carl Schurz only the day before Williamson's opinion on the Indian Territory was delivered. He noted that California was still in a turmoil about a possible A. & P. grant to San Francisco.

> I am so distressed on account of the unsettled condition of our land titles in this state, and the rings that have been and still are robbing the people of their homes, that I can scarcely sleep nights after tiring myself out daytimes trying to defend the homes of these poor people for them. . . . It would take but very little to bring on a terrible civil war, or uprising of the people in this state.[6]

Williamson was appalled at this, and at the gall of the Frisco in continuing to demand the Indian lands even after his pronouncement.[7] The company went so far as to bring suit in the name of the A. & P. against the United States to recover the company's rightful landed inheritance.[8] Little did the commissioner dream that he would within three years be employed by this same company as land agent, and that he would fight these same battles representing the other side. Yet, he was forced to admit that he could not close the California controversy, or give a satisfactory answer to the letter from the senator which Schurz had forwarded him until 1878; the A. & P. still technically had one year to reach the coast and claim the land.[9]

The Frisco thought a transcontinental line built in a year was an unlikely prospect and turned to projects closer at hand. The internal reform helped the road's position in Missouri; at least the Baker administration stopped putting thousands of dollars of the company's money into a mine owned by Joseph Seligman, as Peirce had done. Also the royalty due the company from the Granby Mines was more regularly collected with Judge Baker at the helm, and less fraudulent money was paid the Beaver Branch Railroad for rent of ore cars operating on the short line between the mines and the Frisco main line.[10] But more feeders were needed in Missouri, and eventually some plan had to be devised to build toward the west on a route which would bypass the troublesome tribes along the thirty-fifth parallel in the Indian Territory.

First came an unsuccessful attempt to negotiate a satisfactory contract with the Missouri Pacific, after which the Frisco made a toothless threat to build an independent line into St. Louis. In the year 1877, the Frisco paid the Missouri Pacific $203,473 for the use of the thirty-seven miles from Franklin to St. Louis, even though the Frisco used its own equipment. This amount was regarded by the Frisco as "excessive." Baker argued in the 1877 annual report that for the future, if not at present, an independent road to St. Louis was a necessity. The money paid for rent could be applied instead to construction, and separate terminal facilities in St. Louis "free from the surveillance, exactions, and discrimination" of the Missouri Pacific would give the Frisco the opportunity to seek large increases of business with Kansas and Texas.[11]

This scheme was delayed by a court battle with St. Louis over whether the new corporation, the St. Louis and San Francisco, could claim rights to build in the city which were originally granted to the Pacific of Missouri and claimed by the Atlantic and Pacific only due to its short lease of that company in the early seventies. The case was complicated, in part turning upon whether there was "sufficient proof of the existence of the South Pacific Company." Strangely enough, the Frisco won the case on appeal to the Missouri Supreme Court, but meanwhile attention had again turned elsewhere.[12]

Rogers and Baker were absolutely determined to change the entire financial balance of the income statement. Profits should depend more on the fruits of efficient railway operation and receipts from rail traffic, and less on land speculation and political maneuver. Special care was taken by Rogers to put the road's Missouri mileage in top condition in order to take maximum advantage of traffic possibilities. In 1877 alone forty-six miles of line were relaid with steel rail, the first step in a continuing steel rail replacement program which allowed for the larger engines, longer trains, and higher speeds which Captain Rogers preferred in freight operations. Much of the line had no ballast to cushion great weight; this was added conjointly with the steel rail. A second telegraph wire was strung between St. Louis and Vinita for more accurate dispatching, a large amount of bridge and trestle work was completely renewed, new stockyards were built, and depots and section houses were repaired and repainted.[13] In 1877 Baker made it clear that it was the sense of the board "that a greater development of our mineral, agricultural, and other lands can be secured by pursuing a more liberal course than has hitherto prevailed . . . , and thus contribute to the accomplishment of the end for which your railroad was constructed—i.e. transportation of the products of the lands, and proportionately the articles essential in creating such productions."[14] These statements were important. They indicated the watershed which separated the Fremont era of speculation in a dreamy western venture from the road's later history as a practical if risky business undertaking. The Indies had not been forgotten, but they had been put in proper perspective.

Therefore, rather than counting cars of fictitious California gold dust, the directors meditated on how best to expand their road's traffic area in the immediate vicinity. Two extensions were considered at once: one through Kansas which would skirt the Indian Territory and eventually rejoin the thirty-fifth parallel at Albuquerque, and another south from Pierce City or Springfield through Arkansas and a corner of the Choctaw Nation to Texas, where the cattle trade could be tapped and a connection made with a southern transcontinental. First, however, the line in Missouri needed to be built toward Kansas and to the north of the original route. The directors decided to accomplish this by buying or leasing existing lines rather than embarking on new construction. Most important in the discussions of early 1878 were three short-line railroads, the Missouri and Western, the Springfield and Western Missouri, and the Joplin railroads.

The Missouri and Western, controlled by Seligman and Josiah Macy, had taken over the property of Seligman's old hobby, the Memphis, Carthage and Northwestern. Seligman and Macy represented three large New York investment houses who were eager to get rid of this eighty-two-mile line. The M. & W. would provide the Frisco a link between Pierce City and Oswego, Kansas, where a Kansas Division could commence under Kansas incorporation laws.[15] In January 1878 the Frisco made a traffic agreement with the M. & W. which amounted to a lease.[16]

Seligman formed an elevator company at Oswego to handle grain when the Kansas extension was built.[17] Again he had found himself heavily interested in two competing roads, the Frisco and the M. & W., and again, as in 1872, his solution was to formalize the "consortium" by a lease arrangement. It did accomplish the end desired; C. W. Rogers in an interview in the spring of 1879 was able to advertise the M. & W. as part of the new main line to the Pacific, minus the Indian Territory.[18]

Yet only Seligman was completely satisfied with the lease arrangement. Members of the Frisco board murmured against their most powerful compatriot, while M. & W. officers in an open letter to the Frisco directors stated that they never were satisfied with the agreement, consented to it only in deference to the wishes of Mr. Seligman, and were "very much disappointed and dissatisfied with the arbitrary manner in which your officers interpret its terms."[19] In July 1879 the difficulty was neatly solved by the sale of the M. & W. to the Frisco.[20] This, however, necessitated a $1,000,000 increase in Frisco bonded debt, something which upset the more conservative investors.[21]

Negotiations with the Springfield and Western Missouri were less successful. The line of the S. & W. M. was only nineteen miles long, extending west from Springfield to the little village of Ash Grove.[22] The desire of the Frisco to control it was defensive. The Kansas City, Fort Scott and Gulf Railroad Company, a powerful competitor to the Frisco in eastern Kansas and western Missouri, was interested in using the Springfield short line as a link in its extension eastward toward Memphis, an extension which would lead to rate wars and vicious competition in the Frisco's southwest Missouri traffic area. A traffic agreement was made with the S. & W. M. late in 1877 which guaranteed to the Frisco the "exclusive carrying trade" that might originate on the short line.[23] In return, the Frisco provided cars, engines, and the expert operating advice of C. W. Rogers. In March 1878 the Frisco engine "Thomas A. Scott" steamed out of North Springfield with an S. & W. M. mail car full of dignitaries, and ran over the little line at a speed so tremendous that "the telephone posts all appeared to run together and make one pole."[24]

Financial embarrassment, however, plagued the little road so persistently that the Frisco directors in November were forced to consider either purchasing it outright or allowing it to be controlled by the Gulf road and by that company's Burlington Railroad investors in Chicago.[25] The people at Ash Grove did not like the manner in which the Frisco had treated Springfield, and businessmen there said that any man who supported the Frisco was against the town: "The bird is said to be a dirty one which befouls its own nest."[26] In June 1879 the little road passed into the control of the Kansas corporation.[27] In the Kansas City, Fort Scott and Gulf system the Frisco found a determined competitor which was bothersome until the first years of the twentieth century. It was only then that the Frisco at last gave up trying to reach San Francisco and leased, then bought the entire Fort Scott system complete to Memphis, thus reacquiring the little Springfield and Western Missouri railroad which had been so coveted in the seventies.[28]

The Joplin railroad was also sought by the Gulf system, but the Frisco was determined not to let the rich mining traffic of this short line go to the enemy. The Lone Elm Mining and Smelting Company, with which the Frisco had a lucrative freight contract, was served by the Joplin railroad, which also connected the Frisco with many other rich mining plots in the Joplin, Missouri, area through branches and spurs which the larger company helped the short line to build.[29] In May 1879 Seligman went to Joplin and wrote out a check for over $300,000.[30] The Joplin railroad became a Frisco feeder.

The Joplin road at the moment of its purchase had been in the process of extending its line to Neosho, Missouri, in order to compete with the Frisco at that point. Neosho was therefore especially upset at the sale which raised Joplin railroad freight rates 50 per cent.[31] The Frisco directors, however, were happy that rumors of Missouri trade going to Kansas City were quieted by the purchase. Baker, Rogers, and O'Day submitted to an interview in Pierce City the day of the sale at Joplin. "We bought this road to protect ourselves," said Baker. "They had begun to build that road, and we believed they were just sharp enough to go on and do it; and we bought it to keep it from being built." Rogers simply stated he had to be in St. Louis by six the next morning, "and shaking all round with a good night, amid the flying sparks of the locomotive was whirled into the darkness."[32]

Two local successes in three tries was a better average than the thirty-fifth parallel road was used to. The directors splurged by allowing themselves a $5.00 expense allowance for attending board meetings (there had previously been no allowance) and by making practical and immediate plans for the Kansas line.[33]

In February 1879 the Wichita, Kansas, *Eagle* under the headline "Strike While the Iron Is Hot" notified its readers that Frisco engineers were in south central Kansas and were looking over a route for immediate construction of a railroad from a connection with the Missouri and Western at Oswego to Wichita. Eagle Hall in Wichita filled many a night that winter to listen to the railroad's engineers and executives extol the benefits to Wichita of a second railroad (the Santa Fe had entered town in 1872) and to encourage a large bond subsidy from the city.[34] In March the St. Louis, Wichita and Western railroad was chartered. The plan as stated in the charter was to build to the western boundary of Kansas.[35] This would allow the line then to cut south to Albuquerque, where it could join the Atlantic and Pacific Western Division; the Central Division of the A. & P. could remain stalled in Indian Territory.

The original directors of the St. L. W. & W. were local men headed by Charles Wood Davis of Coronado, Kansas. Davis had been instrumental in convincing Frisco officers to build to Wichita and thereby incidentally to increase the value of the stock of the Oswego and Pittsburg coal companies which he controlled.[36] He was given a contract for providing coal for the new line, but his hopes of being an officer were short lived.[37] In June the local directors resigned and in their place came Judge Baker as president and other Frisco officers as directors. Charles Rogers was elected to fill the place Davis had held, and a Frisco stockholders' meeting was called in July to confirm the lease of the line, called simply the "Kansas Division" by St. Louis officers of the Frisco.[38]

There is evidence that Davis and the other local managers and investors were less than fully prepared for the sudden switch of control and felt they and their local interests had been used as pawns in order to obtain a Kansas charter in the interest of expansion by the larger company. In an 1891 article in the *Arena,* a Populist journal, Davis vented his spleen on railroads in general and especially upon the Frisco's Kansas subsidiaries, charging that there had been a great amount of "hoodooing of accounts" in railroad operations. Also he charged that local interests had been pressured out of existence by big companies once their usefulness was past, and he cited a personal example. In February 1882 C. W. Rogers had written Davis, as president of the Pittsburg Coal Company, the following:

> If we can buy your coal at a low price I think we can possibly make a deal of that basis. As long as you continue shipping coal, it has a demoralizing effect on the trade, and renders the coal business unprofitable, to a certain extent, to the Rogers [C. W. himself] Coal Company.

Davis interpreted the letter as a threat designed to force sale of his coal company to Rogers and the Frisco investors, and he used it in the 1890s to plead for more effective government regulation of corporations. This, he felt, would prevent a repetition of the methods he and his friends encountered as they tried to cash in on the St. Louis, Wichita and Western franchise in the late seventies.[39] Davis's ravings may have been the result of real unfairness or a simple case of sour grapes, but, whether the railroad deserved it or not, his published accusations made it more difficult to maintain a good image.

Similarly damaging to the Kansas project was the antibond phenomenon which developed in April and May of 1879 in Sedgwick County, where Wichita is located. A group of farmers, whom prorailroad opinion accused of being in the pay of the Santa Fe Railroad, became convinced that the St. L. W. & W. was an insidious scheme to tax them unreasonably and that one railroad in the area was quite enough.[40] In a stream of letters to the editor, they made their position clear: the "railroad millennium" which the press promised would not be issued in by

the passage of the bond issue, nor was the $230,000 in bonds which the
Frisco asked "all that stands between us and happiness, prosperity and
freedom." Deflation had made railroad subsidies proportionately more
costly to the taxpayer, and "Heap Big Chief" Seligman and his crowd,
for all their promises, were really nothing but a "new breed of rascals."[41]
It was said that, though Sedgwick County as a whole was voting the
bonds, the road would never be built west of Wichita, leaving only ten
miles of track in the county to show for the subsidy; "Wichita will have
all the road she wants or intended should be built and laugh to think
how easily she duped the county at large." William Ross, the leader of
the antibond movement and the man most often marked as a secret
employee of the Santa Fe, remarked that labor was like Sampson, the
flunky of the "money power," a base Delilah. "Capital is playing a high
handed game," he wrote; "its emissaries are daily becoming more numerous . . . any man who dares to step out from the ranks of labor and
record his protest is immediately singled out as a target for vilification—
is held up before the eyes of his fellow men as a public enemy, every
jackal in their service sets up a howl and the meaner the cur the louder
the noise—always taking care to yelp at a safe distance."[42]

Supporters of the proposed line thought that Ross was the victim of
an exaggerated martyr complex, and that the farmers of western Sedgwick County were reacting unrealistically due to the old country suspicion of cities and city slickers. There was, said railroad writers, no con-
spiracy in Wichita to dupe anyone. The St. Louis, Wichita and Western
had agreed that if the line were not built to the western boundary of
Sedgwick County by August 1881 the road would receive none of whatever county bond subsidy was voted; the full $230,000 would be given
only if the line were built to Wichita by August 1880 and had constructed
two lines to the west boundary of the county by August 1881.[43] That
guarantee was strong enough to silence the county critics while the city
agitators were belittled for daring to say that a great commercial city
like Wichita could get by with one railroad. Wrote one booster in May:

> Who were the men that have built Wichita? Were they inspired
> by that kind of God-forsaken courage, that soft mother milk kind
> of energy that shudders at a shadow . . . no not a whit of it. But
> there is a grade of fellows . . . holding up lamp posts . . . with
> all their weight. . . . If I were king I'd like to give all such
> chronics a passport from Wichita to Medicine Lodge.[44]

On May 20, the Sedgwick County bond issue passed[45] and other counties to the east followed suit.[46] The commencement of construction at Oswego was celebrated on July 4 with a picnic excursion, a matinee of *H. M. S. Pinafore,* a parade of the Veiled Knights, a cornet band, a balloon ascension, and a fireworks display consisting of "everything from a firecracker to Geo. Washington on horseback." One boy was run over by a team and another had his hand burned by a skyrocket; otherwise the ground-breaking for the Kansas Division was orderly.[47]

By September, construction was proceeding at one mile a day,[48] and the quality of the roadbed was so high that Missouri towns had to print exposés of the immoral life of Kansas to prevent a vast exodus in that direction.[49] R. L. VanSant, the principal engineer on the line, achieved an excellent result despite windy cold weather[50] and a shortage of personnel with any experience in operating a transit and level.[51] VanSant's total expense for his surveying party for October was $53.75, of which $12.65 was for stake timber and the ax handles broken trying to drive these into the frozen ground.[52] The railroad employed eight thousand men on the line and by the middle of September material was piled up for two miles west of Oswego ready for the track-laying teams to follow on the heels of the surveyors—a marked contrast to Fremont's operation of thirteen years earlier.[53] "Take a handcar ride on the new line," advised an Oswego paper; "it's immense."[54]

C. W. Rogers traveled behind the track layers in a special car, creating all the while good will in the little towns he visited.[55] Rogers, however, had been sent to Kansas only in November 1879, and by then construction was somewhat behind schedule. For the first few months the job had been in the complete control of Judge Baker. Rogers was authorized to offer opinions and intervened once with the directors in New York to change the original plan of iron rail and wooden bridges to steel rail and iron bridges—this to avoid "a Road which just allows of trains running over it, and one which would be very expensive to operate and building for years to come."[56]

Baker had submitted his resignation as president of the Frisco in July 1878, due to pressure exerted by a "situation of affairs . . . separating the President from the confidence of several directors."[57] He went west, taking the library he had collected with company funds along,[58] and worked for a while as supervisor of the Frisco's mining interests.[59] He retained the position of vice-president, but when he was sent to be president of the Kansas Division it was obvious to him that he was on his way out, and perhaps he did not do the job of which he was otherwise capable. Baker resigned as director of the Frisco in favor of Jesse Seligman in January 1880 and disappeared forever from the affairs of the company with which he had been associated since the 1867 "Home Company" agitation.[60] James Fish became president in February 1879[61] and, after giving Baker a chance in Kansas, called on Rogers.

Rogers was given charge of the road on November 11, 1879. To save the subsidies, he had to complete the first seventy-five miles by January 1. The road was at Neodesha, leaving thirty-four miles to be built in one month and nineteen days. Fish was at that very time trying to negotiate a contract with Thomas Nickerson, president of the Santa Fe railroad, to connect the St. Louis, Wichita and Western with the Santa Fe at Wichita, haul construction materials by the latter line to Albuquerque, and there begin building the Western Division of the Atlantic and Pacific. Fast construction of the Kansas Division would convince the Santa Fe to agree and also give the Frisco a longer haul of the heavy Western Division equipment. Rogers was authorized to increase costs if necessary in the interest of speed.[62]

That he did. He and Kansas Division Chief Engineer James Dun hired audit men to keep the corrupt construction companies from running up large bills against the Frisco and kept the track layers so close behind the grading crews, who were in turn only a few months behind a quick survey, that in the mud and frost a large part of the track layers had from time to time to be diverted to grading.[63]

They worked seven days a week and right through the holidays though it rained almost daily and through much of December the ground was frozen solid. Even building through settled country where town subsidies required the erection of solid depots along the way did not slow progress.[64] Residents of one company-organized town complained that although Rogers was a "wide-awake git up and git" official and had reduced fights in the 140-house town from eight a day to one every other day, the land around was poor, "there not being enough dirt to bury the dead without borrowing from the railroad who have taken up all the dirt in the vicinity for their grade."[65] A Wichita editor noted that the Kansas Division boom was affecting employment in Missouri and that both public and private houses along the line were filled with prospective railroad employees who were "willing to sleep on the floor so as to get a chance to stay."[66]

The subsidies were saved, even the ones on the first section, and by May 1880, three months ahead of schedule, the black and gold passenger cars of the Frisco were rolling between Oswego and Wichita on steel rails and heavy oak ties at a speed of twenty-five miles per hour including stops, the fastest schedule in the state.[67] Special engines with brass-covered cylinders and red wheels were purchased for use on the new road.[68]

The crews which had practiced speed in Kansas were immediately moved to Arkansas to build south from Pierce City toward Texas. The Frisco had intended to build there eventually but not so soon following the expense in Kansas. In 1878, however, the Joplin railroad, backed again by the Kansas City, Fort Scott and Gulf system, had begun buying up franchises in northwest Arkansas.[69] Since there was only one practical route through the Ozarks, the Frisco was forced to press the Arkansas branch immediately in defense of its interest there.[70]

Rogers was in favor of it due to the promise "of working up and securing a part of the through freights to Texas and the Missouri Pacific."[71] Joseph Seligman was also in favor, citing the rich mineral, tobacco, and timber stores of northwest Arkansas left without an outlet.[72] All were aware of the development of Eureka Springs, a newly discovered picturesque health resort that looked as though an "accident wandered out there and happened," but had twelve hundred visitors one Saturday in 1879.[73] Eureka could be connected to the Frisco Arkansas Division by a short branch line.

Several Arkansas charters were secured by the Frisco and consolidated to form the St. Louis, Arkansas and Texas Railroad Company, which like the St. Louis, Wichita and Western was wholly controlled by the Frisco and run by Frisco officers. C. W. Rogers was elected president and promised to ride the rails into Fayetteville for Christmas dinner, 1880.[74] Expansion was by then a familiar process and the ritual of using subsidiary companies had been scientifically formalized. In the Frisco records is found a printed form authorizing consolidation of the various Arkansas companies. The names of these have been struck out and names of Kansas lines written in—the same form sufficed for expansion in all directions.[75]

Joseph Seligman must have been a satisfied man in 1880. The thirty-fifth parallel project, with which he had had so much patience, had risen once again from its own ashes and this time seemed secure and strong. The last of the dishonest managers of the old companies, J. P. Robinson, had been tracked down at a New York hotel in 1878 and part of the securities he held illegally had been recovered.[76] Though Missouri residents still complained that the Frisco cars were "dirty and unkempt" and that their trains looked as though they were "chartered by some western sheriff to carry a full complement of convicts to the state prison,"[77] the farmers' antirailroad movement had died down considerably. Business-men were ecstatic in their praise of the St. Louis, Wichita and Western and of its creator C. W. Rogers. It was, according to most, one of the best built and most efficiently run railroads in the United States. To take notice of the detour around the Indian Territory, the old company trade-mark "The Vinita Route" was removed from the letterhead and replaced with a slogan which would last with some variations to the present day —"Frisco Line."[78]

Seligman, however, was not more satisfied with Fish as president than he had been with Peirce or Baker. For one thing, Fish was presi-dent of the Marine National Bank in New York, a competitor of the Seligman house. More important, Seligman must have known of Fish's shady dealings in the bond market on behalf of former President Ulysses Grant for which he was later sentenced to ten years in prison.[79]

One solution would be to elevate Rogers to the presidency. Rogers's salary was raised to $8,000 immediately,[80] and he was appointed in March 1881 to the position of second vice-president and general manager,[81] an office created especially to take advantage of his particular blend of executive and operating abilities. But the railroad business was not yet ready in the early eighties to obtain its top executives by promotion from within.

Seligman's choice instead was General Edward Winslow, a man from an old New England family who combined a fine war record with a good deal of railroad experience. In January 1879 Joseph Seligman had intro-duced Winslow to the directors and employed him to examine the rela-tions of the Frisco company with the Missouri and Western.[82] In March 1880 he was elected president of the Frisco with the endorsement of Fish and after a nominating speech by Seligman which described the new man as "eminently qualified to discharge the responsible and onerous duties of president of this company."[83]

"Onerous" was the word indeed. Winslow had gone to work build-ing the St. Louis, Vandalia and Terre Haute railroad at the age of nineteen, torn up the Mobile and Ohio during the Civil War, supervised the building of the St. Louis and Southeastern in the early seventies, served as expert inspector for the Union Pacific and as president of the New York, Ontario and Western.[84] Yet never had he assumed so large a responsibility as he faced in 1880 as Frisco president. As he remem-bered it in 1881, his duty upon being elected to the top post was described to him as the securing of the future of the property by special attention to the following items: to coordinate the construction and the operation of the Atlantic and Pacific with the Frisco so as to realize the "expected results" from the thirty-fifth parallel franchise; to extend the Frisco line through Arkansas and Indian Territory to connection with the railways of Texas and Louisiana; to build an independent line from Franklin (by then renamed Pacific Junction) to St. Louis and to obtain independent terminal facilities at St. Louis and on the Mississippi River; to group under the existing organization all subsidiary and leased lines; to increase the equipment and change the roadway so that the cost of maintenance would constantly decrease; and to consolidate the outstanding obligations of the company at a low rate of interest.[85] Winslow accepted the challenge, and remained president for the next ten years, the longest tenure of any of the company's chief executives in the nineteenth century.

The appointment of Winslow, a chief executive who could complement Rogers in ability, was the last and perhaps most important of Joseph Seligman's contributions to the thirty-fifth parallel project. The man who as early as 1867 was dreaming of a "Great National, Atlantic and Pacific Railroad . . . never obstructed by snows,"[86] died in New York in April, mourned by "nearly every banker and broker of prominence in the City," and no doubt by the Frisco directors, whose company owed so much to him.[87] The company had named an engine for Rogers;[88] it was only appropriate to name a town for Seligman. In September 1880 a place along the new southern branch about two miles north of the Arkansas line which was once called Roller's Ridge was renamed Seligman, Missouri.[89] So it remains today.

Joseph Seligman had created a stable management for the thirty-fifth parallel project based on a union of Boston and New York, Yankee and Jew, Winslow and the Seligman family, which he hoped would eliminate the internal difficulties which had so often in the past crippled the corporation at a moment of opportunity.

Winslow wrote to the secretary of the interior in October, used the argument that only the Panic of 1873 and the government's failure to extinguish Indian title had delayed construction on the A. & P. Central Division,[90] and got permission to resume building there with a full right to claim lands under the original 1866 land grant. After a nine-years' halt in construction, fifty miles was built that fall in Indian Territory,[91] while to the west and south the St. Louis, Wichita and Western and the St. Louis, Arkansas and Texas opened new traffic areas.

The St. Louis and San Francisco in the four years following its organization had transformed itself from the laughingstock of the financial world to one of the most desirable investments on the New York

Exchange. Ironically, that earned the company the right to be attacked from the outside just as the internal weaknesses were healed. As the eighties began, the transcontinental interests gathered to turn the Frisco's promise aside before it challenged their great trunk lines, or even possibly reached San Francisco and the Indies trade at last.

9

MR. NICKERSON, MR. HUNTINGTON, AND MR. GOULD: IMPERIALISTS

Jay Gould rode private cars, even private trains, his five-foot frame slouched in a red plush seat. His plain overcoat and red handkerchief tied about the neck sometimes identified him, but he was most easily recognized by a "massive black beard, . . . parrot-like beak, and a pair of jet black eyes piercing and intense in expression."[1] His thoughts, however, were less predictable than his appearance. Using the tactics of taciturnity and surprise, he had risen from a blacksmith's bookkeeper and unsuccessful promoter of a patent mouse-trap of his own invention[2] to one of the most successful manipulators of railway securities on Wall Street. He was much hated for the amount of other peoples' investments he had "squeezed like a sponge into his own coffers,"[3] but was at the same time greatly admired for his "steady application, comparative youth, steady habits, mercilessness and mystery."[4] Most of all it was the mystery that compelled attraction. The railway king moved through the collection of chrysanthemums and orchids that filled the $100,000 conservatory at his Hudson River palace;

119

an enigma even to his closest associates.[5] Yet while his next move was usually unknown, his method was predictable. He traveled. When he came upon a railroad he wanted, he set about obtaining it by money or diplomacy or both. "He is one of the few men who never make a false move," wrote a Kansas editor, "and who consequently never loses. . . . The aid of his open hand or the pressure of his heel is felt throughout most, if not all the lines of intercommunication of this continent."[6]

In 1879 Gould was interested in the Frisco, especially because plans for a line through Arkansas and into Texas threatened his investments there with unwanted competition. In May an unsigned circular appeared on Wall Street claiming that the St. Louis and San Francisco road was in dire financial straits. Since publication of the 1878 Annual Report was over four months late, investors had no way of checking this report;[7] accordingly, Frisco stock went down and Gould bought significant quantities of it. By November 1879 the *Railroad Gazette* reported an unconfirmed story that Gould had control of the road.[8] By November 20 the *Wichita* (Kansas) *Eagle* concluded that there was "no more doubt" that Gould had control. He had gotten it, said the *Eagle*, by buying a large block of stock from the disgruntled Judge Baker.[9] But the paper warned all buyers that

> Kansas knows no king and but one sovereign. The spirit of John Brown . . . goes daily marching across every quarter section of her freedom baptized soil,—nor money kings nor slave kings can intimidate or trample down the spirit of her sovereign power— the people. These prairies are not Wall Street nor does the atmosphere of our homes and legislative halls have any of the intriguing odor of that musty den, the Boston syndicate, a fact that Jay Gould and all other jobbers will find out to their sorrow should they attempt any of their "before high heaven" monopoly squeezing pranks within our borders.[10]

Such a reaction was unnecessary, at least in 1879. A few days following the above stinging editorial the *Eagle* reported that the Frisco had in fact passed under the aegis of the Santa Fe.[11] "Jay Gould & Co.," said the *Boston Herald*, "have been checkmated in their gobbling up career."[12] The Santa Fe, reacting to the threat of the St. Louis, Wichita and Western and the Atlantic and Pacific to its home territory, had made an agreement with the Frisco and its subsidiary A. & P. which provided the Santa Fe with some Frisco directors and a half financial interest in the A. & P. Western Division. Gould, however, was only temporarily defeated. He next tried to gain control of the Santa Fe and thereby the entire enlarged system, and when that failed turned to other devices to stop the Frisco's Arkansas branch. "The power of this one man for good or evil is beyond calculation . . . ," one editor observed. "His death at the moment would work a greater shock in commerce and in stocks . . . than the death of the president with all his cabinet thrown in."[13]

James Fish, then president of the Frisco, and Thomas Nickerson, the agressive president of the Santa Fe, had made a preliminary agreement in November 1879, just as Rogers was sent west to press construction on the Kansas Division.[14] As ratified by the boards of all three companies (the Frisco, the Santa Fe, and the A. & P.) in January 1880, the document was known as the Tripartite Agreement and it much resembled a treaty between nations designating spheres of interest in a newly opened territory. A new company, the Atlantic and Pacific, Western Division, was formed in which stock holding, the directorship, the cost of construction, and the profits were divided between the Frisco and the Santa Fe. Similar arrangements were made for the Central Division, but it was expected by the Santa Fe that this section would never be completed, leaving the Frisco dependent on the Santa Fe lines west of Wichita in order to reach Albuquerque, where the Western Division commenced. It was specifically provided in the Tripartite Agreement of 1880 that the St. Louis, Wichita and Western should not be extended west of Sedgwick County and that "no new lines shall be built by either party in competition with the other except by mutual consent and joint ownership at joint cost."[15]

The new railroad empire was formed apparently as the result of mutual voluntary interest rather than forced by pressure or stock buying by either company. The formalities went smoothly. In March 1880 a number of Frisco directors noted that they wished to spend more time with their families and they resigned from the board to make room for Boston men representing the Santa Fe and for Winslow and Rogers.[16] Winslow, described as a "compromise candidate,"[17] was made vice-president of the Western Division while Thomas Nickerson of the Santa Fe was appointed president.[18] Sedgwick County, Kansas, complained that "we agreed to pay our money for the benefits to be derived from a direct competition and not for an extra track of a monopoly,"[19] but arrangements proceeded for the formation of a "Wichita Pool" to set rates and to divide the traffic administratively rather than competitively.[20]

Financial papers, which a few months earlier had doubted rumors of

Frisco expansion because of the Indian Territory problem and the competition with the Santa Fe west of Albuquerque,[21] must have been amazed at this neat solution. Santa Fe building crews, after a successful fight with the Denver and Rio Grande to gain Rocky Mountain passes, had reached Albuquerque just in time to take advantage of the A. & P. land grant and thirty-fifth parallel franchise to reach the Pacific coast.

Joseph Seligman on his deathbed was not surprised. In May 1872 he had held a conference with J. T. Bird, then vice-president of the Santa Fe, concerning that road's plans to build west to California. Wrote Seligman at that time to A. & P. President Hayes:

> In the conversation I impressed upon Mr. Bird the practicability of their building their line South West in place of West, joining hands with us at Albuquerque. He promised to call upon you tomorrow and get your views on the subject. . . . I think I have made a good impression upon the gentleman and as we don't want additional opposition from any source, I have no doubt you will endeavor to impress him favorably with our scheme, and invite him to join his road with ours at Albuquerque, and also to join hands with us, upon fair and equitable terms, in completing our road to the Pacific.[22]

Seligman knew in 1872 what the Santa Fe only slowly learned through "an interplay between entrepreneurs and situation." That was, as Santa Fe officer William B. Strong wrote in 1882, that "in the United States . . . the power of a Railroad to protect and increase its business depends upon its length, and the extent of the territory it can touch."[23] No better example could be found of Strong's contention that when a railroad ceased to grow it decayed than the fate of the original Atlantic and Pacific Company when construction was stopped in 1871 by the Indian Territory difficulties. Seligman's proposed solution at that time, a tripartite agreement with the Santa Fe, was the one taken in 1880 by a much stronger successor company.

Following election of the new directors, there was a gala reception in St. Louis given by the Merchants' Exchange. Most of the new men were unable to attend, as they had made arrangements to leave immediately on a special Frisco train for Wichita, thence on the Santa Fe into New Mexico. Gould, who was in St. Louis, observing, also declined the invitation. "He is probably the busiest man in the world," wrote a small town reporter.[24]

Five carloads of iron a day went down on the Arkansas branch, and

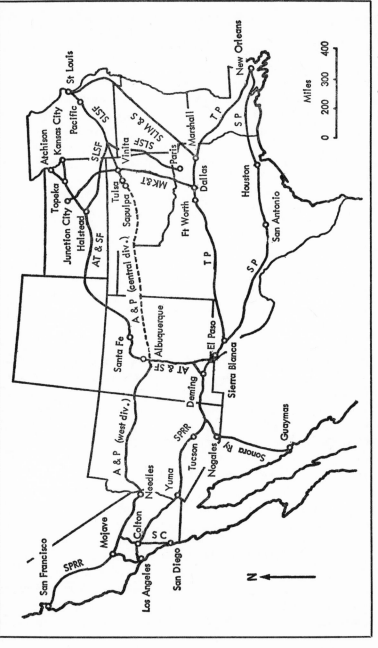

St. Louis and San Francisco Railway Co. 1883

Map by Lewis Armstrong

carpenters began work on one of the largest roundhouses on the line, at Pierce City.[25] Ten to fifteen houses a day went up at the new town of Seligman and daily stages ran between there and the spa at Eureka Springs,[26] where, according to a detailed report by Winslow, a city of one thousand houses had sprung up. Winslow recommended a branch line to Eureka which he scientifically calculated would add $200,000 to traffic receipts of which one half would be net profit.[27] Gone were the days of building based mostly on sentiment. In February 1881, Winslow wrote to the General Land Office: "Our financial Agents Messrs. Seligman & Co. desire to have an official statement of the number of acres of land to which the Atlantic & Pacific R.R. Co. will be entitled upon the completion of its road from the West boundary line of Missouri to San Francisco."[28]

In the years 1880 and 1881, the Santa Fe–Frisco empire was organized to run smoothly, down to the finest detail. In spite of opposition from Clinton Fisk, an erstwhile supporter,[29] the road was extended in Indian Territory and settlement was encouraged in that area. Official reports hinted that the Frisco gave large amounts of money during this period to the support of "Sooners" moving into the Territory and for numerous bills which were presented to Congress as grievances of private citizens.[30] In Arkansas a temporary line was laid until a fourteen-hundred-foot tunnel could be cut in the Boston Mountains at a place called Winslow. By February 1881 James Dun had four surveying parties in the field south of the Boston Mountains locating a route toward Texas.[31] In Kansas a cut-off line was built between Sedgwick and Halstead to connect the Santa Fe and Frisco lines at a point east of Wichita, and the Frisco agreed to "enforce the maintenance of rates" by charging the same rates to Wichita on its St. Louis, Wichita and Western line as did the Santa Fe on its longer route through Kansas City.[32] The two companies built joint stations at many points in Kansas and created numerous "pools" in eastern Kansas counties following the pattern of the "Wichita Pool" of 1880.[33]

Wichitans complained, but they received Charles Rogers on one occasion at their new Turner Opera House with a brass band and proudly showed him their three steam flour mills, their elevators, their banks, and their secret societies.[34] He got the same warm reception in Fayetteville, Arkansas, when in June 1881 he rode the first train into that city. Rogers spoke to a crowd of ten thousand and was then escorted to the tallest tower of Arkansas Industrial University, where in the sunset he surveyed the Choctaw lands to the west.[35] Thirteen toasts were drunk using

"Cook's Imperial," following which a gold-headed cane was given to the vice-president and general manager, and at the request of the ladies all joined in singing "Fine Arkansas Gentlemen Close to the Choctaw Line."[36] Noted one Arkansas observer:

> When Rogers moves he moves like a lightning express train. . . .
> If the gophers burrowing through the mountain don't make a hole large enough for Rogers to run through with a locomotive he will find a way to go over it temporarily, for he is going to the river, and going fast, and don't you fail to recollect it![37]

In October 1881 Rogers brought a consulting engineer from New York to plan a bridge over the Arkansas River at Van Buren.[38] In November James Williamson, now chief attorney for the A. & P. system, wrote to his old colleagues in the General Land Office requesting copies of all official correspondence concerning the right of that company to construct its road through Indian Territory.[39] One D. L. Hansard meanwhile made a good deal of money selling stereoscopic slides showing the beauty and activity along the Frisco's Arkansas line.[40] The contrast in mood between the peaceful Ozark scenery and the spectacle of the men and machines of nineteenth-century enterprise on the move exerted a powerful pull on the imagination.

All, however, was not harmonious. At the top of the list of disagreements between the Santa Fe and the Frisco was the issue of rebates paid to the jointly operated Atlantic and Pacific. In the preliminary negotiations in November 1879, the Santa Fe argued that the two companies should guarantee the A. & P. bonds to the extent of their net earnings on A. & P. interchange business and that this rebate should be entered as a liability on the A. & P. books. To this Judge Baker objected on the grounds that the debt would make A. & P. securities unsalable. The Frisco then made a counter-proposal that the rebate should be 5 per cent on the gross earnings from interchange traffic with no claim for reimbursement. Both sides soon learned that Thomas Nickerson was right in saying that rebates always amounted to "much more than our estimates when our papers were drawn." Nickerson did agree in time to raise the rebate to 15 per cent with no claim of reimbursement but he flatly refused the demand of the Frisco to raise it to 25 per cent; Nickerson felt this move would damage the securities of the Santa Fe and Frisco. When the Santa Fe directors moved into the Frisco board in the spring of 1880, the issue was deadlocked.[41]

Winslow in the next year became quite upset about the rebate, not so much because the A. & P. was in deep trouble as because the refusal of the Santa Fe to take large risks in backing the A. & P. suggested the tentative nature of its managers' commitment to the project. The Santa Fe was surveying several alternative routes to California of which the thirty-fifth parallel line was only one, and it became quite clear to Frisco directors that the Santa Fe was pumping profits out of the Central Division. These it refused to return in the form of rebates for Central Division construction and applied rather to the Western Division, where the Frisco could profit only through use of the Santa Fe line between Wichita and Albuquerque.[42] On April Fool's Day, 1881, Winslow wrote Nickerson that the Frisco was terminating the rebate agreement on the Central Division altogether until some more equitable arrangement could be made.[43] It was, however, too late in the game for that. Santa Fe and Frisco interests were by 1881 so inextricably entwined that Nickerson could send Winslow a cool reply indicating exactly what had been suspected—that profit was the whole of the Santa Fe's interest in the Central Division, and that the land grant and western franchise was the whole of that company's interest in the A. & P.:

> It is evident that this piece of road is worth more to your Co. than any one else and the A. & P. does not wish you to pay more than it is worth. I understand that At. & S.F. agreed to furnish half the money to meet the interest on the bonds on condition that your Co. would allow a satisfactory sum for the use of this property. . . . I wish you would withdraw your letter . . . if you can consistently do so.[44]

It was clear that prospects for a St. Louis–San Francisco thirty-fifth parallel trunk line were not as enhanced by association with the Santa Fe as perhaps the Frisco negotiators had unrealistically hoped in 1879.

There remained the attack on Gould's Texas monopoly, and here the Santa Fe was glad to encourage the Frisco with the hope that thereby two potential transcontinental competitors would become engaged in a battle which, whatever the result, would benefit the Santa Fe. The plat for the extension of the Frisco Arkansas Division into Texas indicated only one major problem: the proposed line ran directly across the Choctaw Nation, which had granted no right of way to any railroad by treaty or otherwise.

When Frisco negotiators visited in the Choctaw capital in October 1881, they took with them Uri J. Baxter, a law clerk from the Department of the Interior. Baxter's role was confusing to the Indians. Two railroads, the Frisco and the Chicago, Texas and Mexican Central, were applying to the Indian Council for rights of way. Did Baxter represent one or the other, or did he represent the United States trying to exercise pressure on the tribe to grant the franchise? Baxter did little to allay their confusion. He addressed Choctaw Principal Chief Jackson McCurtain as "Governor," just as though the area were already a United States Territory,[45] and in a speech to the Choctaw Council he left the impression with some Indians that it was the United States, not the Frisco railway, that was requesting the right of way.[46] On October 25, the Frisco made a deal with the Chicago, Texas and Mexican Central for joint use of any line built, and the latter company withdrew its competing request.[47] On November 18, a bill was passed in the Choctaw legislature granting a right of way through the tribal lands for an extension of the Frisco's Arkansas Division.[48]

It is most likely that the Department of the Interior had sent Baxter as a referee only to make sure there was no foul play. The clerk was asked by Secretary of the Interior S. J. Kirkwood for any reports of "undue influences" used by the Frisco in its dealings with the tribe, and Baxter reported that while "rumor is more or less rife concerning such enterprises" nothing concrete had been discovered by him.[49] Kirkwood in return advised his employee to confine his activity to the protection of the legal and treaty rights of the Choctaws and to the preparation of documents that were fair. "Make no effort to influence decision of Choctaws as to right of way," the secretary telegraphed from Washington.[50]

Many Indians, however, claimed that the bill had been passed "under a misapprehension of the real relation of the Government of the United States in the premises."[51] Choctaw lobbyists went to Washington to block confirmation of the bill by the Senate. They held that Baxter had represented to them in three public speeches that the federal government wanted the concession,[52] that he made motions in the Choctaw Council, though under their constitutions this right was forbidden to noncitizens,[53] and that when objections were raised to Baxter's draft of the bill he had stated that "it was the best and only thing the United States would allow" and that "they would not consent to have it altered." Some objected at the time of the vote that the printed version of the bill was different from that previously presented in manuscript, to which Baxter replied that "it was no use talking that way, that we must come to a vote, that he had not time to stay there."[54] The bill then was defeated in the Choctaw House of Representatives, and only a decision by the tribe's attorney general that the speaker had voted illegally saved it.[55] Baxter signed the bill "in behalf of the United States, just as though this railroad belonged to the United States."[56]

The confrontation over U.S. Senate bill no. 60 to confirm the Frisco right of way was an important one in determining the future rights of the tribes with regard to railroad expansion into Indian Territory. In January 1881 the Committee on Railroads of the United States Senate significantly revised the bill passed by the Choctaws. The changes were for the most part beneficial to the tribe, but the precedent set was not. The theory of self-determination for the Indians, if it had ever been operative during the treaty period, was officially laid to rest. After 1882, power, not possession, became the test of legitimacy in the expanding industrial nation. No Indian legislative consent would again be asked for a railroad right of way; Indians, like U.S. citizens, would be subject to the exercise of the right of eminent domain. The title of Senate bill no. 60 was changed in order to avoid any mention of the Choctaw legislature. The question involved, according to Senator Samuel Maxey, a large landholder at Paris, Texas, where the new Frisco line was headed, was "whether there is an *imperium in imperio* in this country; whether there is a portion of the territory of the United States around which a Chinese wall may be erected to which the right of eminent domain does not apply and thereby intercommunication by railway is forbidden between the states of the Union upon the 'I forbid' of . . . Indians or anybody else."[57] The answer of the Senate, despite the previous passage of numerous treaties guaranteeing complete autonomy of the tribes over their lands, was an emphatic "no." "We will not be penned up," wrote one senator; "we will not be hindered."[58]

Naturally, it would not do to offer either greed or racial prejudice as the reason for this decision. The reason given by Congress was Jay Gould: Gould would benefit from the rejection of the Frisco bill and would retain his Texas rate monopoly. Baxter provided the Committee on Railroads with an opinion of Choctaw Chief McCurtain, a man with scarcely a trace of Indian blood, which implicated Gould as the source of pretended Indian dissatisfaction. McCurtain had written to Baxter:

> It appears that Jay Gould is going to cause a great deal of trouble to the Choctaw and Chickasaw Governments. He is at the bottom of the whole matter of these delegations being got up and sent to Washington. I am satisfied that if an investigation was made in regard to these delegates they would not like to show where their pay comes from.[59]

The Committee on Railroads asked the Indian lobbyist just that, repeatedly and to the exclusion of all other testimony. Isham Walker, clerk of the Choctaw Nation, pulled from his pocket his rough copy of the legislative journal in an attempt to show the original Indian vote. One of the committee members later described him as a "sleepy stupid-looking Indian."[60] The Committee was interested in only one thing: "Who paid your expenses? Don't you know that there are railroads who do not want competing lines that pay your expenses?" Finally from the Indians came the admission that a will finds a way and that a "Mr. Fisher" gave them funds.[61]

Daniel O. Fisher, a member of both the Choctaw and Chickasaw tribes,[62] was in Washington at the time and may well have been in the pay of Gould. At least he complained to his wife that Indians in the pay of the Frisco were constantly accusing him of this, which drove Fisher often to Mass to consult his "God Father."[63] Yet whether or not Daniel Fisher was in the pay of Gould perhaps should not have been the issue before Congress. Fisher was an Indian nationalist who was no doubt willing to use someone else's money to further his own ends. The Congress, however, found in Gould's monopoly an emotional issue with which the real one could be hidden. Those who spoke on behalf of the Indian could be conveniently labeled as being in favor of Gould. That this process was a ruse is best demonstrated by the fact that the appeal was only slightly modified when Gould bought control of the Frisco in late January, thus eliminating it as a potential competitor. The crux of the matter was exactly as Fisher described it in the middle of January:

> Our cause is a good one and our foundation good, if we fail, goodbye to our Government. . . . If the Choctaws are too blind to their own interest and welfare, and will yield, or submit, then I am done with politics. . . . I think every citizen who has a spark of patriotism should raise his voice against tyranny.[64]

Some did and loudly. John Miles, Indian agent for the Cheyenne and Arapahoe tribes in western Indian Territory, wrote in January that there were certain points in the future which would disturb his harmony with his wards if not handled before the critical period arrived. One of these was the expansion of the Frisco railroad both west from Vinita (the A. & P. Central Division) and southwest from Arkansas: "The Indians are alarmed, not only because their land is invaded by the white man and his railroad, but they see in it a deathblow to freighting and consequently a great source of their present revenue cut off entirely and they express their intention to resist this encroachment on their rights, to the bitter End."[65] The Interior Department was plagued by questions from Indian Territory editors concerning the legal position of the Frisco,[66] and Miles himself requested information on which he was unclear.[67] One Irishman, Patrick Shanahan, set up "a sort of fort" across the A. & P. line west of Vinita and, according to his own report, provoked armed retaliation on the part of the railway workers.[68] A Cheyenne chief, "Whirlwind," was more verbose but no less vehement in his talk with Miles:

> I am going to talk good. . . . All our people . . . say to keep back this Rail Road. Our country is getting small enough without R.R.s come the whites to take our country from us. . . . We are not talking any bad words but we think for our own good. Tell Washington we love this country that is ours.[69]

In spite of the agitation, General John Pope at Fort Leavenworth was advised not to interfere with the Frisco surveying parties unless such action was requested by the Interior Department.[70] Jay Gould apparently did not believe such action would ever be requested nor that the agitation would stop the passage of Senate bill no. 60. Late in January 1882, while attention was focused on senators and Indian chiefs, the unpredictable Gould moved from the shadows and bought a controlling interest in the securities of the St. Louis and San Francisco Railway Company.

Gould, Collis Huntington, and officers of the Atlantic and Pacific, Frisco, and Santa Fe railroads had been holding intermittent conferences during the month of January.[71] Huntington for obvious reasons wished to prevent the A. & P., particularly while in league with the Santa Fe, from doing any building in California. In November 1881 Huntington had made a contract with Gould similar to the Tripartite Agreement in that it provided that the two should build no competing lines without consultation and that Gould's Texas and Pacific was to be joined with Huntington's Southern Pacific near El Paso, Texas, to form a joint transcontinental line. The 1881 agreement between the two great southwestern magnates also suggested a plan whereby Gould and Huntington could obtain control of the Frisco and therefore a half-interest in the A. & P. in case negotiations to stop that competitor were unfruitful.[72] Gould in addition to stopping the A. & P. could vote his Frisco stock in favor of either stopping construction into Texas and St. Louis or upping rates on these proposed lines so they would not undercut those on his Missouri

Pacific, Missouri Kansas and Texas, or St. Louis, Iron Mountain and Southern.

In January, the *New York Tribune* quoted Huntington to the effect that "the chances of compromise were about even" in negotiations with the A. & P.[73] On the day this comment was printed Gould and Huntington obtained control of a little less than half the Frisco stock, a controlling interest, by buying it in one transaction from J. & W. Seligman and Company, of whom Gould had been a client since the late sixties.[74] Winslow had indignantly refused to part with his stock,[75] but Joseph Seligman was dead and his brothers had never felt that his large investment in the thirty-fifth parallel road was justified. "Regardless of their opinion of his tactics," reads the official history of the banking house, "the Seligmans were loyal to Gould as a client."[76]

Charles Rogers, who at the January 10 directors' meeting had been positive that a planned independent line into St. Louis and the probable passage of Senate bill no. 60 would make the Frisco line "one of the best in the country, west of the Mississippi,"[77] must have been dizzied as he attended the January 27 meeting and watched four new directors take their places: C. P. Huntington, Jay Gould, Russell Sage, and Leland Stanford.[78] Rogers and Winslow were asked by the new board to retain their offices, but Rogers's plea that he not be forced to discriminate "in favor of any officer or company" was ignored.[79] Winslow, when asked about the bargain, answered rather pitifully: "I am an officer of the company, and, as an officer of the company, I can have no cognizance of bargains between private persons: as an individual I know nothing."[80] Joseph Seligman's idea of an independent thirty-fifth parallel trunk line did not long survive his death. Rogers and Winslow, upon whom Joseph had so heavily depended to make the dream at last concrete, were in the spring of 1882 surrounded and outnumbered at the directors' table by members of syndicates whose interests not only conflicted with the Frisco's interest but with each other. Gould, Huntington, the Seligmans, Winslow, Rogers, and the Santa Fe directors made strange bedfellows indeed.

Journalists and railroad observers in general were spellbound at the speed and intrigue of Gould's remarkable coup. Judge Baker rushed to St. Louis from his home in Springfield to take notes on the situation and to give his opinion to a young reporter who visited him at the LaClede Hotel. Baker said that the sale meant "negation—prevention" and would shut off "all the contemplated and actual progress toward a competitive connection with Texas and California." Gould, he said, had sent the Indian lobby to Washington and had supported bills to disallow the A. & P. Western Division land grant. St. Louis, in his grasp, would be left with no independent outlet, "completely at the mercy of the whims and caprices of two capitalists who have combined to control vast monopolies."[81] The *Commercial and Financial Chronicle,* however, looked at it from a broader perspective and could not but admire the gamesmanship involved:

> It not only emphasizes and strengthens the alliance between these two great railroad operators, but it makes more evident and more certain their purpose to render the combination effective by preventing rivalry and undermining opposition. Where competition threatens to become dangerous, it is to be bought off. Where it cannot be bought off, it is to be deprived of its power for harm.[82]

The *New York Times* regarded the purchase as "a master stroke on the part of the great railway kings,"[83] while the *Cherokee Advocate* in Indian Territory reported the story without enthusiasm.[84] Whatever their perspective, however, most agreed that the temporary alliance between Gould and Huntington had served the interests of those two well. Huntington was for the time perhaps applying the advice he remembered from his father as a boy: "Do not be afraid to do business with a rascal, only watch him; but avoid a fool."[85]

The Santa Fe accepted the change more calmly than might have been expected. Initially its managers were glad to be rid of the aggressive Frisco, especially since it had been unsuccessful in attacking Gould. Yet journalists predicted a battle over the A. & P.:

> While the chuckling of the Atchison, Topeka, and Santa Fe Company was about to explode into uproarious mirth and laughter at Gould's triumph over "Frisco," a cloud appeared on the western horizon on the edge of which were hung in bold letters, "C.P.H." Rex—of the Pacific Slope, the silent partner of Mr. Gould, who had decreed that the Atlantic and Pacific Railroad may be built to the eastern border of the State of California and not one inch further—nous verrons![86]

Southern California real estate dropped 30 per cent on news of the Gould sale,[87] and at San Francisco one million A. & P. ties and enough steel for fifty miles of building piled up, unused, on the wharf.[88] Yet the Santa Fe officials said that finishing the A. & P. to the coast was "a matter in which the people of California are more interested than the stock-

"In the Waiting Room," St. Louis and San Francisco R.R. lithograph, 1899
Photo reproduced from the Collections of the Library of Congress
by J. & W. Seligman & Co.

Logging Crew for A&P near Santa Fe, N. M.
Photo courtesy University of New Mexico

Building of the A&P west from Albuquerque, N. M., in the early 1880s
Photo obtained from Santa Fe Railway by J. & W. Seligman & Co.

holders of the Atchison."[89] It was revealed that the Santa Fe had a chance to buy the Frisco at a much lower figure than Gould paid but considered it a bad risk due to the other alternatives that were available for reaching California.[90] A New York financial paper praised this decision:

> To us . . . this latest action offers renewed evidence of Boston sagacity and good sense. Sentimental considerations do not, and should not, govern in business. An independent line to the Pacific is a pleasing idea, but it would certainly be no proof of business capacity or business skill to jeopardize large amounts of capital. . . . To be able to discriminate and draw the line between ventures of a dubious or not very promising character and those offering a fair measure of success, that is the true test. . . . The railroad fever has subsided, and new undertakings no longer possess the charm they had.[91]

The president of the Santa Fe said that relations with Gould would be harmonious and perhaps the sale would even be a positive advantage to his company "while it is a matter of indifference to the Atchison who controls the San Francisco Road."[92]

Senate bill no. 60 lost much of its importance to the Frisco after January 27, when Gould gained control. Nothing was done about authorizing the Texas line until 1886, and then Sage, Gould's henchman, voted against it while Gould failed to attend the meeting.[93] Yet for the Indians the bill remained of vital importance because of the precedent it would set if passed. In April 1882 the revised bill came out of committee, a large map was set up at the front of the Senate chamber with a red line marking the new route, and debate began in earnest.[94]

The trend was clear. C. J. Hillyer's prorailroad pamphlet was recommended and many senators read it.[95] When in January "the Assyrian came down, like a wolf on the fold, and his cohorts were gleaming in purple and gold," the Indians "folded their tents like the Arabs and as silently stole away."[96] Senators took this as evidence that the tribes were in the pay of Gould. Actually it was more probable that the tribes could not imagine that the bill could possibly pass after the Gould purchase and so withdrew their lobbies. The red man was then denounced more freely:

> When we offer simply to give the right of transit, the right given to the meanest citizen of the United States from his lands to the highway that leads him to market, we are met with the inexor-

able cry, "This is the sacred domain of the five civilized tribes and no white man shall enter it without our consent . . . the sovereignty is in us . . . your railroads shall stop and when you come on bended knees and beg . . . we answer, "You are a nation of robbers, and we will hurl you back from your princely domain as the surf of the ocean is thrown back from the granite rock."[97]

Against this barrage stood Senators George Hoar of Massachusetts and John Ingalls of Kansas. Hoar believed that the Congressional attitude toward economic and political expansion into the Indian Territory resembled the attitude of a small boy who "when he wanted anything that was his father's property, he asked for it as politely as he could; and if his father did not give it to him he generally took it, for fear he should be led to do something wrong for want of it."[98] Ingalls was the Senate gadfly, an eccentric figure who wore a tightly buttoned double-breasted coat, put on two pairs of glasses when he spoke, and even then held his notes under his nose. But he was a no-nonsense debater who meticulously cut out notices of applause for his speeches when they were printed in the *Congressional Globe*.[99] There was no applause when he called the Senators "juggling fiends," and likened their railroad bill to that strange piece of furniture in one of Goldsmith's poems which was "a bed by night, a chest of drawers by day." Senate bill no. 60, Ingalls said,

is a Trojan horse. . . . It pretends that it desires to overthrow monopoly by granting a charter to the line that is named, which belongs to the very person who controls the monopoly. . . . I do not think that is candid; I do not think that is sincere.[100]

A minority, then, opposed the bill, once even going so far as to suggest that "protection does not mean destruction."[101] Yet the minority view was described by one senator as "sickly morbid sentiment," which stood in the way of a great national trade artery.[102] Senate bill no. 60 passed thirty to thirteen; thirty-two senators did not bother to appear for the vote at all.[103] Williamson wrote from the A. & P. offices to Jesse Seligman that the result was "regarded by this company as entirely favorable, being all the company asked for or desired."[104] To the Washington law firm of Britton & Gray Williamson wrote that Colonel H. C. Nutt, new A. & P. president, wished to write the Interior Department for a precise interpretation of the bill. Williamson, however, disagreed:

> I would not write any letter but would go on with the survey
> untill stopped by superior force, and then write what should be
> found necessary. . . . We had much better go on and build our
> road where we want it . . . than to have any adverse decisions
> or opinions expressed.

Britton & Gray were instructed to hold Nutt's letter until they could
"sound out" the secretary of the interior.[105] No letter from Nutt on this
subject is today to be found in Interior Department files.

The thirty-fifth parallel project in 1882 was again the victim of
inimical interests, unfortunate timing, and less than perfect executive
judgment. Just as the Indian Territory difficulty which had haunted the
road since 1870 was removed the company found itself colonized from
two directions by large corporations uninterested in a St. Louis–San
Francisco trunk line. The Frisco had, it seemed, sold its soul to the devil
at the eleventh hour, just before Congress made it unnecessary by ful-
filling its promises of 1866.

Jay Gould was in 1882 making $6.00 a minute from railroad stocks,
yet one paper held that "the man who from one peck of potatoes has by
his own labor caused five bushels to come into existence, has contributed
more in aid of his fellow man than Jay Gould has done in the last fifteen
years."[106] The trend all over the country seemed to be toward centraliza-
tion, consolidation, and colonization—a trend that left little chance for a
new independent transcontinental enterprise at such a late date. Still, the
A. & P. had a western land grant, a franchise, and an abundance of hope
of salvaging at least part of Thomas Benton's 1849 vision. Early in 1882
construction began on the A. & P. Western Division at Albuquerque, and
Williamson, as general solicitor and land agent, settled in his New Mexico
office to try to sell large blocks of the land grant to cattlemen. At the
beginning of the new year, 1882, the Santa Fe and the Frisco issued a circular picturing a huge steam giant traversing the continent. "It is reason-
ably certain," went the text, "that the Atlantic and Pacific will reach
San Francisco by some route independent of the Southern Pacific."[107]

10

THE WESTERN DIVISION

Archibald Sutter, a Scottish visitor traversing the Frisco line in 1881, had little good to say about it. He doubted if a company that could provide no better service for its Missouri passengers had any business trying to build to San Francisco. Sutter was appalled, as had been Anthony Trollope before him, that the porters did not carry his bags. He pointed out also that the sanitary facilities at Frisco stations were less than ideal, that the cars had "a choky feeling not quickly forgot," and that a ride in them at night resulted in "little rest and much shaking." The traveler found Springfield a "dry and dusty" town, felt that the college at Fayetteville was "out of all proportion to the place" and maintained that Eureka Springs was full of "queer people." Between Pierce City and Vinita ("a town on boards") Sutter tried the cuisine on the train only to find he might as well try to take dinner "on board a very small boat, in a good gale of wind, in the Atlantic." The only thing that pleased him was the lemonade, something he had never before encountered.[1]

137

There was no shortage of natives who agreed with the Scotsman in wreathing the Frisco boasts of an eastern and western empire with a heavy air of sarcasm. These cynics, however, were not employees of the companies involved in building the Atlantic and Pacific, Western Division. As early as 1879 a Frisco official had hinted to the press that once the western and central sections were completed, the Frisco probably would be leased to the Atlantic and Pacific, thus forming the elusive thirty-fifth parallel trunk line between St. Louis and San Francisco.[2] Financial analysts granted that, even if this hope was chimerical and Huntington and Gould had stopped the A. & P. in California and the Indian Territory, there was still the possibility of a profitable way traffic, provided the huge A. & P. land grant in New Mexico and Arizona could be sold and traffic-producing industries installed there.[3] James Williamson agreed. When Gould and Huntington entered the Frisco board in 1882, the A. & P. general solicitor and land agent calmly wrote that all suits pending in regard to the western extension should be prosecuted as heretofore—"I am informed and believe that the road will be built to San Francisco."[4]

Construction on the Western Division began in the spring of 1880 and made slow progress. There was a crisis in January 1882, when, due to news of the sale to outside interests, the Frisco was unable to sell its half of the current issue of A. & P. mortgage and income bonds. Prospective investors in A. & P. securities no doubt had heard that Huntington had put a team of Chinese to work extending the Southern Pacific east from Mojave to "the Needles," where Amiel Whipple's old thirty-fifth parallel survey crossed the Colorado River into California.[5] Noted one western paper: "They are expected to gobble up the Atlantic and Pacific, scales, tails and fins."[6]

No "gobbling," however, was done. By early August 1883, an A. & P. bridge spanned the Colorado River and on August 8 the line was completed to a junction with the Southern Pacific at "the Needles." The problem of further California building remained for the time unsettled, but an arrangement with the S. P. to run trains temporarily on its new Mojave line allowed the "Thirty-Fifth Parallel Trans-Continental Line" to be declared officially open.[7] By autumn, 1883, through Pullman sleepers traveled from St. Louis via Wichita to Halstead by the Frisco and St. Louis, Wichita and Western Lines, then to Albuquerque by Santa Fe, on to Needles by Atlantic and Pacific, Western Division, and to San Francisco by Southern Pacific.[8] True, the schedule required nearly twenty-four hours via the "Express" train to traverse the 574 miles be-

tween Albuquerque and Needles,[9] and the bumping and switching involved in changing carriers upset travelers. But cars were running on
the thirty-fifth parallel and it was, as advertised, free from snow in the
winter, when Union Pacific trains across Wyoming were sometimes
delayed for a week.

The financial, legal, and competitive problems unleashed by the construction and operation of this mixed-media line were stupendous and
were complicated by the fact that a majority of the interests involved
were concerned with the line from a strategic point of view only. J. & W.
Seligman, the Frisco, and the Santa Fe advanced money in thirds to
guarantee A. & P. bonds and often requested specific permission from
the United States Trust Company to issue these in advance of construction.[10] By 1884 the Frisco alone had made cash advances to the A. & P.
of $1,724,076 secured by parts of the A. & P. land grant withheld at a
value of fifty cents an acre. In addition both the Frisco and the Santa Fe
tried to buttress A. & P. securities by guaranteeing the interest on the
bonds and making the stock exchangeable to some extent for the stock of
the stronger parent companies.[11]

Although the Frisco annual report for 1884 expressed the hope that
traffic proceeds would soon allow the A. & P. to pay interest on its bonds
without resorting to advances or use of the proceeds from land sales, the
possibility was not good that this would occur. Vast amounts of land,
the very resource on which the A. & P. depended to emerge from its
difficulties, were reserved for the parent companies at fifty cents an acre
to pay off the advances. In addition, the Frisco for its part had acquired
an interest in A. & P. stock nearly as large as the total issue of its own
capital stock.[12]

Both participants in the Tripartite Agreement were afraid by 1884
that support of the A. & P. might cost so much as to endanger their own
companies. The Atchison, Topeka and Santa Fe annual report for 1884
even considered the alternative of abandoning its interest altogether and
leaving "the new road to be wound up in insolvency by its creditors."
The report advised, however, that the loss of prestige, the sacrifice of
money spent, and the possibility that the Southern Pacific would gain
control and make the A. & P. competitive with the Santa Fe, were strong
arguments against this course.[13] The Frisco annual report presented
much the same sort of negative argument in favor of staying in once the
commitment was made. But on the question of whether the Tripartite
Agreement with the Santa Fe should have been negotiated in the first

place, the Frisco report admitted "there may be an honest difference of opinion."[14]

In this atmosphere of doubt, others were quick to seize opportunity. In August 1884 negotiations were concluded with the Southern Pacific. Half of the A. & P. directors, those appointed by the Santa Fe under the Tripartite Agreement, had previously voted to build to California independently of the S. P. while the other half, appointed by the Frisco, followed the Gould-Huntington line in advising conciliation.[15] The problem was solved in the ambiguous manner typical of a company which had no directors to call its own and to the advantage of Huntington's road. A vote was passed to extend the road to the Pacific (that was to sell securities), while at the same time a contract was negotiated with the S. P. for lease of its Mojave-Needles line with an option to buy; the agreement also contained a clause specifying that no further independent line would be built by the A. & P.[16] The A. & P. did eventually buy the S. P. branch line from Mojave to Needles, thus paying the California company for the track Huntington had built specifically to head it off. But the S. P. all the while retained control of traffic both ways from San Francisco and could discriminate at will against the A. & P. on eastbound traffic and in favor of its own thirty-second parallel transcontinental. From November 1, 1883, to June 30, 1897, the A. & P. operations showed a $14,000,000 deficit, all of which had to be made up by the Frisco and Santa Fe.[17]

Nor was this the only headache. The rush and intrigue involved in the construction of the road and the bargaining with the Southern Pacific resulted in neither a high-quality roadbed nor good feeling either within the organization or with the public and the government. When a shipper filed a damage claim, he was not thrilled to be informed, as he often was, that sudden cloudbursts in the territories made it impossible for the company always to be informed on the condition of the track.[18] Nor were the government commissioners, sent to inspect the construction, pleased when the company argued that the mileage expenses they submitted were too high.[19] Contractors complained that the company was paying them too little for hauling water to the crews and that it was paying different rates in different areas.[20]

Some of these charges were no doubt justified. The correspondence of Williamson and other Western Division employees is full of attempts to stretch the law to its limit and at times the railroad policy trod the thin line between cleverness and dishonesty. Writing to A. & P. President H. C. Nutt in 1882, the land agent proposed issuing bonds on the side track as well as the main line even though Santa Fe officials had informed him that the mortgage specifically prohibited this. Williamson justified striking out the offending words in the mortgage by noting that he thought "this is clearly a case where contemporaneous history and facts may be sought and referred to, in order to enable the Corporation to arrive at a just conclusion as to what it may or ought to do."[21]

This situation ethic applied to other activities of the land office as well, notably to the taking of construction materials, mostly timber and coal, from the government sections of the land grant rather than those the railroad owned, a policy which Williamson consistently advised.[22] He and his clerks went over the 1866 land grant act carefully and seized upon words such as "and so forth" which could be used as elastic clauses. Thomas Sedgwick, one of Williamson's clerks at Albuquerque, once ended a letter full of such justifications with only a shade of doubt: "Is it not so? Certainly in time of War!"[23]

Not all agreed that it was. H. R. Holbrook, an A. & P. engineer who would leave his name on a railroad town in Arizona, wrote to his comrade Lewis Kingman in 1883:

> Have been out of the world as it were for the past four months . . . have been looking over the country west to Pacific for a railroad enterprise—Don't know yet what it will amt. to. I think the President of your road should know there is an "irrepressible" conflict between honesty and rascality and that the two elements cannot work together "harmoniously." . . . I sincerely hope you will get through all right and soon be rid of *all* the damned outfit.[24]

Edward Winslow was aware of the financial problems and the expedients that had been chosen to deal with them when he wrote his 1884 report to the stockholders. Yet he maintained that the sale of the land grant could still salvage the A. & P. situation. The regions traversed by the Western Division were "sparsely settled and comparatively unknown," a situation which land sales and railway communication could rapidly change. "The location and physical conditions of the line," the Frisco president wrote, "will make it a desirable one for fast freight."[25] To convert several million acres of Arizona and New Mexico wasteland into a source of this freight was the assignment of James Williamson. His responsibility perhaps excused his overeagerness.

Williamson had accepted the position of land commissioner for the Atlantic and Pacific on June 1, 1880, and set up a small office in Albuquerque. By September of the same year, the company, short on trained personnel, asked him to assume in addition the duties of general solicitor for the company; also his experience in government made him a frequent choice to lobby on behalf of the company in Washington. To properly attend to this multiplicity of duties would have required the travel facilities of the twentieth century. The best Williamson could do was alternate fairly regularly between Washington and the company's general offices at 87 Milk Street, Boston. He was able to travel to Albuquerque all too seldom and was forced to run the land department by correspondence with his none-too-reliable clerk, Col. Thomas S. Sedgwick, who remained in the West.[26]

The constant, uncertain communications, the travel, and the rapid switches from political to legal to land business wore away at Williamson's health, jangled his nerves, and probably affected his judgment as well as his moral sense. Once he wrote Sedgwick that the latter's letters from Albuquerque had piled up for a month unanswered: "My time is so divided between this place [Boston] and Washington that delays in answering your communications are unavoidable. In Washington I have no office, no clerks, no books, etc. and can not answer communications from there."[27] Williamson was always restive about the scarce communication between himself and President Nutt, which left him unsure he knew how to advise Sedgwick on company policy even if he could contact him. He, for example, was kept ill-informed on construction progress and plans, and, to one seeker of information from Albuquerque, had to admit, "I know nothing except what the President chooses to tell me, and that is very little."[28]

Added to the logistic difficulties involved in running the land office was the financial malaise which affected the whole corporation. Salaries were wildly inconsistent. In October 1882, a lawyer for New Mexico business was hired by the A. & P. land office for $24,000, which President Nutt admitted was "high for the present business," but which Williamson justified on the grounds that a sharp eye in the offices of the surveyor general at Santa Fe could save the company that much in fraudulent homestead entries within the grant.[29] Yet the very next month a lawyer employed by the company at Winslow, Arizona, was dismissed on the grounds that "the Land Department of this Company has not yielded any revenue and it had been deemed best to reduce the expenses of the same to a minimum." That minimum, according to Williamson's letter, was the salaries of two employees at the Albuquerque office, so it may be assumed that the lawyer just hired at the fabulous salary was immediately fired—a situation indicating some confusion as to either policy or the state of the company's finances.[30]

By 1883 finances were so strained that clerk Thomas Sedgwick, after advising a prospective office employee of his duties, was forced to write him a long dissertation on the cost of living at Albuquerque, presumably so that he could decide whether the meager salary would be enough. Beef was brought from Kansas at twenty-five cents a pound, potatoes were three cents a pound, but garden supplies were cheap and most employees apparently supplemented their food supply from gardens.[31] A clerk in the A. & P. land office was a rugged character who had to become used to his pay being as much as six months behind and weather which could vary from 28° in the morning to 96° at noon.[32] The atmosphere was sometimes enlivened further by a smallpox epidemic, as in February 1883, when Sedgwick found it convenient to visit Washington and leave the land office entirely in the hands of itinerant dayworkers.[33]

Sedgwick, on the spot at Albuquerque, bore all this patiently, complaining only that it was "not reasonable" to ask him to pay expenses out of his own pocket when his salary was six months in arrears, and that "many land cases are accumulating by default for [lack] . . . of funds to bear the expense of investigation."[34] Yet the parsimonious budget of the land department affected more than the personal comfort of its employees. There was not, for example, an adequate means to show prospective buyers the land until March 1884, when the land department was allowed to buy a used army ambulance at Ft. Leavenworth for the purpose. Even then, the Santa Fe charged almost as much to ship the colorful contraption as it had cost, a tactic which Sedgwick found "unusual as between connecting roads fostered by the same financial promoters."[35] The land clerk thought advertising the lands in Texas, Colorado, Kansas, Iowa, and Missouri would help sales but admitted that "our eleven inch 'Ad' is to [sic] expensive for such use." Advertising was confined to Santa Fe, Albuquerque, Prescott, Deming, and Flagstaff papers, where capital necessary to buy large cattle ranches was rare. Even the budget required for this—$81.67 a month—was soon found to be more than the company could bear.[36] Williamson was forced late in 1885 to order complete discontinuance of the newspaper advertising when sickness in his family prevented him from making the $1,000 personal contribution that had allowed the ads to continue that year.[37]

The financial contributions of Williamson and Sedgwick, as well as their willingness to stretch the law on occasion, demonstrated at least an intense loyalty to the company. Williamson went so far as to question the U. S. Land Office Circular of 1875 which limited A. & P. rights in Indian Territory, a circular which he himself as U. S. land commissioner had had a leading role in writing. In November 1881 Williamson wrote to Sedgwick that the A. & P. grant was not "modified in any of its provisions or conditions" by the 1875 decision and that he hoped to convince the current commissioner of the General Land Office that the decision "is in some respects wrong and unauthorized by law."[38]

This loyalty was no doubt buttressed by Williamson's rather well conceived plan for disposing of the railroad's land and getting it out of debt. It was clear that the land was not suitable for agriculture, at least as practiced in Missouri. One Rolla farmer rode the A. & P. west from Albuquerque and concluded that there was no place within the grant a white man could live: "You can bet your last nickle I am not going to live here until I die unless I die pretty soon."[39] Williamson had enlightened ideas on irrigation, which he thought might save a portion of the grant for sale in small tracts for agricultural purposes but did not expect these sales to be very important in extent. He concluded, therefore, that the "first and main revenue to the company" would be provided by the sale of grazing land in large blocks to cattlemen or cattle companies.[40]

The original idea was to sell grazing land in tracts of no less than 11,520 acres,[41] but this was later changed to 100,000 acres.[42] Williamson knew and informed the company officers that nearly all sufficiently watered grazing lands in the public domain were appropriated "according to the ethics rules and regulations existing among stock raisers, or ranch men; which rules and regulations are carefully observed and when necessary enforced by the shot-gun and revolver." Stockmen had used the tactic of getting control of large acreages by buying up 160-acre tracts controlling the water supply, often hiring bogus settlers to make the claims under the homestead law. The A. & P. grant was not watered and could not be except at great expense. Williamson, however, believed that the opportunity to acquire a large compact body of land cheaply, as was no longer possible elsewhere, would draw the cattlemen to New Mexico and Arizona and induce them to procure water by artificial means. These cattlemen would then own alternate sections and could, by grazing freely over the government sections also, "enjoy the use of double the area they own, with no one to interfere but the United States." Selling to cattlemen at a price lower than the government preemption price within the grant of $2.50 an acre would have the additional advantage, according to Williamson, of "stopping statesmen from crying out in the halls of

Congress against this as a 'soulless corporation' and 'monopoly' which robs the people of their heritage in the public lands."[43] The price was set therefore at one dollar an acre on four-year terms,"[44] but large sales were made for as little as fifty cents an acre.

Flaws in this plan became immediately obvious. For one thing, all prospective buyers, especially cattlemen buying large acreages, demanded a good title to the land. The A. & P., however, was hampered in securing this by delay on the part of the General Land Office in surveying the lands and giving the patents to the company. Recent scholarship on the subject of the railroads and the General Land Office has concluded that the administration of laws providing for withdrawal, survey, and patenting of land grants "had a direct bearing on the political position of the roads."[45] This was no more than the A. & P. office at Albuquerque was aware of in the early eighties. Engineers waited in the Indian Territory "at heavy expense" while politics was played in Washington over a resurvey of the Central Division line.[46] Of 840 A. & P. townsites in Arizona only 40 had been surveyed by June 1882, and Williamson was worried that changes in the law governing payment would make contracts for the public surveys so undesirable that further delay would result.[47] The problem became serious enough that Williamson in 1883 was asked to write a long letter to Jesse Seligman in New York explaining the mysteries of the public survey system,[48] and settlers along the line were requested by the company to petition for the completion of the surveys under existing laws.[49] The A. & P. was again in the right place at the wrong time. Land reform was popular with the constituents of members of Congress in the eighties, and there was talk of requiring the railroads to forfeit all unearned portions of their land grants and restore them to the public domain. The General Land Office was therefore slow to act, anticipating a change in the political wind.[50] Wrote Williamson early in 1882: "I can get nothing done at the General Land Office without delay and trouble. . . . There is now in that office a strong prejudice against all land grant railroads."[51]

Still Williamson maintained confidence in his decision on policy. Inquiries from farmers were frequent, but the railroad was so perfectly honest with prospective agricultural buyers about the poor prospects that most were discouraged from buying even the small acreages that A. & P. was willing to sell for irrigated agricultural lands. This honesty was no doubt motivated as much by imagined self-interest as genuine concern for the welfare of the farmer. The railroad land office employees knew that "sod-busters" and cattlemen got along poorly together and that fences broke up the range land on which the A. & P. was depending for profit. In the summer of 1882 Williamson refused Sedgwick's request to subscribe $500.00 to the New Mexico Agricultural Association on behalf of the company.[52] The title of those farmers already settled within the grant was examined as carefully as company funds would permit, and on occasion posses were formed to enforce the rules.[53] It was the company view that "many, if not most of the entries made & attempted to be made, are fraudulent & that the allegations as to date of settlement & improvements are false & fraudulent, & mainly with a view to securing springs of water timber or coal."[54]

Williamson and his small staff worked almost constantly for a time on fraudulent homestead entries and enclosed a pamphlet in all correspondence which quoted the attorney general of California to the effect that the A. & P. land grant had not lapsed by nonperformance in construction as many settlers claimed.[55] Still, by 1885, losses within the limits of the land grant to homestead and preemption entries as well as sometimes questionable Mexican land grants were 4,346,720 acres, only about half of which could be made up by selecting indemnity lands outside the primary grant limits.[56] The general feeling was that "a 'squatter' is without color of title and as he can purchase only one hundred and sixty acres ($\frac{1}{4}$ of a section), he cannot cause trouble except as a ruffian, & be suppressed by law."[57]

Colonists, that is those groups who wished to buy a large tract and subdivide it, occupied a middle ground between "squatters," whom the railroad discouraged, and cattlemen who were cultivated. Many of the colonies whose representatives wrote to Williamson were to be agricultural and that discouraged him. However, the prospect of the sale of really significant blocks of land caused a certain ambiguity in the attitude toward colonies of certain directors of the A. & P., Frisco, and Santa Fe. While the company never had a highly organized colonization program such as the Burlington or the Santa Fe, it did on occasion provide free transportation to interested parties and offer information on irrigation systems which could be built by colonists.[58]

The Seligmans, who had banking houses in Europe, were eager to establish offices in London and Frankfurt to solicit European colonists to settle in the American West, and preliminary steps were taken in this direction.[59] The A. & P. land office, however, objected to this policy, even though Europe had to be exploited if colonization were to succeed. Sedgwick noted that until the survey had been completed "only a very small part of the lands in Arizona could be described" much less offered to

European colonists.[60] Williamson was also against the encouragement of European colonization, but for slightly different reasons. Regarding plans to colonize persons from England and Scotland he wrote:

> They want to have everything their own way. I do not believe that any sale can be made at anything like fair prices. . . . I have always maintained that the lands could be better sold to Americans who understand how to use them, and my opinion is strengthened from day to day.[61]

Without the support of the two key members of the land department, attempts at colonization on the land grant could not help but fail.

That left the company fortunes exclusively dependent upon whether the cattlemen acted as Williamson predicted they would when offered large quantities of arid land in a checkerboard pattern at less than one dollar an acre. In August 1882 Williamson wrote to a friend that "in regard to the cattle business, it seems that the whole world has a craze upon it." Williamson was so enthusiastic that he invested a good deal in the cattle business himself although he granted that "for persons in my circumstances there is absolutely no chance." He hoped, however, to supplement his salary by investing also in the cattle shipping business on the A. & P.[62] For this reason partly he made a thorough study of stock-raising and in letters to possible investors he outlined quite scientifically the number of acres needed per head, the type of cattle best suited to the area of the land grant, and the salary necessary to obtain a good supervisor for a western ranch. Referring to these western ranch supervisors in a letter to New York, the land agent boasted: "These men are gentlemen in our western classification and can hold up their end of an intelligent conversation with any member of Congress but may not be quite up with Sam Cox or Belford in *classical* humor."[63]

Thomas Sedgwick in letters to associates made gentle sport of his superior's fervor about the cattle business. In 1884 he wrote to the A. & P. San Francisco agent: "Gen'l Williamson has a big deal on hand with some eastern people, which will not probably reach so far eastward as Holbrook."[64] Rumors from time to time of large sales boosted the price of A. & P. bonds temporarily, but in general Sedgwick's satirical outlook was well justified.[65] Many of Williamson's schemes were almost wholly chimerical. In February 1884, for example, he was sanguine that a bill could be pushed through Congress providing that in sales of railroad land for grazing purpose the government land could be sold along with the railroad sections. "The discussion that would be provoked," he wrote, "would be an entering wedge that would be kept moving until the knot would be rifted."[66] Once Williamson soothed the doubts of a Chicago man by claiming that U. S. statutes against fencing or occupying government lands were "a dead letter," and that persons fencing in government land with their own would not be prosecuted. In the summer of 1884 he wrote: "While the Company can guarantee nothing as to what the Government will do about the even sections it is most probable that it will do nothing for many years to come and that stock men will have the use of it without cost or hindrance during that time."[67] This last assumption especially took too little account of the wave of sentiment in the government for land reform.

Serious trouble for the railroad in its relation with the government began in 1883 and climaxed in 1884 and 1885. Territories through which the road ran, especially Arizona Territory, made attempts to tax it. Williamson was advised of the possible tax advantages of abandoning the A. & P.'s federal charter of 1866 on the Arizona section and incorporating under Arizona's general incorporation laws as the Southern Pacific had done. He, however, felt this too dangerous and instead sent lobbyists to the Arizona legislature: "What would this company gain? Can the territorial legislature, the child and creature of Congress . . . add to or take away from what Congress has done?"[68]

Taxation, however, was only one problem. Bogus agents appeared in 1884 who abused the company's fare allowances for inspection parties, offered good prices for the land, and then were revealed as men with little capital playing a "brokerage trick."[69] The railroad land office could only express amazement at the "audacity and cheek" of this class of operators.[70] To add to the crisis the winter of 1883–84 was particularly severe, snowing in trains on the line advertised as free from snow, piling cuts to a depth of fourteen feet and washing out large sections of the rapidly built line.[71] Edward Winslow, president of the Frisco, expressed interest in buying a fifty-thousand-acre ranch[72] but when Winslow's wife and some friends were taken on a bumpy tour of the lands in a spring wagon a sudden storm came up. Williamson had to admit that he thought "her impressions of the country are not highly favorable."[73]

These various difficulties, however, Williamson strongly felt could be overcome in time. But in Congress in the mid-eighties developed a serious sentiment to require the railroad to forfeit much of its grant and to restore the portion unearned by construction to the public domain. This meant not only the loss of expected revenue but the end of all hope to

Building a bridge at Johnson's Canyon, Ariz.
Photo courtesy University of New Mexico

Flagstaff, Ariz., shortly after completion of A&P
Photo courtesy University of New Mexico

Locomotive Capt. C. W. Rogers
Photo courtesy St. Louis-San Francisco Railway Co.

Locomotive C. P. Huntington
Photo courtesy St. Louis-San Francisco Railway Co.

complete the gaps in the St. Louis–San Francisco thirty-fifth parallel trunk line.

Forfeiture had been discussed in Congress as early as April 1879 and a bill introduced charging that since the A. & P. would fail to complete its road by the date required in the grant (July 4, 1879), all lands not earned by construction to that date would be forfeited.[74] In December 1880 there was a resolution asking an inquiry and charging that the company had "sold or pretended to sell" unearned lands "in prejudice of the rights of the people of the United States."[75] A spate of forfeiture bills were pushed by Gould and Huntington in an attempt to weaken the Frisco before they bought it in January 1882.[76]

All these were ignored by the A. & P., which interpreted them as so much congressional bluster. In 1883, however, Williamson began to view the traditional series of forfeiture bills with more concern. In December he wrote to President Nutt that the make-up of the three Senate committees in which the railroad was interested—Judiciary, Pacific Railroads, and Public Lands—was not favorable to the company. The Committee on Public Lands, he wrote, "could not be worse for our interests than it is," and its chairman "is perhaps the bitterest man in the American Congress against land grant roads."[77] Williamson, in conjunction with lobbyists for the Northern Pacific, which had a similar grant and a similar fear of forfeiture, had been able in previous Republican Congresses to exercise some control over appointments to these vital committees. But the 1882 elections had brought a Democratic Congress elected on a reform platform.[78] Williamson recommended that his associate lobbyist John Harris be given $1,000 extra for his services in the future,[79] and advised Nutt that it "will now be necessary to organize some line of defense."[80]

The prospects were discouraging. Williamson concluded that the House would pass any forfeiture bill that came before it, so he concentrated on the Senate. Even there it was clear by January 1884 that nothing could prevent an adverse bill from being reported from committee. Williamson therefore worked on securing a minority report, which "is our only chance to get our side of the question before the country." He also worked on a clever bit of reverse psychology. So long as a bill would be reported anyway, he decided to encourage those who wished to make it very radical:

> The Committee was organized for a purpose and it will not fail to fulfill the purpose. . . . The more sweeping and reckless the

bill or bills reported, the better it will be for the roads. In the hot haste to do acts of spoilation the committee will I think do things which will react for the benefit of the roads.[81]

In an appearance before the Committee on Public Lands early in 1884,[82] Williamson argued that the A. & P. was in a special position due to the Indian Territory problem, which was really the fault of the United States. He tried hard to rebutt the current rumor that the A. & P. did not intend to build to San Francisco and revealed a "secret" agreement with the Santa Fe for extending the Western Division toward its stated goal.[83] The congressional reformers, unfortunately for the railroad, had the perfect counter. They had discovered a fraudulent contract between the A. & P. and the Western Union Telegraph Company. The best the company could do was claim the present management had only inherited the contract. "People who are willing to do this Company an injury may catch at almost any pretense to assist them,"[84] Williamson wrote. ". . . Our case is desperate."[85]

A forfeiture bill passed both houses in July 1885, but Williamson's tactic of promoting divisions within the Congress as to the exact form of the bill resulted in a Senate version which suspended the effect of the measure until the question could be tested in court. Yet simultaneously a new administration arrived in Washington which was "in all respects . . . hostile to all land grant railroads," and a reforming commissioner of the General Land Office, William Andrew Jackson Sparks, refused categorically to grant the A. & P. patents on lands already earned.[86] Williamson advised the management in July 1885 that it would be best to pay the amount owed to the company's Washington law firm, Britton and Gray, in order to retain their services: "From this time forward, there is nothing but a continuous fight in prospect."[87]

While forfeiture was delayed in effect, the blow had been struck, and between congressional sessions during the summer of 1885 the vultures began to gather around the stricken carcass of the thirty-fifth parallel project. Among these were the Indian tribes, a familiar opponent. The A. & P. pressed especially hard for a rule to allow settlement of lands in Indian Territory in an attempt to save something of the Central Division plan.[88] This and continued differences over damage claims caused trouble with the tribes. The railroad sent Frisco attorney John O'Day into Indian Territory to adjust claims while holding that it needed "no terrorizing to cause it to pay to every Indian what is due to him."[89] O'Day, however, was not known for his tact or even temper and the methods used upset the Indians so much that they favored forfeiture all the more strongly. Wrote the Cherokees to the Indian office:

> This Company kills our Stock, has it undervalued by their own section men, and then a stock agent who arbitrarily shaves down this already low estimate. We are compelled to submit to his dictation or lay out of the money for years & spend so much in the collection by employing an attorney to *write* & *write* to the Indian Bureau which for some reason seems *peculiarly* and most *singularly* slow in such cases for causes to us unknown.[90]

The Indians were, however, unable to do the railroad any further damage. Not so with Land Commissioner Sparks. In July 1885 Williamson could say "I do not attach very grave importance to the action of this officer,"[91] but by December, when the Congress again considered forfeiture, he was in a fury at Sparks. Through November, A. & P. lobbyists had tried to convince the secretary of the interior to dismiss his land commissioner on the grounds that he was "an obstructionist and from a political point of view, injuring the administration with its own party."[92]

Williamson continued to address polite letters to Sparks asking patent of the lands and beginning, "I have the honor to respectfully request," but by December his letters to other railroad officials took on a different tone:

> There is no common sense rule that can be applied to the business of the General Land Office under the Commissioner. When all his other objections fail for want of any common sense or law to sustain them, he falls back upon what Congress may do or upon what objections might be urged against him for patenting lands while Congress is in session. The arguments that should be conclusive against his foolish objections, go for nothing with him as he has not the sense or the disposition to do right. His prejudice and enmity against railroads is boundless and controlling. . . . He promised me today that he would soon take up the case and see me again. Of course I know that he does not intend to do anything very soon, but I will not allow him to forget his promise, and I must in the mean time deal with him as if he were an irresponsible child or an idiot. It should be a humiliation and disgrace to the government of the United States to have this man in office.[93]

The day before Christmas, the *New York Tribune* printed an interview with Williamson which quoted him as saying that Sparks was "only three or four removes from an idiot."[94] Williamson in a private letter to Nutt denied that the interview had ever taken place but declined to say so publicly: "I have not asked him for any favors I have only asked for justice, but he denies justice and favors alike, and I do not see any object in placating or trying to soothe his feelings."[95]

The winter of 1885–86 was difficult in every way. Williamson's daughter died in December,[96] and the bills proceeded apace through the legislative process. In February 1886 the forfeiture bill passed the House with no discussion, only a dozen votes for it and none against—"not a very good thing to go to the Senate with," was Williamson's comment.[97] Senate passage was equally routine and a last-minute attempt by the company to influence the president to veto the bill failed.[98] In late summer, 1887, the General Land Office made the bill yet harder to swallow by restoring all indemnity lands to the public domain. Secretary of the Interior L. C. Lamar was not kind in announcing this to the A. & P.:

> Criticism upon the alleged shortcomings of the government with respect to this grant comes with an ill grace from this company. The people, whom the government represents, had some rights under the grant, as well as the company.

The secretary indicated that the act of 1866 was not passed for the sole benefit of the company and that the A. & P. could not construct "such fragments, or to and from such points as pleased its management," and expect the government to keep the lands "in a state of infinite withdrawal to wait the pleasure or convenience of the company."[99] In 1888 began the notices in the Boston papers which would become so familiar in the next ten years: "Atlantic & Pacific was flat at 10."[100]

These events left the thirty-fifth parallel project at the end of 1887 in desperate condition as regarded its transcontinental franchise.[101] The improvement reported in local traffic was of little encouragement following the loss of all but about fourteen million acres of the grant of forty-nine million that was expected by Fremont in 1866.[102] Even of the lands remaining sales were slow and by the end of 1887 the A. & P. land office had a dismal accounting to show of total sales. The total receipts since the opening of the office in 1880 were $1,110,159. Of that $500,000 had come from the sale of one million acres at fifty cents to the Aztec Land and Cattle Company, which was owned by the Seligmans; that sale was partially a payment for the bank's advances. The second largest sale, $164,984.00, was to E. B. Perrin,[103] a sheepman who complained constantly about the price of the land (seventy cents an acre) and the provisions of the contract and refused to make his last payment of $50,000.[104] The other buyers were few: S. G. Little ($98,143), Arizona Cattle Company ($121,450), William Crane ($594), Cebolla Cattle Company ($20,795), and Arizona Lumber Company ($400). Seven sales excepting town lots and a million dollars revenue in seven years was a poor record, especially when the expenses for the land office in 1887 after they had been pared considerably amounted to $213,572.[105] "For several years past," wrote Williamson in the spring of 1888, "there has been, & still is, a bitter and unreasonable prejudice against land grant R.R.s & we are compelled to defend the title to the grant against each separate branch of the government as well as against vicious men who draw their inspiration to do wrong from the example and advice of subordinate representatives of the gomt as well as from their superiors."[106]

11

SIEGE AND CAPITULATION

As the thirty-fifth parallel project died, so did one of its champions. In January 1886 Charles W. Rogers was forced by illness to resign his post as general manager, though he remained a vice-president.[1] In May, amidst optimistic reports of his recovery by newspapers along the line,[2] the Frisco company granted him a complete leave of absence "from business cares and duties."[3] Less than a year later, in February 1887, Rogers died at a South Pasadena, California, hotel of severe bronchitis.[4] The funeral at St. Louis's exclusive Lafayette Park Presbyterian Church was elaborate. Carriages belonging to every important member of the Frisco board and of many competing railroads lined the street as their owners respectfully filed past a casket surmounted by the complete floral engine and string of passenger cars, the engine's fragrant drive shaft broken to indicate unfinished work.[5]

His life, some said, had been cut short at fifty-three years because of the "unending round of toil, physical and mental," to which Joseph Seligman had appointed him in 1880 by elevating him to the status of

155

Frisco executive officer.[6] The company recognized Rogers's contribution with a two-page memorial to the "sterling qualities" of the man.[7]

Perhaps the sentiment at Rogers's death was prompted as much by a sense of guilt as a sense of loss, for he had lived long enough to recognize that the business goals to which he had devoted his career would not be realized. The forfeiture of the Atlantic and Pacific land grant made it certain that the Central Division and California section of that road would not be built. Farther east the Frisco had decided in 1886 to "enter aggressively" upon the construction of branches and extensions "to prevent the construction and operation of new lines of railroad into territory virtually belonging to the company."[8] This resolve resulted in the building of the long-delayed line to Texas under the name Paris and Great Northern Railroad Company and the sale of some bonds and town lots by the Frisco in Paris, Texas.[9] This, however, was defensive building only and succeeded mostly in arousing further enmity toward the Frisco by Texas citizens who resented being duped into subscribing to what they thought was a local enterprise while all the time John O'Day was masterminding the scheme for the Frisco.[10]

Far from maintaining transcontinental schedules, the management spent much of its time in the late 1880s answering such charges as townsite speculation,[11] mule-killing,[12] and failure of its engines to ring a bell instead of blowing a whistle within the city limits of Carthage, Missouri.[13] The extension into St. Louis was completed, but only to initiate a conflict with the Missouri Pacific over location of a freight depot.[14] The high freight rates of the golden years were forced down by new competition just as the road could least afford it,[15] and the new six-drivered freight locomotives which Rogers had ordered to pull up to sixty freight cars at a time pulled short trains as traffic from the Western Division dwindled.[16] By 1886 visitors were appalled at the air pollution and dirt as they boarded the Frisco at St. Louis,[17] and their impression of the line was not enhanced as they dined with begging pigs surrounding the station platform at the Newburg, Missouri, lunch stop[18] or took the next morning's breakfast on a desolate siding in the Choctaw Nation.[19] The deterioration of the track caused accidents that ruined the Frisco's sterling passenger safety record despite the constant claim by management that all the wrecks were due to sabotage.[20]

By the time of Rogers's death the A. & P. Western Division land office was reduced to going through the motions of conducting business. The operating department of the Western Division was run entirely by the Santa Fe after 1887.[21] Williamson abandoned his Washington office for lack of hope to do anything further there and suggested that the land office at Albuquerque need not be maintained as "there are no buyers there; not one acre has ever been sold there. . . . No sale has ever been closed outside of New York."[22] Frisco stockholders objected to further plans to guarantee A. & P. stock for fear that it would endanger their own securities,[23] while President William Strong of the Santa Fe expressed the opinion that any A. & P. line built in the Indian Territory would be nothing but a burden to the parent companies.[24] An engineering party reported in 1888 a rapid deterioration of ties on the Western Division due to a too narrow base for the rail and use of too light rail and too few ties in the hurry of construction. The A. & P. bridge over the Colorado River obstructed navigation and was so poorly built that it often washed away. Even the company cottages, intended to boost employee morale, could not turn the desert into the profit of which many had dreamed.[25] Scandals arose in connection with the A. & P.'s role in the building of a feeder line, the Arizona Mineral Belt Railway,[26] and residents of the area warned the railway managers that "if they intend to do an honest upright business, they need not buy up any legislatures . . . and they need issue no passes to politicians."[27] In 1888 the company-planned town of Holbrook burned to the ground,[28] and open warfare broke out between cattle and sheep men on A. & P. sections.[29] Wrote James Williamson: "I am more afraid of doing a foolish act, or one that would justly subject one to ridicule than I am of anything else that a man is supposed to ever fear."[30]

Hard times were reflected in the attitude of labor. The Frisco, which had kept the loyalty of its workers during the 1877 strikes, did so again during the 1886 strike by the Knights of Labor against Gould roads.[31] In 1888, however, a threatened strike over fireman's pay and working conditions forced the road to compromise its position and agree to an expense which many in the management felt the company could not afford.[32]

The Frisco found that its policy of allowing employees to become stockholders in the corporation's township companies helped to make them conservative but did not guarantee docility.[33] In 1889 an investigation revealed that Chief Superintendent D. H. Nichols was receiving a kickback from conductors under threat of dismissing them and that he was often drunk, profane, and violent in carrying out his duties.[34] This sort of behavior by supervisory personnel, combined with the declining financial fortunes of the road, could not help leading to a worsening labor problem for management.

Added to these general difficulties was a series of specific battles in which the Frisco became embroiled in the late 1880s, conflicts that weakened the corporate structure further by generating suspicion and irresponsible charges between a group of officers who had previously worked together in relative harmony. Representative of these are the so-called Surface Track Fight of 1886, the Oppenheim Stock Fight in 1887, and the O'Day imbroglio of 1889–90. Each of these resulted in a loss of public confidence in the line, a decline in stock prices, and an embarrassment to the Santa Fe by virtue of its being connected with such an organization.

The surface track fight of 1886 was the last battle in which Charles Rogers was involved. The issue was whether the Frisco had the right to build spur tracks within the city of St. Louis to serve local industries. The Gould roads—the Missouri Pacific and the St. Louis, Iron Mountain and Southern—had such lines crisscrossing the city and often left engines or trains upon them in such a fashion as to block city traffic and flout city ordinances. It was, however, the management of these very railroads that pressed the passage of a bill in the City Council to deny the Frisco opportunity for a similar privilege.

Calm heads in St. Louis realized that it was unfair to deny surface track privileges to the Frisco alone when that road's violations were comparatively insignificant, but these same men recognized that if the city continued unregulated growth it would have by 1900 a population of eight hundred thousand and a terrible traffic problem due to a snarl of switch engines shuttling cars across public streets. The feeling was growing that St. Louis's policy toward railroads, formed in a frenzy to attract them when the city had none, had been "short-sighted" and was out of date in the 1880s. The only sane solution proposed was the formation of a belt railway line to be shared by all roads entering the city. This would prevent both duplication of facilities and monopolizing of the trade of certain businesses by the railroad which built a spur to their locations. The Iron Mountain and the Missouri Pacific, however, had arranged backing for their position from the Merchant's Transportation Committee and the Wholesale Grocers' Association and were in no humor to compromise this chance of doing away with the Frisco as competitor; Gould, after all, did not have decisive control of the newest St. Louis road.

John O'Day, the company attorney, late in February 1886, collected a "very solid array of facts and figures" and faced the Council with the Frisco's case. The Frisco, O'Day stated, had obeyed all city ordinances, had bought up $1,500,000 worth of city property that would be made valueless if its side tracks were taken away, had reduced fares for St.

Louis commuters by 50 per cent since entering the city, and had so benefited St. Louis in other ways that the proposed ordinance would be "an enormous injustice."[35] O'Day succeeded in stopping the surface track bill and then he, Rogers, and Winslow proceeded to join with the lobbyists for the Iron Mountain and Missouri Pacific in insuring that any belt line built or regulated by the city would not impair business already established by the respective lines under the old system.[36]

The victory was won for the Frisco, yet at least a portion of the public viewed the surface track manipulations and the role played by the Frisco with disgust. Many interests used the occasion for a recital of collected grievances, damaging further the railroad's failing prospects. Editorialized the St. Louis Post-Dispatch:

> The proverbial irony of fate could hardly bring about a stranger situation than that of the St. Louis and San Francisco Road appealing to the Municipal Assembly to save it from the encroachment of a rival corporation. That road has turned the Constitution of the State into a mockery, has defied its statutes, violated its charter, despised the city ordinances, bought up Legislatures, handled slush funds to elect Governors, has persecuted private competition out of existence, has escaped the taxation which other property must bear, has gone into business as a coal dealer, has imposed on the traffic all that it would bear, and has managed its business generally on the public-be-damned principle. Now it comes asking protection from the Municipal Assembly. We invite attention to the spectacle.[37]

Another instance of unfortunate timing had placed the thirty-fifth parallel project in this awkward situation just at the height of the antirailroad political fervor of the 1880s.

Bearing the brunt of this political wave of reform was John O'Day. He had been elected second vice-president of the Frisco in May 1886, and many charged that his role as an executive officer of the railroad became in these years too thoroughly mixed with his position of leadership in the Democratic party of Missouri.[38] Rogers, sick though he was, was alert enough to send clippings to Winslow in New York which attacked O'Day and by implication the Frisco. O'Day, said the clippings, was the leader of an alliance of "shrewd and unscrupulous manipulators, masters of finesse, false pretense and dark-horse strategy" who were trying to prostitute the honest rural delegates at state conventions to the railroad monopolies.[39] O'Day, it was said, dictated the choice of State Supreme

Court justices year after year, bribed delegates to the state convention,[40] and lobbied unscrupulously in the state legislature against bills for railway regulation.[41] The Frisco vice-president was pictured in the press as a "Swamp Angel" who was corrupting the "Mountain Maid" (that is, honest delegates),[42] and with the baton of party control in his hands would "spit contemptuously and murmur softly to himself: 'What fools these rustics are!' "[43] The reputation of neither O'Day nor the company he represented was aided when in July 1887 O'Day's nephew Ed, who was employed by the Frisco as a telegraph line repairer between Rolla and Springfield, kidnapped a Rolla prostitute and an extensive unpaid-for wardrobe, then abandoned the girl in Pierce City to return to his wife and children in Kansas City.[44] The O'Day family assailed Victorian morality from all directions and provided a stereotyped shyster Irish lawyer whose image could be invoked with every thought of the St. Louis and San Francisco Railway Company. After Rogers's death O'Day's reputation seemed to dominate the public mind when the subject of the railroad was introduced. It was unfair and unfortunate but true and understandable. Equally understandable was the friction which developed between O'Day and the rest of the Frisco management.

Again Jay Gould took advantage of the situation. On March 6, 1887, the *New York Times* printed a report that Gould had obtained some of the remaining Seligman holdings in the Frisco and so had upped his share of six of the thirteen directors to a number that would represent a majority after the elections at the next annual meeting. The headline read, "A Control for Which He Has Been Working for Years Secured at Last."[45] Gould quickly denied the rumor, saying that he would "prefer to keep my money yet awhile." Winslow told reporters that Gould had not even a six-thirteenths hold on the board and that his votes, usually by proxy, were most often in agreement with the rest of the board. Winslow was insulted that the newspapers would question his word when as president of the Frisco he told them Gould had no plans for a change in management. The papers, however, had interviewed one of Gould's Wall Street associates. While this anonymous informer could not say whether the scheme had been accomplished yet, he did indicate to the *New York Times* that in conversations with Gould since the surface track fight the possibility of joining the Frisco with the Iron Mountain and Missouri Pacific "to insure greater harmony in management" had been often mentioned.[46]

The exact relation of these Gould purchase rumors and the Oppenheim stock fight which immediately followed is unclear except by reasoned inference. Yet it appears likely that E. L. Oppenheim & Company was working with Gould as financial agents just as the Seligmans worked with Winslow and the existing management. Newspaper advertisements, placed in the financial sections of leading newspapers in mid-April 1887, solicited the proxies of stockholders for use at the Frisco annual meeting on May 11 to change the directorate of the road. The board, went the argument, had been formed since 1882 by a combination of Gould, Huntington, and Seligman interests, the last predominating while the outside stockholders, who held the majority of the stock, had no voice in the management. If the directors recommended by Oppenheim were elected, read the advertisements, the First Preferred stockholders would be paid dividends as soon as they were earned rather than watching the company reinvest the profits in extensions, branches, and upkeep as previously. The Frisco board discussed the issue and resolved to declare a dividend on the First Preferred immediately and thereby hopefully dampen the threat to their positions.[47]

To financial analysts, the situation was not difficult to decipher. The *Financier,* a New York Wall Street paper, reported that the general feeling in Boston was that Oppenheim and Company were acting for Gould and Huntington and against the Santa Fe. The strategy was to "bottle up" the Frisco in its present local territory and then to "milk" the corporation by neglecting its condition and paying high dividends for the enrichment of speculators. All this was well-known Gould strategy. Many responsible railroad people believed that the declaration of a dividend "took much of the wind out of the sails of the opposition." William B. Strong, president of the Santa Fe, and his directors were generally regarded as relatively honest men, at least as builders rather than speculators, and it was hoped that their union with the Frisco would not yield to "the evil influence of the arch railroad wrecker." There was, as an afterthought, the A. & P. to consider: "They [the Frisco and the Santa Fe], together, are the parents of the Atlantic & Pacific, and if divorced, who can tell what will become of the child?"[48]

Apparently members of the Frisco management were too frightened to depend upon the stock dividend alone to save them and so resorted to a subterfuge that saved their positions but perhaps damaged the company almost as much as if Oppenheim and Gould had won the fight. In April Oppenheim and Company made a routine request for a statement of their holding of stock in the Frisco and when the reply disagreed with Oppenheim's own records the statement was sent back to the Frisco treasurer for correction. Not only would the Frisco not change the statement but it would not allow Oppenheim's representatives to look at the stock transfer books to find how it happened that they had suddenly lost so much of their interest. Winslow pled lack of jurisdiction and said the transfer books were not in the possession of the New York office and that he had no access to a list of stockholders.[49] The Oppenheim party found this "tenebrious ignorance" phenomenal especially since the Frisco stock certificates plainly read "transferable only at the transfer agency of the company in New York City."[50] The challenging group suspected that the books had been altered so as to prevent voting of the Oppenheim stock at the annual meeting and to deny E. L. Oppenheim and others chosen by him or by Gould seats in the Frisco directorate. A suit was therefore instituted by Oppenheim's attorney Walter DelMar in the Supreme Court of New York, the purpose of which was to acquire a writ ordering the railroad company to allow examination of its stock-holder record books.[51]

In the course of the court battle the Frisco officers made spectacles of themselves. Many of them including Winslow were fined for contempt of court because of their failure to appear or to testify meaningfully to a judge who was determined that the enforcement of court orders would not be obstructed by "some gentlemen from Wall Street."[52] Frisco Treasurer Frank Butler, who was in charge of the transfer books, at first demonstrated to the court a "reticence . . . of that close and masterly quality which distinguishes the Egyptian sphinx and the cast-iron watch dog." He could not say if there was a stock transfer book in the New York office and if he had seen it he could not remember. "I am not sure I ever wrote in it," he testified, "I may have done so without knowing it." The prosecuting attorney did finally wring from Butler the admission that the stock transfer book in question was in the company's New York safe and that he personally had made up a list of stockholders which he refused to produce for the court. This admission, however, came only after the lawyer had directed inquiries to Butler concerning "his sanity, his membership in the Episcopalian church, his knowledge of its dogmas, his belief in a hereafter, and his appreciation of the nature of an oath."[53] All this was a delight to newspaper editors across the country who found a chance to reveal to their rural pre-Populist readers that Wall Street was a center of idleness and corruption peopled by audacious "Robber Barons." Elaborate word pictures were drawn at the expense of the Frisco portraying a scene in which "the hosts of Oppenheim beleagured the general of the Seligmans in his castle and there was battle long and fierce between men who panted and sought each other's neckties hot-blooded."

The press found its perfect example of the rapacious predator of the business world in none other than Edward Winslow, who had been a relatively sober operator throughout his career but chose this least opportune moment to make an absolute fool of himself. Winslow, as did other officers, refused to testify, but in addition to that he locked himself in his office of the seventh floor of the Mills Building and left instructions with the personnel that should anyone call "he was busy and would continue to be busy indefinitely." When two deputy sheriffs called on April 23 to serve subpoenas on Winslow they were forced to resort to a complicated stratagem lest by reason of their failing to see him the general claim a technical immunity from appearing in court. One of the deputies diverted the clerk while the other slipped through to Winslow's office. He tried the door, found it blocked with a chair, and when he tried to open it met with President Winslow pushing on the other side. The deputy broke in and Winslow jumped him, knocking down a decorative screen in the process. The scene as the two crushed the screen and "wrestled around on the floor like two aspiring leg twisters in an athletic club" greatly amused the readers of the next morning's *New York Times*. The description of Winslow's face "white with anger" and his bombastic threats to do something irresponsible if his office were forced again was comic.[54] Winslow was forced to testify and the court ordered the company to open its books for inspection.[55] Oppenheim later said that even after this he was shown only a list of stockholders and not the original transfer books.[56]

The final ignominy, however, was yet to come. Several members of the Oppenheim group were drawn for jury duty in New York immediately after the trial. Had they served it would have prevented them from going to the Frisco annual meeting in St. Louis, and they protested loudly that the railroad was somehow responsible.[57] They were allowed to go to St. Louis after some wrangling but neither that nor the fact that the open books showed Jay Gould a much larger Frisco stockholder in his own name than Wall Street had expected caused the "lively shaking up of dry bones" that all the fanfare implied.[58]

The annual meeting on May 11, 1887, went smoothly, due partly to the "warlike appearance" of the sixth floor of the Roe Building in St. Louis where the stockholders met. The word "Private" had been freshly cut on all the glass doors of company offices, and around them stood rather sinister-looking brakemen.[59] When Oppenheim rose to vote he was told that a protest had been filed by the Seligmans which disallowed his vote. Oppenheim charged that the managers of the company had "conspired against the stockholders."[60] Later a Circuit Court held that the transfer books had been altered to give Seligman Oppenheim's stock and that the election of Russell Sage to the board at that meeting had been illegally conducted. The court then restored Sage's place on the board to Oppenheim.[61] But on the day of the annual meeting, it was a "cut-and-dried affair," the only sign of strife being "a broken pane of the President's office as if somebody had thrown a law book from the general attorney's office opposite." After the meeting Winslow slipped off quietly to the Southern Hotel for dinner[62] with James Seligman, who told a reporter only that "we had so many votes that we could easily have spared a few. The Oppenheims did not have a show."[63]

The "victory" made what was left of the hopes of the thirty-fifth parallel project a laughingstock to many who had restrained their laughter before. How was a company which found it necessary to resort to such antics to promote a transcontinental trunk line? The titters must have turned to guffaws when it was recognized how little of positive value the fight accomplished. Before the court's installation of Oppenheim the only change was the substitution of George Gould on the directorate for his ailing father Jay and the belated decision by the Frisco board to strike the words "at its Transfer Agency in the City of New York" from its stock certificates.[64] That the Oppenheim challenge was a clever maneuver by Gould and a serious threat to the Frisco is doubtless. The public, however, saw only the comic side, since according to a business code that had existed from the time Fremont and other taciturn officers entered railway management after the Civil War "the inner current of events which turned the tide of ballots to the reelection of the old Directory, was kept a profound secret."[65] To this day the old minute books and the stockholders' record books that were the object of the cataclysmic affray hide forever in their "suitable and uniform style" the true dynamics of the Oppenheim stock fight.

An unexpected result of the annual meeting was an open power struggle among the Frisco officers. Until May 1887, John O'Day was the "head and foot" of the Frisco organization. He was vice-president, general manager, and general attorney and no doubt expected to be elected president (Winslow was losing interest in the job and spending much of his time in Europe). At the annual meeting, however, the stockholders in addition to squelching the Oppenheim threat dampened as well the power of the vociferous O'Day.[66] Henry Morrill, a "sturdy

Maineite" who was known for being close-mouthed,[67] replaced O'Day as vice-president and general manager, and the Irishman from that point forward chose to vent his considerable spleen on the Frisco instead of in its behalf. In the process he brought the management into an impossible squabble and the corporation into a quandary which it could not solve independently.

At first O'Day's opposition and jealousy was a private affair felt mostly by the reformed management personally. By 1890, however, it had become public and laughable. The governor of Missouri, David Francis, instituted a suit against the Frisco for $300,000, presumably owed the state by the old South Pacific railroad. The full "moral weight and influence of the State" was thrown into the case just a few days before the statute of limitations on the debt would have run out.[68] Why had the state ignored their interest for twenty years and then suddenly put the attorney general's office into a flurry to try it? The Frisco found the answer in O'Day, who as general attorney knew the problem intimately and as few others did. Winslow was called back from Europe in February 1890 to investigate the "$300,000 case" and the allegations that an insider had tipped off the governor's office. The first man he spoke with in New York was John O'Day.

The result of Winslow's investigation was that on March 1, 1890, O'Day was dismissed from his employment with the company. Winslow gave reporters a synopsis of his thinking on the subject:

> My idea of a railroad is that it is a business concern and should be run as such and not as a political machine or lever to aid some man or party. Mr. O'Day is a Democratic partisan and full of political ambition. Mr. Morrill is an equally zealous Republican and does not take kindly to being subservient to Mr. O'Day.

The Seligmans, who had been responsible for first introducing O'Day into the management, agreed reluctantly to his dismissal but still spoke of him as "a remarkable man," which surely he was.[69]

The tact and explanations did not, however, hide the damage. O'Day made an elaborate defense of himself which contained in part the allegation that he was a martyr who was persecuted for standing up to Jay Gould. This the St. Louis papers found humorous. They called it a "clever dodge" designed to give O'Day "a soft place to land . . . with the Gould knife sticking out from his breast."[70] Winslow came to St. Louis early in March but avoided reporters and closeted himself all day in the

Frisco offices in the Roe Building conferring with Jay and George Gould and his officers. He told a reporter who called:

> If you gentlemen of the press will kindly give the Frisco a chance to attend to its business we shall hear very little more of factional troubles in the management. . . . I have neither the time nor the inclination to notice any assertions in the newspapers made by a retired officer in criticism of the management. There is only one answer in that regard. The directors have accepted Col. O'Day's resignation, and that ends the trouble.[71]

O'Day's tragedy, however, was completed only in April, when his inadequately insured Queen Anne mansion on the outskirts of St. Louis burned to the ground. The elegant immigrant who had enjoyed the warmth of two furnaces, a wine cellar, a cook, maid, gardener, coachman, and the hopes of great power, business and political, was at last reduced to a man in borrowed clothes looking at the ashes of his home and his career and suffering from nervous prostration.[72]

The Santa Fe at this point moved boldly. Four years earlier Santa Fe President William B. Strong had noted in a speech to his directors that "railroading is a business wherein progress is absolutely necessary. . . . A railroad cannot stand still; it must either get or give business; it must make new combinations, open new territory, and secure new traffic." The Frisco in 1890 definitely did not fit Strong's description of a thriving railroad, and the directors in analyzing their course remembered Strong's advice that "costly as a war always is, peace can be bought at too great a price."[73] From 1886 on, rumors circulated that the Santa Fe would formally absorb the Frisco and as early as 1888 the *New York Times* reported that the deal was close to consummation.[74] Then in April 1890, immediately after O'Day's resignation, came rumors that Gould and Huntington were manipulating the stock market and had been buying lots of Frisco stock and that "railroad men must hereafter . . . figure upon the Frisco as a part of the Missouri Pacific or Southern Pacific system, or perhaps of both."[75] But in May, when Winslow suddenly resigned, his place was taken not by Gould but by Allen Manvel of the Santa Fe.[76] The "mysterious buyer" who had been affecting the price of Frisco stock since the O'Day imbroglio had been the Atchison road. The Frisco became part of the Atchison, Topeka and Santa Fe system, adding 1,442 miles to that company's 7,706 and making it, next to the Prussian government, the largest owner of railway mileage in the world. For a time even the Frisco name disappeared.[77]

Resignations came in quickly as the Frisco directors were replaced entirely by Santa Fe officers. Winslow in his letter expressed the belief that operating the two railroads jointly would allow both to earn more money than when the fiction of separation had been maintained under the Tripartite Agreement. He did not, however, look forward to a sojourn in Europe caring for his ill wife: "I find myself for the first time during twenty consecutive years, no longer the executive officer of any railroad corporation and about to 'turn over a new leaf' in a life more than ordinarily filled with railroad work."[78] Winslow returned from his self-imposed exile on the continent only at the outbreak of World War I, and his return was quickly followed by his death in 1914 at age seventy-seven.[79]

Jesse Seligman's resignation letter contained a short history of the thirty-fifth parallel project and expressed "regret" at having to sever the family connection with the road which his brother Joseph had fostered. The truth was never more truly spoken than in Seligman's closing sentences, which were perhaps laced with a touch of irony:

> It is . . . a great source of satisfaction to me to be able to state that neither myself, nor my firm, nor (so far as I know) any of the officers or directors of this Company has at any time ever derived any profit from the construction of its thousand miles of roads, or in any speculation in its lands, or in any contracts for the supply of coal or any materials required by the road.

Perhaps it was not from want of trying.

Seligman wrote that the time had arrived when it was in the interest of stockholder and public alike for large corporations to unite.[80] This particular union of the Frisco and the Santa Fe was, however, unwise. Even as the sale was announced Wall Street papers warned that the deal would only add to the danger of the market being glutted with Atchison stock of which there was already an "enormous amount."[81] Exactly that happened, and when the financial panic of 1893 was added (the Santa Fe apparently inherited the bad timing that had haunted the thirty-fifth parallel project), the whole Santa Fe system went to the receivers. In 1896 the reorganized St. Louis and San Francisco Railroad Company bought the old Frisco and the A. & P. Central Division at a foreclosure sale while the Western Division became part of the Santa Fe.[82] Thus was the thirty-fifth parallel transcontinental trunk line project formally and finally laid to rest.

The foreclosure sales were drab affairs—no cigars, no clandestine deals and no Clinton Fisk. Fisk had once imagined that the "firery steed of steam whose breath is flame, whose sinews are brass and steel, whose neck is clothed with thunder, whose 'eyes are as the eyelids of the morning,' whose hoofs are iron" would quickly span the continent from St. Louis to San Francisco and show man's complete mastery of his environment. Perhaps he more than anyone should have realized that before the "crooked places" along the thirty-fifth parallel could be "made straight," account would have to be taken of those forces which Fisk blamed for his own defeat as a Prohibition candidate; that is, "partisan trickery, organized appetite, banded agencies of disorder . . . and the selfishness of sin."[83] In 1895 the ruined John O'Day seriously claimed that he had gained control of the St. Louis and San Francisco Railway Company, once aspirant to the continent.[84] Atlantic and Pacific advertising in the same year became aware too late of an important attraction along its route and began advertising the Grand Canyon for tourists "In Search of a New Sensation."[85] Maybe some of the old Frisco managers stopped there, tired as they were of the sensation that had occupied their lifetimes.

In the late 1960s Frisco diesels running freight trains west to Lawton, Oklahoma, or east into Tennessee had only the old abandoned Pacific of Missouri five-foot six-inch gauge tunnel west of St. Louis to remind their engineers of the reason for the corporate name lettered on the metal sides. Even the black and gold colors had disappeared in favor of red and white and in response to a safety campaign. Due to a vast change in corporate goal and the railway system's configuration in the twentieth century, the question of the meaning of the old name often still arises, and few know the full explanation. Much has certainly disappeared from memory since Henry Morrill went to San Francisco in 1888, the hopes of the thirty-fifth parallel project and its ruin fresh in his mind. Asked a reporter: "When is the St. Louis and San Francisco Railroad going to build into San Francisco?" With the infinite optimism of his predecessors since the South-West Branch began building at Franklin in 1853, Morrill replied: "Oh, that is something I cannot say. It won't be this year or next, but some day I suppose we will go there."[86]

APPENDIX

Corporate History of the Frisco System to 1890

Atlantic and Pacific Railroad Company	July 27, 1866 Act of Congress	Property in Missouri sold under foreclosure Sept. 8, 1876; acquired by St. Louis and San Francisco Ry. Co., Nov. 2, 1876; property in Indian Territory sold under foreclosure Dec. 18, 1897; acquired by St. Louis and San Francisco R.R. Co., Dec. 18, 1897
Fort Smith and Southern Railway Company	Feb. 13, 1886 Arkansas	Deeded to Frisco, Feb. 23, 1887
Fort Smith and Van Buren Bridge Company	March 23, 1885 Arkansas	Deeded to Frisco, July 17, 1907
Joplin Railroad Company (Kansas)	Dec. 22, 1875 Kansas	Consolidated with Joplin R.R. Co. (Mo.) as Joplin R.R. Co. (Consolidated) Feb. 25, 1876
Joplin Railroad Company (Missouri)	July 25, 1874 Missouri	Consolidated with Joplin R.R. Co. (Kans.) as the Joplin R.R. Co. (Consolidated) Dec. 28, 1881
Joplin Railroad Company (Consolidated)	Feb. 25, 1876 Missouri & Kansas	Consolidated with Joplin and Galena Ry. Co. (of Kans.) and Joplin and Galena Ry. Co. (of Mo.) to form Joplin Ry. Co. Dec. 28, 1881
Joplin Railway Company	Feb. 23, 1882 Kansas Feb. 25, 1882 Missouri	Property in Missouri deeded to St. Louis, and San Francisco Ry. Co., Mar. 17, 1882; Property in Kans. deeded to St. Louis and San Francisco Ry. Co., Mar. 27, 1882

Joplin & Galena Railway Company (of Kansas)	Sept. 28, 1880 Kansas	Consolidated with Joplin and Galena Ry. Co. (of Mo.) and Joplin R.R. Co. (Consolidated) to form Joplin Ry. Co. Dec. 28, 1881
Joplin and Galena Railway Company (of Missouri)	Sept. 28, 1880 Missouri	Consolidated with Joplin & Galena Ry. Co. (of Kans.) and Joplin R.R. Co. (Consolidated) to form Joplin Ry. Co. Dec. 28, 1881
The Kansas Midland Railway Company	Feb. 8, 1886 Kansas	Property sold at foreclosure July 25, 1900; deeded to the Kans. Midland R.R. Co., Oct. 1, 1900
Memphis, Carthage & Northwestern Railroad Company	July 24, 1871 Missouri	Consolidated with The State Line, Oswego and Southern Kans. Ry. under name of Memphis, Carthage and Northwestern R.R. Co. (Mo. and Kans.), Apr. 12, 1872
Memphis, Carthage & Northwestern Railroad Company	April 12, 1872 Kansas April 13, 1872 Missouri	Deeded to the Mo. and Western Ry. Co., Feb. 7, 1877
Missouri, Arkansas and Southern Railway Company of Arkansas	Sept. 10, 1880 Arkansas	Consolidated with St. Louis, Ark. & Tex. Ry. Co. (of Mo.), and St. Louis, Ark. and Tex. Ry. Co. (of Ark.) under name of St. Louis, Ark. and Tex. Ry. Co. (Consolidated), June 28, 1881
The Missouri and Western Railway Company	Mar. 19, 1875 Kansas Mar. 22, 1875 Missouri	Deeded to St. Louis and San Francisco Ry. Co., July 26 & 29, 1879
Oswego and State Line Railroad Company	Feb. 16, 1875 Kansas	Consolidated with The Pierce City and Kans. R.R. Co. under the name of The Mo. and Western Ry. Co., Mar. 19, 1875

Ozark Land Company	June 19, 1871 Missouri	Corporation dissolved, Sept. 2, 1903
Pacific Railroad (of Missouri)	Mar. 12, 1849 Missouri	That part of the property of this Co. known as Southwest Branch R.R. was sold under foreclosure by the State of Mo., on May 28, 1866, and conveyed to John C. Fremont by deed dated June 14, 1866. Deeded to South West Pacific R.R. Sept. 12, 1866
Paris and Great Northern Railroad Company	July 28, 1881 Texas	Deeded to St. Louis, San Francisco and Tex. Ry. Co., June 1, 1928, Corporation dissolved, July 21, 1928
Peirce City Real Estate Company	July 18, 1872 Missouri	Liquidated. Charter expired July 18, 1902
The Pierce City and Kansas Railroad Company	Feb. 11, 1875 Missouri	Consolidated with Oswego and State Line R.R. Co. under name of The Mo. and Western Ry. Co., Mar. 19, 1875
St. Louis, Arkansas and Texas Railway Company (of Arkansas)	July 17, 1880 Arkansas	Consolidated with Mo., Ark. and Tex. Ry. Co. (of Arkansas) and St. Louis, Ark. and Tex. Ry. Co. (of Mo.) under name of St. Louis, Ark. and Tex. Ry. Co. (Consolidated), June 28, 1881
St. Louis, Arkansas and Texas Railway Company (of Missouri)	June 4, 1880 Missouri	Consolidated with Mo., Ark. and Tex. Ry. Co. (of Ark.) and St. Louis, Ark. and Tex. Ry. Co. (of Ark.) under name of St. Louis, Ark. and Tex. Ry. Co. (Consolidated) June 28, 1881
St. Louis, Arkansas and Texas Railway Company (Consolidated)	June 28, 1881 Missouri and Arkansas	Deeded to St. Louis and San Francisco Ry. Co., Jan. 21, 1882

St. Louis, Wichita and Western Railway Company	Feb. 4, 1879 Kansas	Deeded to St. Louis and San Francisco Ry. Co. Mar. 28, 1882
St. Louis and San Francisco Railway Company	Sept. 10, 1876 Missouri	Property sold under foreclosure June 27, 1896; deeded to St. Louis and San Francisco R.R. Co., June 30, 1896
St. Louis and Western Railroad Company	————— Missouri	Property purchased during May 1887 by St. Louis and San Francisco Ry. Co. and subsequently abandoned
South Pacific Railroad Company	May 12, 1868 Missouri	Deeded to Atlantic and Pacific R.R. Co., Oct. 26, 1870
Southwest Branch Railroad	Not a Corporation	Constructed by Pacific R.R. (of Mo.) under act of the State of Mo., approved Dec. 25, 1852. Sold under foreclosure by the State of Mo. on May 28, 1866, and conveyed by John C. Fremont by deed dated June 14, 1866. Conveyed by Fremont to South West Pacific R.R., Sept. 12, 1866
South West Pacific Railroad	Aug. 24, 1866 Missouri	Property seized by State of Mo. on June 21, 1867. Deeded to South Pacific R.R. Co., June 15, 1868
Springfield Western & Southern Railroad Company	Sept. 9, 1875 Missouri	Name changed to Springfield & Western Mo. R.R. Co., Oct. 29, 1877
Springfield and Northern Railway Company	May 3, 1884 Missouri	Deeded to St. Louis and San Francisco Ry. Co., Dec. 29, 1885
Springfield and Southern Railway Company	June 10, 1882 Missouri	Deeded to St. Louis and San Francisco Ry. Co., Dec. 29, 1885

Springfield and Western Missouri Railroad Company	Sept. 9, 1875 Missouri	Incorporated as Springfield, Western and Southern R.R. Co.; name change Oct. 29, 1877. Deeded to Kans. City, Springfield & Memphis R.R. Co. (Consolidated) June 3, 1888
The State Line, Oswego and Southern Kansas Railway	Apr. 5, 1872 Kansas	Consolidated with Memphis, Carthage and Northwestern R.R. Co. (Mo.) under name of Memphis, Carthage and Northwestern R.R. Co. (Mo. & Kans.), Apr. 12, 1872

NOTES

CHAPTER 1
A HAUNTED JOURNEY

1. [Heinrich] Baldwin Mollhausen, *Diary of a Journey from the Mississippi to the Coast of the Pacific with a United States Government Expedition,* trans. Mrs. Percy Sinnett, 2 vols. (London: Longman, Brown, Green, Longmans, & Roberts, 1858), I, 1.
2. Muriel H. Wright and George H. Shirk, eds., "The Journal of Lieutenant A. W. Whipple," *Chronicles of Oklahoma,* XXVIII, No. 3 (Autumn, 1950), 240–41.
3. U.S. Congress, Senate, *Reports of Explorations and Surveys to Ascertain the Most Practicable and Economical Route for a Railroad from the Mississippi River to the Pacific Ocean,* Sen. Ex. Doc. 78, 33d Cong., 2d Sess., III, Pt. I, 3 (Serial 760). Hereafter cited as *Pacific Railroad Reports.* Most of the material from the Whipple expedition appears in Vols. III and IV of this twelve-volume set.
4. "Instructions from Jefferson Davis," *ibid.,* p. 1.
5. George L. Albright, *Official Explorations for Pacific Railroads, 1853–1855* (Berkeley, Calif.: University of California Press, 1921), pp. 29–32.
6. U.S. House, Speech of Rep. Thomas Bayly, 32d Cong. 2d Sess., March 1, 1853, *Congressional Globe,* XXII, 999.
7. Speech of Rep. James Strother, *ibid.,* 998.
8. William Goetzmann, *Army Exploration in the American West, 1803–1863* (New Haven: Yale University Press, 1959), p. 267.
9. For evidence of Whipple's reading, see *Pacific Railroad Reports,* III, Pt. I, 35, 64, 72.
10. Francis R. Stoddard, "Amiel Weeks Whipple," *Chronicles of Oklahoma,* XXVIII, No. 3 (Autumn, 1950), 226.
11. Wright and Shirk, eds., "The Journal of Lieutenant A. W. Whipple," p. 239.
12. *Pacific Railroad Reports,* III, Pt. I, 48.
13. Introduction by Alexander von Humbolt, in Mollhausen, *Diary,* I, xxi–xxii.
14. A discussion of these different ways of viewing the West is in William Goetzmann, *Exploration and Empire: The Explorer and the Scientist in the Winning of the American West* (New York: Alfred A. Knopf, 1966), p. 181.
15. Compare Mollhausen, *Diary,* I, 106, 153 with Whipple's entries in Wright and Shirk, eds., "The Journal of Lieutenant A. W. Whipple," p. 274, and *Pacific Railroad Reports,* III, Pt. I, 34.

16. Mollhausen, *Diary*, I, 2-3, 11.

17. Goetzmann, *Army Exploration*, pp. 248, 265.

18. *Jefferson Inquirer* (Jefferson City, Mo.), Sept. 16, 1854.

19. Goetzmann, *Army Exploration*, p. 286.

20. Wright and Shirk, eds., "The Journal of A. W. Whipple," pp. 243-44.

21. Mollhausen, *Diary*, I, 14-15.

22. *Pacific Railroad Reports*, III, Pt. I, 5-6, 9.

23. Mollhausen, *Diary*, I, 136, 220.

24. *Pacific Railroad Reports*, III, Pt. I, 12, 132.

25. Mollhausen, *Diary*, I, 106, 65, 75.

26. Wright and Shirk, eds., "The Journal of Lieutenant A. W. Whipple," pp. 255-56.

27. Robert Riegel, *The Story of the Western Railroads* (Lincoln: University of Nebraska Press, 1964), pp. 20, 23. First published in 1926.

28. Wright and Shirk, eds., "The Journal of Lieutenant A. W. Whipple," pp. 266, 271.

29. Mollhausen, *Diary*, I, 97, 107, 111.

30. Wright and Shirk, eds., "The Journal of Lieutenant A. W. Whipple," p. 259.

31. Mollhausen, *Diary*, I, 109-10, 113, 153-54.

32. *Pacific Railroad Reports*, III, Pt. I, 33.

33. Mollhausen, *Diary*, I, 241, 270; II, 7-8.

34. *Pacific Railroad Reports*, III, Pt. I, 132.

35. "Preliminary Report," *ibid.*, p. 5. The men of the fifties were as sure that trade would follow the natural lines of geography as they were of the wealth of the Orient.

36. Mollhausen, *Diary*, I, 268-69, 278, 284; II, 33, 121.

37. *Pacific Railroad Reports*, III, Pt. I, 59, 62, 67. A small wolf in the area was called by the natives "Coyota" from the Aztec word "Coijotl" meaning wolf.

38. Mollhausen, *Diary*, II, 23.

39. *Pacific Railroad Reports*, III, Pt. I, 69.

40. Mollhausen, *Diary*, II, 70-71.

41. *Pacific Railroad Reports*, III, Pt. I, 78, 82, 84, 88, 109.

42. *Ibid.*, pp. 134-35; Mollhausen, *Diary*, II, 301.

43. John Million, *State Aid to Railways in Missouri*, Economic Studies of the University of Chicago, No. 4 (Chicago: University of Chicago Press, 1896), p. 85; *Pacific Railroad Reports*, III, Pt. I, 62.

44. *Pacific Railroad Reports*, III, Pt. I, 106; Pacific Railroad Company, Minutes of the Board of Directors, Feb. 13, 1854, location 1170801, security vault, Missouri Pacific Building, St. Louis, Mo.

45. Million, *State Aid*, p. 77.

46. "Preliminary Report," *Pacific Railroad Reports*, III, 31.

47. Stoddard, "Amiel Weeks Whipple," p. 229.
48. *Rolla Express* (Rolla, Mo.), Jan. 7, 1861.

CHAPTER 2
THE SOUTH-WEST BRANCH

1. Frederick A. Cleveland and Fred Wilbur Powell, *Railroad Promotion and Capitalization in the United States* (New York: Longmans, Green & Co., 1909), pp. 136, 140–41.
2. *Ibid.,* p. 133.
3. Pacific Railroad Company, Minutes of the Board of Directors, Oct. 14, 1852, location 1170801, security vault, Missouri Pacific Building, St. Louis, Mo. Hereafter cited as Mo.Pac. Archives. These archives are organized by section only.
4. Quoted in John W. Million, *State Aid to Railways in Missouri,* Economic Studies of the University of Chicago, No. 4 (Chicago: University of Chicago Press, 1896), p. 90.
5. *Jefferson Inquirer* (Jefferson City, Mo.), Sept. 16, 1854.
6. U.S. Congress, Senate, 30th Cong., 2d Sess., Feb. 7, 1849, *Congressional Globe,* XVIII, 470, 472.
7. Patrick E. McLear, "The St. Louis Cholera Epidemic of 1849," *Missouri Historical Review,* LXIII, No. 2 (Jan. 1969), 177.
8. Robert S. Cotterill, "The National Railroad Convention in St. Louis 1849," *Missouri Historical Review,* XII, No. 4 (July 1918), 211.
9. The best work on the St. Louis/Chicago duel for railroad supremacy is Wyatt W. Belcher, *The Economic Rivalry between St. Louis and Chicago,* Studies in History, Economics and Public Law, No. 529 (New York: Columbia University Press, 1947).
10. *Missouri Weekly Patriot* (Springfield, Mo.), March 26, 1868.
11. James P. Kirkwood, *Report on Gauge of Track to the Board of Directors of the Pacific Railroad, Mo.,* pp. 4, 6–7, 9–10, bound in Reports of the Pacific Railroad Company, 1851–1872, Missouri Historical Society, Columbia, Mo., Vol. I. Hereafter cited as Reports.
12. Missouri Pacific Lines, *The First 112 Years* (n.p.: printed for the company, 1963), p. IV. The unloading scene is captured in a painting commissioned by the Missouri Pacific which now hangs in its offices in St. Louis.
13. *Missouri Republican* (St. Louis), July 21, 1853, clipping in box 5, Division "F," Railroad Right of Way and Reclamation, Records of the General Land Office, Record Group 49, National Archives. Hereafter cited as Div. "F," R.G. 49, N.A.
14. Million, *State Aid,* pp. 83, 76–77, 68.

15. *Missouri Republican* (St. Louis), July 21, 1853, clipping in box 5, Div. "F," R.G. 49, N.A.

16. *Missouri Republican* (St. Louis), July 6, 1851.

17. Missouri Pacific Lines, *The First 112 Years,* p. IV. Thomas Allen wrote in his annual report for 1853, that due to the national surveys "it now behooves us to push both our lines with increased energy, so that we shall be in a position to reach that road whatever route for it may be adopted." Pacific Railroad Company, *Third Annual Report . . . 1853,* p. 11, in Reports, Vol. I.

18. *Missouri Republican* (St. Louis), July 21, 1853, clipping in box 5, Div. "F," R.G. 49, N.A.

19. Pacific Railroad Company, Minutes of the Executive Committee, Feb. 13, 1854, location 1170801, Mo.Pac. Archives. The division points changed many times as construction proceeded and new towns grew up to claim the honor. Originally, the first division was to be from Franklin to the Gasconade River valley, the second from there to Springfield and the third from Springfield to the western boundary of the state. Million, *State Aid,* p. 85.

20. Million, *State Aid,* p. 85.

21. Letters, Thomas Allen to John Wilson, March 11, 1854, and April 8, 1854, box 5, Div. "F," R.G. 49, N.A.

22. Letter, John S. Phelps to John Wilson, Nov. 11, 1854, *ibid.*

23. Letter, R. M. Clelland to the President, Nov. 27, 1854, *ibid.*

24. Quoted in James Neal Primm, *Economic Policy in the Development of a Western State: Missouri 1820–1860* (Cambridge, Mass.: Harvard University Press, 1954), pp. 1, 43.

25. Million, *State Aid,* pp. 62, 65, 69.

26. *An Act to Expedite the Construction of the Pacific Railroad, and of the Hannibal and St. Joseph Railroad, Laws of Missouri 1850–51,* 16th Gen. Assem., 1st Sess., pp. 265–68, in Clair V. Mann, ed. "Frisco First: A Source Materials History of the St. Louis & San Francisco Railroad, 1845–1945," Vol. II: Book of Statutes (unpublished collection, Phelps County Historical Society, Rolla, Mo.), pp. 13–18. A less complete collection of statutes relating to the railroads in this study before 1873 is Atlantic and Pacific Railroad Company, *Laws and Documents. Atlantic & Pacific Railroad and Leased Lines* (St. Louis: Levison & Blythe, 1873).

27. Million, *State Aid,* p. 107.

28. *An Act to Amend the Act Entitled "An Act to Incorporate the Pacific Railroad," Laws of Missouri 1850–51,* 16th Gen. Assem., 1st Sess., pp. 268–73. *An Act to Authorize the City of St. Louis to Subscribe Stock in the Pacific Rail Road Company, and for Other Purposes, ibid.,* pp. 721–22. These laws are in Mann, Book of Statutes, pp. 19–26, 27–30.

29. *An Act to Accept a Grant of Land Made to the State of Missouri by the Congress of the United States, to Aid in the Construction of Certain Railroads in This State, and to Apply a Portion thereof to the Pacific Railroad, Laws of Missouri 1852*, 17th Gen. Assem., 1st Sess., pp. 10–14, in Mann, Book of Statutes, pp. 38–45.

30. *An Act to Secure the Completion of Certain Railroads in This State, Laws of Missouri 1855–56*, 18th Gen. Assem., Adj. Sess., pp. 472–84, in Mann, Book of Statutes, pp. 68–82.

31. *The Pacific Railroad* v. *the Governor* (1856), *Missouri Reports*, XXIII, 353–71.

32. Million, *State Aid*, p. 103.

33. *An Act to Amend "An Act to Secure the Completion of Certain Railroads in This State, and for Other Purposes,"* Approved Dec. 10, 1855, *Laws of Missouri 1857*, 19th Gen. Assem., pp. 85–91, in Mann, Book of Statutes, pp. 87–95.

34. Million, *State Aid*, p. 112.

35. *An Act Supplemental to "An Act to Amend 'An Act to Secure the Completion of Certain Roads in This State, And for Other Purposes,'"* Approved March 3, 1857, *Laws of Missouri 1857*, 19th Gen. Assem., Adj. Sess., pp. 69–73, in Mann, Book of Statutes, pp. 98–105.

36. *An Act to Expedite the Completion of the South-West Branch of the Pacific Railroad, and in Relation to the Pre-Emptions Upon Railroad Land, Laws of Missouri, 1859*, pp. 63–66, in Mann, Book of Statutes, pp. 109–13.

37. Million, *State Aid*, p. 103.

38. *St. Louis Globe Democrat*, Nov. 1, 1885, in *Rolla Weekly Herald* (Rolla, Mo.), Nov. 12, 1885. A thirtieth anniversary account of the disaster.

39. Edward Miller, *Address, Delivered by Request, Before a Railroad Meeting of the Citizens of Cooper County* (St. Louis: George Knapp, 1858), pp. 6, 8, 12, 11.

40. *Ibid.*, pp. 11–12.

41. *Pacific Railroad* v. *Hughes* (1855), *Missouri Reports*, XXIII, 291–309.

42. Pacific Railroad Company, Minutes of the Board of Directors, Nov. 18, 1856, location 1170801, Mo.Pac. Archives.

43. Deeds No. 381 and No. 624 in files of St. Louis–San Francisco Railway Co., St. Louis, Mo.

44. Letter, Edward Miller to Sam J. Reeves, Oct. 26, 1857, Missouri Historical Society, St. Louis, Mo.

45. *Ibid.*, Oct. 22, 1857. Pacific Railroad Company, Minutes of the Board of Directors, April 21, 1857, location 1170801, Mo.Pac. Archives.

46. Edward Miller in Pacific Railroad Company, *Eighth Annual Report . . . 1858*, pp. 25–26, in *Reports*, Vol. I.

CHAPTER 3
DISUNION AND DISRUPTION

1. Anthony Trollope, *North America* (5th ed.; London: Chapman & Hall, 1866), pp. 117, 111.
2. *Rolla Express* (Rolla, Mo.), July 30, 1860.
3. William Fayel, quoted in *Rolla Weekly Herald* (Rolla, Mo.), Oct. 1, 1891.
4. *Rolla Express,* Dec. 24, 1860.
5. Trollope, *North America,* pp. 111–13.
6. *Ibid.,* pp. 112–13.
7. *Rolla Express,* Feb. 18, 1861.
8. *Ibid.,* Dec. 3, 1861.
9. *Ibid.,* Aug. 6, 1860. In August 1860, only eight months after the founding of Rolla and four months before railroad service began, lots in Bishop's Addition, the most exclusive suburb, were selling for $100 each.
10. *Ibid.,* Aug. 13, 1860; Feb. 25, 1861. Barrel sugar was 10¢ a lb., beeswax 40¢ a lb., "Machanaw" fish 6½¢ a lb., and eggs 10¢ a dozen. After the first train, prices were down to 8½¢, 25¢, 2¢, and 8¢ respectively.
11. *Ibid.,* Oct. 1, 1860.
12. *Ibid.,* Nov. 30, 1861.
13. *Marshfield Express,* quoted in *ibid.,* Sept. 10, 1860.
14. Letter, E. B. Brown to O. D. Greene, Feb. 21, 1864, in *Records of the Rebellion,* Series I, XLVIII, Pt. II (Washington: G.P.O., 1896), p. 389.
15. Richard Brownlee, *Gray Ghosts of the Confederacy: Guerrilla Warfare in the West, 1861–1865* (Baton Rouge: Louisiana State University Press, 1958), p. 15.
16. *Rolla Express,* Aug. 31, 1961.
17. Brownlee, *Gray Ghosts,* p. 226.
18. *Rolla Express,* Sept. 27, 1862; June 24, 1861.
19. *Ibid.,* Aug. 31, 1861.
20. Letter, George Taylor to John C. Fremont, Aug. 30, 1861, Taylor Collection, Missouri Historical Society, St. Louis.
21. Letter, D. R. Garrison to Col. Chester Harding, Jr., May 9, 1865, in *Records of the Rebellion,* Series I, XLVIII, Pt. II (Washington: G.P.O., 1896), p. 370.
22. Brownlee, *Gray Ghosts,* pp. 42–53.
23. Letter, A. Lincoln to Maj. Gen. William S. Rosecrans, March 10, 1864, in *Records of the Rebellion,* Series I, XXXIV, Pt. II (Washington: G.P.O., 1891), p. 349.
24. Paul Plato in *Daily Missouri Democrat* (St. Louis), Jan. 1, 1861, p. 2, col. 3.
25. *Rolla Express,* Aug. 27, 1860.
26. *Ibid.,* April 4, 1863.

27. Pacific Railroad Company, Minutes of the Executive Committee, June 18, 1862, location 1170801, security vault, Missouri Pacific Building, St. Louis, Mo. Hereafter cited as Mo.Pac. Archives.

28. Letter, Henry L. Patterson, Daniel R. Garrison, and George R. Taylor to Pacific railroad directors, March 19, 1870, Taylor Collection, Missouri Historical Society, St. Louis; U.S. Congress, *Joint Resolution in Regard to Certain Railroads in Missouri,* 37th Cong., 2d Sess., March 6, 1862, *Congressional Globe,* XXXII, Appendix, p. 420.

29. *An Act Authorizing a Change of Gauge of Railroads in the State of Missouri, Laws of Missouri,* 1866, 23d Mo. Gen. Assem., Adj. Sess., p. 101, in Clair V. Mann, ed. "Frisco First: A Source Materials History of the St. Louis & San Francisco Railroad, 1845–1945," Vol. II: Book of Statutes (unpublished collection, Phelps County Historical Society, Rolla, Mo.), pp. 141–42.

30. "A Sketch History of the Missouri Pacific and Southwest Branch," in *ibid.,* Vol. I: Early & General Frisco History, p. 124.

31. *Cheyenne Daily Leader* (Cheyenne, Wyo.), Feb. 22, 1872.

32. Walter Ehrlich, "Was the Dred Scott Case Valid?" *Missouri Historical Review,* LXIII, No. 3 (April 1969), 320.

33. *Missouri Weekly Patriot* (Springfield, Mo.), Sept. 16, 1875.

34. Pacific Railroad Company, *Eighth Annual Report . . . 1858,* p. 10, bound in Reports of the Pacific Railroad Company, 1851–1872, Missouri Historical Society, Columbia, Mo., Vol. I.

35. *Missouri Republican,* quoted in *Missouri Weekly Patriot* (Springfield, Mo.), Oct. 19, 1865.

36. *Missouri Weekly Patriot* (Springfield, Mo.), Oct. 12, 1865.

37. Letter, Henry T. Blow to Ellis G. Evans, S. Grayson, P. T. Mettai, and E. W. Bush, Jan. 22, 1866, inserted in scrapbook of the Southwest Pacific Railroad, in possession of Mr. Andrew Niemeier, Ass't. Sec., St. Louis–San Francisco Railway Co., St. Louis, Mo. Hereafter cited as SWP Scrapbook.

38. *Rolla Weekly Herald,* May 14, 1885.

39. *Missouri Weekly Patriot* (Springfield, Mo.), Nov. 23, 1865.

40. *Ibid.,* May 3, 1866.

41. *Ibid.,* Oct. 5, 1865.

42. *Missouri Republican,* quoted in *ibid.,* April 19, 1866.

43. *Journal* (Springfield, Mo.), Sept. 25, 1865, in SWP Scrapbook.

44. *Rolla Express,* Aug. 20, 1860.

45. Pacific Railroad Company, Minutes of the Board of Directors, March 3, 1866, location 1179891, Mo.Pac. Archives.

46. *An Act Granting Lands to Aid in the Construction of a Railroad and Telegraph Line from the States of Missouri and Arkansas to the Pacific Ocean, Statutes at Large,* XIV, 292–99 (1866).

47. Cardinal Goodwin, *John Charles Fremont: An Explanation of His Career* (Palo Alto, Calif.: Stanford University Press, 1930), pp. 240, 260.

CHAPTER 4
JOHN C. FREMONT AND THE ATLANTIC AND PACIFIC RAILROAD COMPANY

1. *Lebanon Advocate* quoted in *Missouri Weekly Patriot* (Springfield, Mo.), May 10, 1866.
2. *St. Louis Republican,* Aug. 3 [1866], clipping in scrapbook of the Southwest Pacific Railroad Company, in personal possession of Mr. Andrew Niemeier, Ass't. Sec., St. Louis–San Francisco Railway Co., St. Louis, Mo. Hereafter cited as SWP scrapbook.
3. Allan Nevins, *Fremont, Pathmarker of the West* (New York: D. Appleton-Century Co., 1939), pp. 583–87.
4. Herbert Bashford and Herr Wagner, *A Man Unafraid: The Story of John Charles Fremont* (San Francisco: Herr Wagner Publishing Company, 1927), frontispiece caption, p. 4.
5. *Missouri Weekly Patriot* (Springfield, Mo.), Nov. 23, 1865.
6. *Ibid.,* Oct. 26, 1865.
7. *Ibid.,* Feb. 22, 1866.
8. *Daily Missouri Democrat* (St. Louis), July 16, 1866, p. 1, col. 2.
9. *St. Louis Press,* quoted in *Missouri Weekly Patriot* (Springfield, Mo.), June 28, 1866.
10. *Missouri Weekly Patriot* (Springfield, Mo.), Nov. 16, 1865.
11. Letter, Thomas Fletcher to R. J. Mc Elhany, Jan. 13, 1866 in *ibid.,* Jan. 25, 1866.
12. Letter, Thomas Fletcher to Henry C. Young, Feb. 12, 1866, in *ibid.,* March 1, 1866.
13. *An Act Granting Lands to Aid in the Construction of a Railroad and Telegraph Line from the States of Missouri and Arkansas to the Pacific Ocean, Statutes at Large,* XIV, Sec. 1, 292 (1866).
14. *St. Louis Times,* quoted in *Weekly People's Tribune* (Jefferson City, Mo.), March 4, 1868.
15. *Missouri Weekly Patriot* (Springfield, Mo.), March 7, 1867.
16. *Daily Missouri Democrat* (St. Louis), July 17, 1866, p. 2, col. 2.
17. *St. Louis Press,* quoted in *Missouri Weekly Patriot* (Springfield, Mo.), June 28, 1866.
18. *Charter and By-Laws of the Atlantic and Pacific Railroad Company, . . .* July 21, 1853 (New York: John F. Trow, 1853), pp. 1, 5.
19. Cornelius Glen Peebles, *Exposé of the Atlantic and Pacific Railroad Company (Extraordinary Developments)* (New York: New York Examiner, 1854), pp. 6, 9–10.

20. U.S. Congress, Senate, 39th Cong., 1st Sess., March 1, 1866, *Congressional Globe*, XXXVI, 1100–03.
21. *An Act to Provide for the Sale of Certain Railroads and Property by the Governor, to Foreclose the State's Lien Thereon, and to Secure the Early Completion of the Southwest Branch Pacific, the Platte County, the St. Louis and Iron Mountain and the Cairo and Fulton Railroads of Missouri, Laws of Missouri, 1866*, 23d Mo. Gen. Assem., Adj. Sess., pp. 107–14, in Clair V. Mann, ed. "Frisco First: A Source Materials History of the St. Louis & San Francisco Railroad, 1845–1945," Vol. II: Book of Statutes (unpublished collection, Phelps County Historical Society, Rolla, Mo.), pp. 128–36.
22. Letter, R. J. Mc Elhany to Editors, *Missouri Democrat*, June 21, 1866, quoted in *Missouri Weekly Patriot* (Springfield, Mo.), June 28, 1866.
23. Deed, John C. Fremont and Jessie Benton Fremont to South West Pacific Railroad Company, Sept. 12, 1866, Deed #19875, secretary's vault, St. Louis–San Francisco Railway Co., St. Louis, Mo. Hereafter cited as Frisco Archives.
24. *New York Tribune*, June 23, 1866, in SWP Scrapbook.
25. Letter, R. J. Mc Elhany to Editors of *Missouri Democrat*, quoted in *Missouri Weekly Patriot* (Springfield, Mo.), June 28, 1866. Another story had it that Freeman & Co. asked for a $300,000 bribe from Fremont to withdraw, and was prepared to let Fremont then buy the road on his own. *St. Louis Press*, quoted in *ibid*.
26. Letter, R. J. Mc Elhany to *Missouri Weekly Patriot*, May 28, 1866, in *Missouri Weekly Patriot* (Springfield, Mo.), May 31, 1866.
27. Letter, A. W. Maupin to ?, July 26, 1866, SWP Scrapbook.
28. Letter, Henry L. Patterson, Daniel R. Garrison, and George R. Taylor to Pacific Railroad Directors, March 19, 1870, Taylor Collection, Missouri Historical Society, St. Louis, Mo.
29. *San Francisco Bulletin*, June 1, 1866, SWP Scrapbook.
30. *An Act Granting Lands to Aid in the Construction of a Railroad and Telegraph Line from the States of Missouri and Arkansas to the Pacific Ocean, Statutes at Large*, XIV, Sec. 1, 292 (1866).
31. *Missouri Weekly Patriot* (Springfield, Mo.), Jan. 11, 1866; Oct. 19, 1865.
32. *Ibid.*, March 8, 1866.
33. *An Act Granting Lands to Aid in the Construction of a Railroad and Telegraph Line from the States of Missouri and Arkansas to the Pacific Ocean, Statutes at Large*, XIV, Sec. 3, 294–97 (1866).
34. *Daily Missouri Democrat* (St. Louis), Oct. 2, 1866, p. 2, col. 2.
35. *Missouri Weekly Patriot* (Springfield, Mo.), Oct. 4, 1866.
36. *St. Louis Democrat*, Aug. 17, 1866, SWP Scrapbook.
37. U.S. Interstate Commerce Commission, "Valuation Docket Number 400 —St. Louis–San Francisco Railway Company et al., July 8, 1932," *Valuation Reports*, XLI (Washington: G.P.O., 1933), 495.

38. Proposal of John C. Fremont for the purchase of the South West Pacific Railroad, May 18, 1866, filed with Deed #19875, Frisco Archives.

39. Certificate of Incorporation of the South West Pacific Railroad, Aug. 24, 1866, *ibid*.

40. Pacific Railroad Company, Minutes of the Board of Directors, June 14, 1866, location 1170801, security vault, Missouri Pacific Building, St. Louis, Mo.

41. Interstate Commerce Commission, *Valuation Reports,* XLI, 499.

42. Gov. Thomas Fletcher's annual message to the legislature, Nov. 3, 1865, quoted in *Missouri Weekly Patriot* (Springfield, Mo.), Nov. 9, 1865.

43. *Daily Missouri Democrat* (St. Louis), April 3, 1867.

44. Mortgage of the Southwest Pacific Railroad to John P. Yelverton and Charles Ward, Sept. 15, 1866, in Southwest Pacific Railroad Company, *Southwest Pacific Railroad Company. Atlantic & Pacific Railroad Company. Statutes, Conveyances and Documents* (New York: Stockholder Job Printing Office, 1867), pp. 67–68.

45. John Million, *State Aid to Railways in Missouri,* Economic Studies of the University of Chicago, No. 4 (Chicago: University of Chicago Press, 1896), p. 169.

46. Interstate Commerce Commission, *Valuation Reports,* XLI, 495.

47. Southwest Pacific Railroad Company, Minutes of the Board of Directors, Sept. 11, 1866, basement vault, Frisco Archives.

48. *Stockholder,* New York, Sept. 11, 1866, SWP Scrapbook.

49. *Ibid.,* Sept. 18, 1866.

50. *New York Tribune,* June ?, 1866, SWP Scrapbook.

51. Southwest Pacific Railroad Company, Minutes of the Board of Directors, Sept. 14, 1866, basement vault, Frisco Archives.

52. *St. Louis Democrat* quoted in *Missouri Weekly Patriot* (Springfield, Mo.), Sept. 27, 1866.

53. Contract, Southwest Pacific Railroad Company and American Emigrant Aid and Homestead Company, Sept. 26, 1866, S.L.&S.F. contract #323, basement vault, Frisco Archives. The contracts in the four black boxes marked "S.L.&S.F. contracts" have been destroyed, but there are summaries of their content on the cover envelopes yet existing.

54. Contract, Southwest Pacific Railroad Company and John J. Sturg, Nov. 16, 1866, S.L.&S.F. contract #320, basement vault, Frisco Archives.

55. *St. Louis Democrat* quoted in *Missouri Weekly Patriot* (Springfield, Mo.), Sept. 27, 1866.

56. Southwest Pacific Railroad Company, Minutes of the Executive Committee, Dec. 6, 1866, basement vault, Frisco Archives.

57. Charlotte Erickson, *American Industry and the European Immigrant, 1860–1885* (New York: Russell & Russell, 1957), pp. 79–80.

58. *St. Louis Democrat,* quoted in *Missouri Weekly Patriot* (Springfield, Mo.), Jan. 17, 1867.

59. *Ibid.*, Jan. 31, 1867.

60. *Missouri Weekly Patriot* (Springfield, Mo.), Supplement, May 23, 1867.

61. *St. Louis Democrat* quoted in *Missouri Weekly Patriot* (Springfield, Mo.), June 27, 1867.

62. *Lebanon Advocate,* quoted in *Missouri Weekly Patriot* (Springfield, Mo.), April 18, 1867.

63. Southwest Pacific Railroad Company, Minutes of the Executive Committee, Dec. 14, 1866, basement vault, Frisco Archives.

64. Southwest Pacific Railroad Company, Minutes of the Board of Directors, Dec. 15, 1866, *ibid.*

65. Southwest Pacific Railroad Company, Minutes of the Stockholders, Jan. 17, 1867, *ibid.*

66. Southwest Pacific Railroad Company, Minutes of the Board of Directors, May 18, 1867, *ibid.*

67. *St. Louis Democrat,* quoted in *Missouri Weekly Patriot* (Springfield, Mo.), June 27, 1867.

68. *Rolla Express,* June 17, 1867.

69. Southwest Pacific Railroad Company, Minutes of the Board of Directors, May 18, 1867, basement vault, Frisco Archives.

70. *St. Louis Democrat,* quoted in *Missouri Weekly Patriot* (Springfield, Mo.), June 27, 1867.

71. Southwest Pacific Railroad Company, Minutes of the Board of Directors, May 18, 1867, basement vault, Frisco Archives.

72. Southwest Pacific Railroad Company, Account Book, March 1, 1866–Dec. 31, 1867, Missouri Historical Society, St. Louis.

73. Southwest Pacific Railroad Company, Minutes of the Board of Directors, May 18, 1867, basement vault, Frisco Archives.

74. George Anderson, *Kansas West* (San Marino, Calif.: Golden West Books, 1963), p. 14. This early map clearly shows the projected connection.

75. H. Craig Miner, "The Border Tier Line: A History of the Missouri River, Fort Scott and Gulf Railroad, 1865–1870" (unpublished M.A. thesis, Wichita State University, 1967), p. 35.

76. *St. Louis Democrat,* quoted in *Missouri Weekly Patriot* (Springfield, Mo.), June 27, 1867.

77. *Daily Missouri Democrat* (St. Louis), July 9, 1867, p. 1, col. 1.

78. *Ibid.,* June 27, 1867, p. 1, col. 1.

79. *Missouri Weekly Patriot* (Springfield, Mo.), June 27, 1867.

80. Quoted in Bashford and Wagner, *A Man Unafraid,* p. 386.

81. *John Charles Fremont,* p. 259.

82. Alice Eyre, *The Famous Fremonts and their America* (Boston: The Christopher Publishing House, 1961), pp. 346, 14.

83. *Rolla Herald of Liberty,* quoted in *Missouri Weekly Patriot* (Springfield, Mo.), April 11, 1867.

CHAPTER 5
THE SOUTH PACIFIC RAILROAD COMPANY

1. U.S. Interstate Commerce Commission, "Valuation Docket Number 400 —St. Louis–San Francisco Railway Company et al., July 8, 1932," *Valuation Reports,* XLI (Washington: G.P.O., 1933), 498, 497, 494, 407.

2. Letter, James Baker to editor, July 1, 1867, quoted in *Missouri Weekly Patriot* (Springfield, Mo.), July 4, 1867.

3. *History of Greene County, Mo.* (St. Louis: Western History Company, 1883), p. 742; *Pictorial and Geneological Record of Greene Co., Mo. together with Biographies of Prominent Men. . . .* (Chicago: Goodspeed Brothers, 1893), p. 195; *Missouri Weekly Patriot* (Springfield, Mo.), July 14, 1867.

4. *Missouri Weekly Patriot* (Springfield, Mo.), July 18, 1867.

5. *Ibid.,* Oct. 17, 1867.

6. Letter, M. Blair to James B. Eads, Aug. 21, 1867, J. B. Eads papers, Missouri Historical Society, St. Louis.

7. *Arizona Silver Belt* (Globe, Arizona), Jan. 17, 1879.

8. *Missouri Weekly Patriot* (Springfield, Mo.), Nov. 14, 1867.

9. *Ibid.,* Nov. 21, 1867.

10. *Ibid.,* Dec. 19, 1867.

11. *Atlantic and Pacific Railroad Company, Route to the Pacific Ocean on the 35th Parallel, Extracts from Reports of E. F. Beale, Esq., and Lieut. Whipple to the War Department Showing the Features of the Route* (New York: Stockholder Job Printing Office, 1897), p. 8.

12. Memphis newspaper, quoted in *Missouri Weekly Patriot* (Springfield, Mo.), Jan. 2, 1868.

13. Fletcher's address to Mo. House, Jan. 20, 1868, quoted in *Missouri Weekly Patriot* (Springfield, Mo.), Jan. 30, 1868.

14. *Missouri Weekly Patriot* (Springfield, Mo.), Feb. 6, 1868.

15. "U.V.R." in *Daily Missouri Democrat* (St. Louis), Feb. 15, 1868, p. 2, col. 2.

16. *Missouri Weekly Patriot* (Springfield, Mo.), Feb. 6, 1868.

17. *Ibid.,* Feb. 20, 1868.

18. *Daily Missouri Democrat* (St. Louis), Feb. 15, 1868, p. 1, col. 1.

19. *Ibid.,* March 2, 1868, p. 1, col. 2.

20. South Pacific Railroad Co., Articles of Association, March 17, 1868, secretary's vault, St. Louis–San Francisco Railway Co., St. Louis, Mo. Hereafter cited as Frisco Archives.

21. South Pacific Railroad Co., Minutes of the Board of Directors, May 19, 1868, basement vault, Frisco Archives.

22. Interstate Commerce Commission, *Valuation Reports,* LXI, 495.

23. *Missouri Weekly Patriot* (Springfield, Mo.), April 1, 1869.

24. South Pacific Railroad Co., Minutes of the Board of Directors, May 19, 1868, basement vault, Frisco Archives.
25. *Ibid.,* June 4, 1868.
26. Letter, Francis B. Hayes to Charles J. Morrill, Dec. 11, 1868, Folder labeled "South Pacific Railroad Co.," Steam Railroads Collection, Baker Library, Harvard University. Hereafter cited as Harvard Collection.
27. Interstate Commerce Commission, *Valuation Reports,* XLI, 488.
28. Letter, W. H. Coffin to Uriel Crocker, Jan. 18, 1869, South Pacific folder, Harvard Collection.
29. Letter, Francis B. Hayes to Uriel Crocker, Jan. 27, 1870, South Pacific folder, Harvard Collection; South Pacific Railroad Company, Minutes of the Board of Directors, June 4, 1868, basement vault, Frisco Archives.
30. South Pacific Railroad Co., Minutes of the Board of Directors, Sept. 29, 1870, basement vault, Frisco Archives.
31. *St. Louis Times,* May 1, 1870, in Scrapbook of the Southwest Pacific Railroad Co., in possession of Andrew Niemeier, Ass't. Sec., St. Louis–San Francisco Railway Co., St. Louis. Hereafter cited as SWP Scrapbook.
32. South Pacific Railroad Co., Minutes of the Board of Directors, Nov. 9, 1869, basement vault, Frisco Archives.
33. Letter, James Baker to Francis Hayes, Oct. 4, 1869, box 1, Division "F," Railroad Right of Way and Reclamation, Records of the General Land Office, Record Group 49, National Archives.
34. Letter, Thomas C. Fletcher to Joseph Wilson, Feb. 18, 1870, *ibid.*
35. Letter, Clinton Fisk to Francis Hayes, Feb. 4, 1869, *ibid.*
36. Letter, H.T.B. [Henry T. Blow] to James Eads, Dec. 22, 1868, James B. Eads papers, Missouri Historical Society, St. Louis.
37. Alphonso A. Hopkins, *The Life of Clinton Bowen Fisk with a Brief Sketch of John A. Brooks* (New York: Funk & Wagnalls, 1888), pp. 24, 99, 111.
38. *Missouri Weekly Patriot* (Springfield, Mo.), July 9, 1868.
39. *Ibid.,* July 23, 1868.
40. Hopkins, *Life of Fisk, passim.*
41. *Missouri Weekly Patriot* (Springfield, Mo.), July 23, 1868.
42. Letter, Jacob Sleeper to Colored M. E. Church, Springfield, Mo., Oct. 12, 1868, quoted in *ibid.,* Dec. 17, 1868.
43. Letter, Clinton Fisk to Uriel Crocker, Jan. 12, 1869, South Pacific folder, Harvard Collection.
44. Letter, Andrew Peirce to Uriel Crocker, Aug. 1, 1868, *ibid.*
45. Letter, W. H. Coffin to Uriel Crocker, Dec. 10, 1868, *ibid.*
46. Letter, Francis Hayes to Charles Morrill, Dec. 11, 1868, *ibid.*
47. Letter, Francis Hayes to Uriel Crocker, Feb. 10, 1869, *ibid.*
48. *Ibid.,* Feb. 18, 1869.

49. Letter, W. H. Coffin to Uriel Crocker, Jan. 18, 1869, *ibid.*
50. Letter, Francis Hayes to Uriel Crocker, Feb. 18, 1869, *ibid.*
51. Letter, Clinton Fisk to Uriel Crocker, Feb. 1, 1869, *ibid.*
52. *Missouri Weekly Patriot* (Springfield, Mo.), Oct. 1, 1868.
53. Letter, Francis Hayes to Uriel Crocker, Sept. 29, 1869, South Pacific folder, Harvard Collection.
54. Letter, Francis Hayes to Uriel Crocker, Sept. 28, 1869, *ibid.*
55. Letter, Francis Hayes to Uriel Crocker, Sept. 28, 1869, *ibid.*
56. *St. Louis Democrat,* Oct. 7, 1869, in SWP Scrapbook.
57. *Missouri Weekly Patriot* (Springfield, Mo.), Dec. 16, 1869.
58. *Ibid.,* May 5, 1870.
59. *Weekly People's Tribune* (Jefferson City, Mo.), May 11, 1870.
60. Federal Writers' Project, *Missouri: A Guide to the "Show Me" State* (New York: Hastings House, 1854), pp. 332–33.
61. In 1876, the company held $339,000 worth of stock in town companies. Interstate Commerce Commission, *Valuation Reports,* XLI, 487.
62. *Ibid.,* 489.
63. Justin Kaplan, *Mr. Clemens and Mark Twain* (New York: Simon & Schuster, 1966), p. 188.
64. Quoted in Bryant M. French, *Mark Twain and The Gilded Age* (Dallas: Southern Methodist University Press, 1965), p. 163.

CHAPTER 6
PLAYED OUT

1. Letter, William Tweed to Commissioner of the General Land Office, July 6, 1871, marked "Private and Immediate," box 1, Division "F," Railroad Right of Way and Reclamation, Records of the General Land Office, Record Group 49, National Archives. Hereafter cited as Div. "F," R.G. 49, N.A.
2. Letter, J. B. Andrews to Sec. of Interior, May 25, 1871, railroad package 11, Lands and Railroads Division, Records of the Department of the Interior, Record Group 48, National Archives. Hereafter cited as L&RR, R.G. 48, N.A. See also Jacob Siever to Sec. of Interior, April 17, 1871, *ibid.,* and James Smith to U. S. Grant, Sept. 11, 1870, railroad package 10, *ibid.*
3. Letter, Amos Tuck to Willis Drummond, June 3, 1871, box 1, Div. "F," R.G. 49, N.A.
4. *Missouri Weekly Patriot* (Springfield, Mo.), Feb. 1, 1872.
5. *Ibid.,* Oct. 5, 1871.
6. *Ibid.,* Aug. 3, 1871.
7. *Ibid.,* Jan. 25, 1872.
8. *Ibid.,* May 30, 1872.

9. *Weekly People's Tribune* (Jefferson City, Mo.), Nov. 23, 1870.

10. *Rolla Express* (Rolla, Mo.), Nov. 15, 1873.

11. *Parmley v. St. Louis, I.M. & S.R. Co. Paul v. Pacific R.Co. Bailey v. Atlantic & P.R. Co. St. John v. Missouri K. & T. Ry. Co. Courtright v. Clark et al.* (1874), *Federal Cases,* XVIII, 1228.

12. *Baily v. Atlantic & P.R. Co. et al.* (1874), *Federal Cases,* II, 366.

13. "H," in *Missouri Weekly Patriot* (Springfield, Mo.), March 3, 1870.

14. *Ibid.,* June 1, 1871.

15. *Weekly Peoples' Tribune* (Jefferson City, Mo.), May 11, 1870.

16. Letter, Francis B. Hayes to J. D. Cox, Aug. 1, 1870, railroad package 10, Lands and Railroads Division, Records of the Department of the Interior, Record Group 48, National Archives. Hereafter cited as L&RR, R.G. 48, N.A.

17. *Missouri Weekly Patriot* (Springfield, Mo.), Feb. 15, 1872.

18. F. S. Hodges, Report of Surveys for the Atlantic & Pacific R.R. Co., Missouri to Arizona, 1870 & 1871, MSS. in library of the Oklahoma Historical Society, Oklahoma City.

19. "An Act in Regard to the East and West Railway Company, that may be Authorized to Construct the East and West Railroad through the Cherokee Nation," Dec. 15, 1870, Cherokee Vol. 258, 71, Indian Archives Division, Oklahoma Historical Society. Hereafter cited as IAD.

20. Letter, Lewis Downing to Francis Hayes, Nov. 29, 1869, Cherokee Vol. 253, 158–59, IAD.

21. Letter, Lawrence Kellitt to C. J. Hillyer, Nov. 22, 1871, Quapaw Railroad File, IAD.

22. Morris L. Wardell, *A Political History of the Cherokee Nation, 1838–1907* (Norman: University of Oklahoma Press, 1938), p. 259.

23. Angie Debo in *Oklahoma City Times,* April 1, 1954, p. 7.

24. Wardell, *Political History,* p. 259.

25. *Missouri Weekly Patriot* (Springfield, Mo.), May 18, 1871.

26. *Ibid.,* Feb. 29, 1872.

27. Letter, John B. Jones to C. Delano, Sept. 1871, in *Report of the Secretary of the Interior,* H. Exec. Doc. 1, Pt. 5, 42d Cong., 2d Sess., 1872, p. 980, 982 (Serial 1505).

28. Letter, F. A. Walker to Enoch Hoag, Dec. 12, 1871, with accompanying papers, Quapaw Railroad File, IAD.

29. C. J. Hillyer, *Atlantic and Pacific Railroad and The Indian Territory* (Washington: McGill & Witherow, 1871), pp. 1–2, 26, 36, 39, 42, 52.

30. Letter, Jas. Harlan to C. Delano, June 10, 1872, railroad package 12, L&RR, R.G. 48, N.A.

31. V. V. Masterson, *The Katy Railroad and the Last Frontier* (Norman: University of Oklahoma Press, 1952), pp. 128–29.

32. Letter, A. Peirce, Jr., to Gen. Wm. Vanderveer, C. W. Babcock and M. Hilton, Dec. 27, 1871, railroad package 333, L&RR, R.G. 48, N.A.

33. Letter, Joseph Seligman to Francis Hayes, Sept. 18, 1871, Private Letter Book of J. & W. Seligman & Co., New York. Hereafter cited as PLB.

34. Andrew Peirce, Jr., *The Atlantic and Pacific Railroad Company. Report of the General Manager to the Directors, December, 1873* (New York: Union Printing House, 1874), p. 12.

35. South Pacific Railroad Co., Minutes of the Executive Committee, Nov. 13, 1869, basement vault, St. Louis–San Francisco Railway Co., St. Louis, Mo. Hereafter cited as Frisco Archives.

36. Ross Muir and Carl White, *Over the Long Term: The Story of J. & W. Seligman & Co.,* 1964), pp. 24, 65.

37. Letter, Joseph Seligman to Seligman Bros. (London), Oct. 10, 1868, PLB.

38. Muir and White, *Over the Long Term,* pp. 99–100.

39. Letter, Joseph Seligman to Seligman & Stettheim (Frankfort), March 29, 1869, PLB.

40. Muir and White, *Over the Long Term,* p. 99.

41. *San Francisco Chronicle,* Jan. 3, 1872.

42. Letter, Joseph Seligman to Hon. Joseph Brown, Feb. 3, 1872, PLB.

43. *St. Louis Republican,* quoted in *San Francisco Chronicle,* Feb. 24, 1872, p. 1, col. 3.

44. *Missouri Weekly Patriot* (Springfield, Mo.), Feb. 8, 1872.

45. Letter, Joseph Seligman to Jos. Brown, April 6, 1872, PLB.

46. *Ibid.,* May 19, 1871.

47. Letter, Joseph Seligman to Andrew Peirce, April 8, 1872, PLB.

48. Letter, Joseph Seligman to Seligman & Stettheim (Frankfort), March 8, 1872, PLB.

49. Letter, Joseph Seligman to C. J. Morrill, April 6, 1872, PLB.

50. Letter, Joseph Seligman to Seligman & Stettheim (Frankfort), March 8, 1872, PLB.

51. Letter, Joseph Seligman to C. B. Fisk, May 18, 1872, PLB.

52. Letter, Joseph Seligman to A. Peirce, Feb. 8, 1872, PLB.

53. Letter, [Joseph Seligman] to Andrew Peirce, April 2, 1872, PLB. The only reason Seligman did not go to California with them was that the marriage of his daughter was to take place at that time. Letter, Joseph Seligman to C. J. Morrill, April 2, 1872, PLB.

54. Letter, Francis Hayes to C. Delano, April 6, 1872, railroad package 12, L&RR, R.G. 48, N.A.

55. *Ibid.,* April 8, 1872.

56. Letter, C. J. Hillyer to Columbus Delano, April 13, 1872, railroad package 12, L&RR, R.G. 48, N.A.

57. Letter, Cherokee Delegation to B. R. Cowen, May 14, 1872, *ibid.*

58. Letters, B. R. Cowen to Francis Hayes, April 10, 1872 and April 11, 1872; to C. J. Hillyer, April 20, 1872; to W. P. Rose *et al.,* May 16, 1872,

Pacific Railroads, Letters Sent, Records of the Department of the Interior, Record Group 48, National Archives.

59. Bancroft, Hubert H., *History of California,* Vol. XXIV of *The Works of Hubert Howe Bancroft,* VII, pp. 607, 609.

60. Letter, Francis Hayes to C. Delano, April 6, 1872, railroad package 12, L&RR, R.G. 48, N.A.

61. Letter, Joseph Seligman to Seligman Bros. (London), May 14, 1872, PLB.

62. *Rural World,* quoted in *Missouri Weekly Patriot* (Springfield, Mo.), Sept. 12, 1872.

63. Letter, Joseph Seligman to Andrew Peirce, Jr., April 15, 1872, PLB.

64. Peirce, *Report of the General Manager, 1873,* p. 8; Receipts to A. Peirce, March 20, 1871, W. H. Coffin, Feb. 7, 1871, Francis Hayes and Oliver Ames, March 8, 1871, Hudson Bridge Collection, Missouri Historical Society, St. Louis.

65. *Annual Report. Atlantic and Pacific Railroad Company to the Stockholders, For the Fiscal Year Ending December 31, 1874* (New York: Evening Post Steam Presses, 1875), p. 43.

66. *Commercial and Financial Chronicle* (New York), Feb. 1, 1873.

67. U.S., Interstate Commerce Commission, "Valuation Docket Number 400 —St. Louis–San Francisco Railway Company et al., July 8, 1932," *Valuation Reports,* XLI (Washington: G.P.O., 1933), 363, 362.

68. Peirce, *Report of the General Manager,* 1873, p. 18.

69. Masterson, *Katy,* pp. 94, 105.

70. Letter, Joseph Seligman to Capt. Jos. Brown, May 18, 1872, PLB.

71. Letter, Joseph Seligman to A. Peirce, May 20, 1872, PLB.

72. *Ibid.;* Letter, Uriel Crocker to Andrew Peirce, Jr., and William A. Hayes, June 20, 1872, Atlantic and Pacific folder, Steam Railroad Collection, Baker Library, Harvard University. Hereafter cited as Harvard Collection.

73. *New York Times,* Aug. 30, 1873, p. 8, col. 3.

74. Letter, J. B. Henderson to C. Delano, March 10, 1873, railroad package 12, L&RR, R.G. 48, N.A.

75. *Commercial and Financial Chronicle* (New York), Feb. 1, 1873.

76. *Missouri Weekly Patriot* (Springfield, Mo.), Jan. 30, 1873.

77. *Commercial and Financial Chronicle* (New York), Feb. 1, 1873.

78. *Rolla Express,* Dec. 7, 1872.

79. *Ibid.,* Dec. 7, 1872.

80. "Piquad Abroad" in *Missouri Weekly Patriot* (Springfield, Mo.), Jan. 30, 1873.

81. A. M. Strong, "When the Frisco System Was Young," *Frisco System Magazine,* II, No. 5 (June 1903), 48.

82. *Chicago Tribune,* quoted in *Rolla Express,* Aug. 23, 1873.

83. Letter, William A. Hayes to Uriel Crocker, March 7, 1873, Atlantic and Pacific folder, Harvard Collection.

84. *Missouri Weekly Patriot* (Springfield, Mo.), Aug. 11, 1873.

85. Samuel Hayden Church, "Thomas Alexander Scott," in *Dictionary of American Biography,* ed. Dumas Malone, XVI (New York: Charles Scribners and Sons, 1936), 501.

86. *Cheyenne Daily Leader* (Cheyenne, Wyo.), June 29, 1871.

87. Quoted in Julius Grodinsky, *Transcontinental Railway Strategy, 1869–1893: A Study of Businessmen* (Philadelphia: University of Pennsylvania Press, 1962), p. 23.

88. Robert Riegel, "The Missouri Pacific Railroad to 1879," *Missouri Historical Review,* XVII (October 1923), 16.

89. *Commercial and Financial Chronicle* (New York), Feb. 1, 1873.

90. *New York Times,* May 28, 1873, p. 9, col. 1.

91. *Ibid.,* May 3, 1872, p. 5, col. 3.

92. Grodinsky, *Strategy,* p. 16.

93. *New York Times,* Aug. 21, 1874, p. 2, col. 4.

94. *Cheyenne Daily Leader,* June 29, 1871.

95. *Missouri Weekly Patriot* (Springfield, Mo.), April 24, 1873.

96. *Ibid.,* July 17, 1873.

97. *New York Times,* May 28, 1873, p. 9, col. 1.

98. Letter, Joseph Seligman to Paris office, Aug. 20, 1872, PLB.

99. Muir and White, *Over the Long Term,* p. 102.

100. Letter, Joseph Seligman to Paris office, Aug. 26, 1872, PLB.

101. Memphis, Carthage and Northwestern Railroad Co., Minutes of the Board of Directors, Oct. 1, 1874, Dec. 20, 1873, basement vault, Frisco Archives.

102. *New York Times,* May 28, 1873, p. 9, col. 1.

103. Peirce, *Report of the General Manager,* 1873, p. 23.

104. *Annual Report, Atlantic and Pacific, 1874,* p. 49.

105. Letter, Joseph Seligman to William Seligman, June 1, 1872, PLB.

106. Letter, Joseph Seligman to Seligman Bros. (London), July 25, 1872, PLB.

107. Letter, Joseph Seligman to William Seligman, July 20, 1872, PLB.

108. Letter, Joseph Seligman to J. Seligman & Co. (San Francisco), Aug. 19, 1872, PLB.

109. Letter, Joseph Seligman to Seligman Bros. (London), Oct. 7, 1872, PLB.

110. *Missouri Weekly Patriot* (Springfield, Mo.), May 20, 1875.

CHAPTER 7
THE ST. LOUIS AND SAN FRANCISCO RAILWAY COMPANY

1. U.S. Interstate Commerce Commission, "Valuation Docket Number 400 —St. Louis–San Francisco Railroad Company et al., July 8, 1932," *Valu-*

ation Reports, XLI (Washington: G.P.O., 1933), 478; Foreclosure Decree, June 6, 1876, filed with deed #19872, secretary's vault, St. Louis–San Francisco Railway Co., St. Louis, Mo. Hereafter cited as Frisco Archives.

2. U.S. Congress, Senate, *Memorial of the Texas & Pacific Railway Co. and the Atlantic and Pacific Railroad Co.,* Sen. Misc. Doc. 6, 43d Cong., 2d Sess., 1874, pp. 2–5 (Serial 1653); *Cheyenne Daily Leader* (Cheyenne, Wyo.), Dec. 1, 1874.

3. Letter, A. A. Sargent of C. Delano, March 28, 1875, railroad package 13, Lands and Railroads Division, Records of the Department of the Interior, Record Group 48, National Archives. Hereafter cited as L&RR, R.G. 48, N.A.

4. Letter, W. Townsend to Willis Drummond, April 15, 1874, box 2, Division "F," Railway Right of Way and Reclamation, Records of the General Land Office, Record Group 49, National Archives.

5. Letter, C. P. Huntington to David Colton, Dec. 13, 1875, quoted in *San Francisco Chronicle,* Dec. 23, 1883, p. 9, col. 11.

6. *Missouri Weekly Patriot* (Springfield, Mo.), Sept. 9, 1875.

7. *New York Times,* Dec. 7, 1874, p. 1, col. 2.

8. Protest of Cherokee Delegation against the Revival of Certain Land Grants Therein Named 7c., Dec. 29, 1876, Cherokee File Ixa, pp. 2, 5, Indian Archives Division, Oklahoma Historical Society, Oklahoma City. Hereafter cited as IAD.

9. U.S. Congress, Senate, *Memorial of the Citizens of the Chickasaw Nation . . . ,* Sen. Misc. Doc. 34, 42d Cong., 2d Sess., 1875, p. 1 (Serial 1630).

10. U.S. Congress, Senate, *Protest of the Osage Nation of Indians . . . ,* Sen. Misc. Doc. 72, 42d Cong., 2d Sess., 1875, pp. 1–2, 5 (Serial 1630).

11. *Commercial and Financial Chronicle* (New York), April 19, 1873.

12. Robert Riegel, "The Missouri Pacific Railroad to 1879," *Missouri Historical Review,* XVII (October 1923), 16–17.

13. *New York Times,* Oct. 13, 1875, p. 12, col. 3.

14. Interstate Commerce Commission, *Valuation Reports,* XLI, 488.

15. *New York Times,* Oct. 13, 1875, p. 12, col. 4.

16. *Ibid.,* Nov. 2, 1875, p. 10, col. 1.

17. *Ibid.,* Nov. 4, 1875, p. 8, col. 1.

18. *Ibid.,* Dec. 30, 1875, p. 2, col. 4.

19. *Ibid.,* Jan. 8, 1876, p. 2, col. 3.

20. Stockholders list, item 57, Atlantic and Pacific folder, Steam Railroads Collection, Baker Library, Harvard University. Hereafter cited as Harvard Collection; *Railroad Gazette* (New York), May 12, 1876.

21. Letter, Jos. Seligman to Uriel Crocker, May 3, 1876, Atlantic and Pacific folder, Harvard Collection.

22. *Railroad Gazette* (New York), June 16 and 21, 1876.
23. Letter, W. H. Coffin to Uriel Crocker, June 7, 1876, Atlantic and Pacific folder, Harvard Collection.
24. Letter, J. R. Robinson to Uriel Crocker, July 7, 1876, *ibid.*
25. Stockholders list, item 57, *ibid.*
26. Letter, J. R. Robinson to Uriel Crocker, July 7, 1876, *ibid.*
27. Letter, Uriel Crocker to Clinton B. Fisk, Aug. 15, 1876, *ibid.*
28. *Railroad Gazette* (New York), Sept. 1, 1876.
29. *St. Louis Globe-Democrat,* Sept. 9, 1876, p. 7, col. 2.
30. *Ibid.,* Sept. 7, 1876, p. 3, col. 3.
31. *Ibid.,* Sept. 9, 1876, p. 8, col. 3.
32. *Ibid.,* Sept. 10, 1876, p. 4, col. 6.
33. *Ibid.,* Sept. 19, 1876, p. 3, col. 1.
34. *Ibid.,* Sept. 9, 1876, p. 8, col. 3.
35. *Springfield Weekly Patriot-Advertiser* (Springfield, Mo.), Oct. 18, 1876.
36. *Rolla Weekly Herald* (Rolla, Mo.), April 4, 1878.
37. *Missouri Weekly Patriot* (Springfield, Mo.), March 23, 1876.
38. *Ibid.,* March 9, 1876.
39. *Ibid.,* Feb. 17, 1876.
40. Letter, Clinton B. Fisk to Uriel Crocker, Sept. 21, 1876, Atlantic and Pacific folder, Harvard Collection.
41. Letter, W. H. Coffin to Uriel Crocker, Oct. 6, 1876, *ibid.*
42. St. Louis and San Francisco Railway Co., Minutes of the Board of Directors, Sept. 11, 1876, secretary's vault, Frisco Archives.
43. *Ibid.,* Sept. 12, 1876.
44. *Ibid.,* Oct. 7, 1876.
45. *Ibid.,* Dec. 5, 1876.
46. *Ibid.,* Dec. 27, 1876.
47. *Springfield Weekly Patriot-Advertiser,* Dec. 28, 1876.
48. *New York Tribune,* Feb. 23, 1887, clipping in St. Louis and San Francisco Railway Scrapbook, 1886–99, in personal possession of Mr. Andrew Niemeier, St. Louis. Hereafter cited as Frisco Scrapbook. Like the Southwest Pacific scrapbook previously cited, this volume was kept by the managers themselves and often includes notations concerning who sent in the clipping. It is an excellent guide to which newspaper coverage the officials felt was important.
49. *St. Louis Globe-Democrat,* Feb. 23, 1887, Frisco Scrapbook.
50. Letter, C. W. Rogers to H. W. Jones, June 16, 1877, Quapaw Railroad File, IAD.
51. Letter, C. W. Rogers to J. M. Haworth, June 2, 1879, *ibid.*
52. *St. Louis Republic,* quoted in *Rolla Weekly Herald,* May 2, 1889.
53. *Rolla Weekly Herald,* June 10, 1886.
54. J. A. Dacus and J. W. Buel, *A Tour of St. Louis; or The Inside Life of a Great City* (St. Louis: Western Publishing Company, 1878), p. 159.

55. *Rolla Weekly Herald,* Feb. 27, 1877.

56. *Ibid.,* Jan. 11, 1877.

57. St. Louis and San Francisco Railway Co., Minutes of the Board of Directors, April 13, 1877, secretary's vault, Frisco Archives.

58. St. Louis and San Francisco Railway Co., Minutes of the Executive Committee, April 25, 1878, *ibid.*

59. St. Louis and San Francisco Railway Co., *Annual Report, 1877,* pp. 10–11, secretary's office, Frisco Archives.

60. St. Louis and San Francisco Railway Co., Minutes of the Board of Directors, May 5, 1877, secretary's vault, Frisco Archives.

61. St. Louis and San Francisco Railway Co., Minutes of the Executive Committee, Sept. 29, 1877, *ibid.*

62. St. Louis and San Francisco Railway Co., Minutes of the Board of Directors, Dec. 27, 1876, *ibid.*

63. *Ibid.,* Sept. 13, 1877.

64. *Ibid.,* Sept. 14, 1877.

65. *Ibid.,* Dec. 3, 1877.

66. *Ibid.,* Dec. 1, 1877.

67. *Ibid.,* Nov. 22, 1877.

68. *Ibid.,* May 5, 1877.

69. Robert Bruce, *1877: Year of Violence* (New York: Bobbs-Merrill, 1959), pp. 254–75.

70. St. Louis and San Francisco Railway Co., *Annual Report, 1877,* pp. 10–11, secretary's office, Frisco Archives.

71. *Springfield Weekly Patriot-Advertiser,* July 26, 1877.

72. The wreck got wide publicity. Principal sources are *Railroad Gazette* (New York), June 8, 1877; *St. Louis Daily Globe-Democrat,* July 10, 1877, p. 3, col. 3, July 11, 1877, p. 1, col. 3, July 12, 1877, p. 1, col. 3; *Rolla Weekly Herald,* June 7, 1877; St. Louis and San Francisco Railway Co., *Annual Report, 1877,* pp. 23–24, secretary's office, Frisco Archives.

73. *St. Louis Daily Globe-Democrat,* July 24, 1877, p. 4, col. 5.

CHAPTER 8
EXPANSION

1. Leslie Decker, "The Railroads and the Land Office: Administrative Policy and the Land Patent Controversy, 1864–1896," *Mississippi Valley Historical Review,* XLVI, No. 4 (March 1960), 679.

2. Letter, W. H. Coffin to Rutherford B. Hayes, Aug. 28, 1877, railroad package 13, Lands and Railroads Division, Records of the Secretary of the Interior, Record Group 48, National Archives. Hereafter cited as L&RR, R.G. 48, N.A.

3. Letter, J. P. Robinson to Carl Schurz, Oct. 12, 1877, *ibid.*

4. Testimony in U.S. Congress, Senate, Sen. Rep. 744, 45th Cong., 3d Sess., 1878, Appendix, pp. 5–6 (Serial 1839).

5. Letter, J. A. Williamson to Carl Schurz, Oct. 13, 1877, *ibid.*, p. 2.

6. Letter, James Stuart to Carl Schurz, Oct. 12, 1877, marked "Private," railroad package 13, L&RR, R.G. 48, N.A.

7. Letter, James Baker to Carl Schurz, Nov. 13, 1877, *ibid.*

8. Letter, J. A. Williamson to Carl Schurz, Oct. 13, 1877, *ibid.*

9. *Ibid.*, Sept. 20, 1877.

10. St. Louis and San Francisco Railway Co., Minutes of the Executive Committee, Sept. 29, 1877, secretary's vault, St. Louis–San Francisco Railway Co., St. Louis, Mo. Hereafter cited as Frisco Archives.

11. James Baker in St. Louis and San Francisco Railway Co., *Annual Report, 1877*, pp. 11, 15, secretary's office, Frisco Archives; *Railroad Gazette* (New York), Oct. 26, 1877.

12. *Atlantic and Pacific R.R. Co., Appellant* v. *City of St. Louis et al., Missouri Reports*, LXVI, pp. 228–60 (1877).

13. Rogers's report in St. Louis and San Francisco Railway Co., *Annual Report, 1877*, pp. 20–23, secretary's office, Frisco Archives.

14. Baker's report in *ibid.*, pp. 13–14.

15. U.S. Interstate Commerce Commission, "Valuation Docket Number 400 —St. Louis–San Francisco Railroad Company et al., July 8, 1932," *Valuation Reports*, XLI (Washington: G.P.O., 1933), 502.

16. St. Louis and San Francisco Railway Co., Minutes of the Board of Directors, Jan. 7, 1878, secretary's vault, Frisco Archives.

17. *Ibid.*, March 21, 1878.

18. *Arkansas Sentinel* (Fayetteville), May 21, 1879.

19. St. Louis and San Francisco Railway Co., Minutes of the Board of Directors, Jan. 7, 1879, secretary's vault, Frisco Archives.

20. Interstate Commerce Commission, *Valuation Reports*, XLI, 501.

21. *Railroad Gazette* (New York), May 30, 1879.

22. Interstate Commerce Commission, *Valuation Reports*, XLI, 673.

23. St. Louis and San Francisco Railway Co., Minutes of the Board of Directors, Jan. 12, 1878, secretary's vault, Frisco Archives.

24. *Springfield Weekly Patriot-Advertiser* (Springfield, Mo.), March 7, 1878.

25. St. Louis and San Francisco Railway Co., Minutes of the Board of Directors, Nov. 19, 1878, secretary's vault, Frisco Archives.

26. *Springfield Weekly Patriot-Advertiser*, May 29, 1879.

27. Springfield and Western Missouri Railroad Co., Minutes of the Board of Directors, June 19, 1879, basement vault, Frisco Archives.

28. Interstate Commerce Commission, *Valuation Reports*, XLI, 300. For detail on Springfield's railway and her relations with the Frisco, see Craig Miner, "Hopes and Fears: Ambivalence in the Anti-Railroad

Movement at Springfield, Missouri, 1870–1880." *Bulletin of the Missouri Historical Society*, XXVII (Jan. 1971), 129–46.

29. Joplin Railroad Co., Minutes of the Board of Directors, May 26, 1879, basement vault, Frisco Archives.

30. *Springfield Weekly Patriot-Advertiser*, May 29, 1879.

31. *Ibid.*, June 12, 1879.

32. *Arkansas Sentinel* (Fayetteville), May 28, 1879.

33. St. Louis and San Francisco Railway Co., Minutes of the Board of Directors, March 11, 1879, secretary's vault, Frisco Archives.

34. *Wichita City Eagle* (Wichita, Kansas), Feb. 27, 1879.

35. St. Louis, Wichita and Western Railroad Co., Articles of Incorporation, in St. L.W. & W. Minute Book inside front cover, basement vault, Frisco Archives.

36. *Ibid.*, *Wichita City Eagle*, May 1, 1879.

37. St. Louis and San Francisco Railway Co., Minutes of the Board of Directors, July 9, 1879, secretary's vault, Frisco Archives.

38. *Ibid.*, St. Louis, Wichita and Western Railroad Co., Minutes of the Board of Directors, June 24, 1879, basement vault, Frisco Archives.

39. C. Wood Davis, "The Farmer, the Investor, and the Railway," *The Arena*, XV (Feb. 1891), 292, 299, 304.

40. Letter, Jno. Kelley to editors, April 7, 1879, quoted in *Wichita City Eagle*, April 10, 1879; Jno. Hufbauer in *ibid.*, May 15, 1879.

41. Letter, William Ross to editors, April 10, 1879, quoted in *ibid.*, April 17, 1879.

42. Letter, William Ross to editors, April 10, 1879, quoted in *ibid.*, May 15, 1879.

43. *Wichita City Eagle*, May 15, 1879.

44. W. C. Weedman in *ibid.*

45. *Wichita City Eagle*, May 23, 1879.

46. *Oswego Independent* (Oswego, Kansas), May 17, 1879.

47. *Ibid.*, June 28 and July 12, 1879.

48. *Wichita City Eagle*, Sept. 4, 1879.

49. An example is found in *Rolla Weekly Herald* (Rolla, Mo.), Aug. 14, 1879.

50. Letter, R. L. VanSant to J. F. Hinkley, Sept. 6, 1879, R. L. VanSant Letter Copy Book, 1879–1882, Missouri Historical Society, Columbia, Mo.

51. Letter, R. L. VanSant to Jas. Dun, Sept. 6, 1879, *ibid.*

52. Letter, R. L. VanSant to J. F. Hinkley, Oct. 1, 1879, *ibid.*

53. *Wichita City Eagle*, Sept. 11, 1879.

54. *Oswego Independent*, Sept. 6, 1879.

55. *Neodesha Free Press* (Neodesha, Kansas), Oct. 10, 1870; *Wichita City Eagle*, Nov. 13, 1879.

56. Letter, C. W. Rogers to E. F. Winslow, June 26, 1880, copied in St. Louis and San Francisco Railway Co., Minutes of the Board of Directors, Aug. 3, 1880, secretary's vault, Frisco Archives.

57. St. Louis and San Francisco Railway Co., Minutes of the Board of Directors, July 24, 1879, secretary's vault, Frisco Archives.

58. *Ibid.*, Oct. 29, 1878.

59. *Ibid.*, July 24, 1878.

60. *Ibid.*, Jan. 6, 1880.

61. *Railroad Gazette* (New York), Feb. 7, 1879.

62. Letter, C. W. Rogers to E. F. Winslow, June 26, 1880, copied in St. Louis and San Francisco Railway Co., Minutes of the Board of Directors, Aug. 3, 1880, secretary's vault, Frisco Archives.

63. Letter, James Dun to C. W. Rogers, June 26, 1880, *ibid.*

64. Letter, C. W. Rogers to E. F. Winslow, June 26, 1880, *ibid.*

65. *Neodesha Free Press,* Feb. 20, 1880. The reference is to the new town of Severy, Kansas.

66. "Jim," in *Wichita City Eagle,* Nov. 27, 1879.

67. *Ibid.*, Oct. 14, 1880.

68. *Ibid.*, June 3, 1880.

69. *Arkansas Sentinel* (Fayetteville), Dec. 4, 11, 18, 1878.

70. St. Louis and San Francisco Railway Co., Minutes of the Executive Committee, Dec. 21, 1878, secretary's vault, Frisco Archives.

71. *Ibid.*, July 11, 1878.

72. *Ibid.*, Nov. 14, 1878.

73. *Arkansas Sentinel* (Fayetteville), Oct. 8, 1879; June 2, 1880.

74. *Ibid.*, Aug. 4, 1880.

75. The form is inserted loose in the second volume of the Frisco minute books.

76. St. Louis and San Francisco Railway Co., Minutes of the Executive Committee, July 11, 1878, secretary's vault, Frisco Archives.

77. H.F., in *Springfield Weekly Patriot-Advertiser,* Oct. 30, 1879.

78. *Wichita City Eagle,* Oct. 28, 1880.

79. *Rolla Weekly Herald,* July 9, 1885.

80. St. Louis and San Francisco Railway Co., Minutes of the Board of Directors, June 2, 1880, secretary's vault, Frisco Archives.

81. *Ibid.*, March 9, 1881.

82. *Ibid.*, Jan. 21, 1879.

83. *Ibid.*, March 16, 1880.

84. Philip D. Jordan, "Edward Francis Winslow," in Dumas Malone, ed., *Dictionary of American Biography* (New York: Charles Scribners Sons, 1936), XX, 395–96.

85. E. F. Winslow in St. Louis and San Francisco Railway Co., *Annual Report, 1881,* p. 14, secretary's office, Frisco Archives.

86. Quoted in Stephen Birmingham, *Our Crowd: The Great Jewish Families of New York* (New York: Harper & Row, 1967), p. 140.
87. *New York Times,* April 27, 1880, p. 2, col. 3.
88. Information taken from a photograph of the engine in files of Frisco operating Dept., Springfield, Mo.
89. Ross Muir and Carl White, *Over the Long Term: The Story of J&W Seligman & Co.* (New York: J&W Seligman & Co., 1964), 107.
90. Letter, E. F. Winslow to Carl Schurz, Oct. 14, 1880, railroad package 14, L&RR, R.G. 48, N.A.
91. *Commercial and Financial Chronicle* (New York), Oct. 30, 1880.

CHAPTER 9
MR. NICKERSON, MR. HUNTINGTON, AND MR. GOULD: IMPERIALISTS

1. *Rolla Weekly Herald* (Rolla, Mo.), April 14, 1881.
2. *Ibid.,* Dec. 8, 1892.
3. *New York Times,* May 14, 1883, p. 4, col. 3.
4. *Cheyenne Daily Leader* (Cheyenne, Wyo.), April 29, 1875.
5. *Rolla Weekly Herald,* Dec. 8, 1892.
6. *Wichita City Eagle* (Wichita, Kansas), Dec. 29, 1881.
7. *Commercial and Financial Chronicle* (New York), May 3, 1879.
8. *Railroad Gazette* (New York), Nov. 21, 1879.
9. *Wichita City Eagle,* Nov. 20, 1879.
10. *Ibid.,* Dec. 4, 1879.
11. *Ibid.,* Dec. 11, 1879.
12. *Boston Herald,* quoted in *St. Louis Globe-Democrat,* Dec. 22, 1879, p. 10, col. 3.
13. *Wichita City Eagle,* Dec. 11, 1879.
14. Preliminary Agreement, Nov. 14, 1879, in *Atlantic & Pacific R.R. Co. and Atchison, Topeka & Santa Fe R.R. Co. Contracts, Deeds, and Other Documents as Between the Two Companies Together with the Charter of the Atlantic & Pacific R.R. Co. and Legislation Subsequent Thereto* (Boston: Alfred Mudge & Son, 1887), p. 1.
15. Tripartite Agreement, Jan. 31, 1880, *ibid.,* p. 31.
16. St. Louis and San Francisco Railway Co., Minutes of the Board of Directors, March 2, 1880, secretary's vault, St. Louis–San Francisco Railway Co., St. Louis, Mo. Hereafter cited as Frisco Archives.
17. *Neodesha Free Press* (Neodesha, Kansas), Feb. 13, 1880.
18. *Commercial and Financial Chronicle* (New York), Feb. 7, 1880.
19. *Wichita City Eagle,* Oct. 9, 1879.
20. Wichita Pool Agreement, Dec. 1, 1880, Records of the A.T. & S.F. Board of Directors, Box 21, Case 6, Shelf F, Bay 9, Sec. Treas. Floor,

unclaimed freight warehouse, Topeka, Kansas. Hereafter cited as Santa Fe Archives.

21. *Commercial and Financial Chronicle* (New York), Oct. 25, 1879.
22. Letter, [Joseph Seligman] to Francis B. Hayes, May 23, 1872, Private Letter Book of J. & W. Seligman & Co. New York Office, 1867–73, Archives of J. & W. Seligman & Co., New York.
23. Arthur E. Johnson and Berry E. Supple, *Boston Capitalists and Western Railroads* (Cambridge: Harvard University Press, 1967), pp. 288, 304.
24. *Rolla Weekly Herald,* March 4, 1880.
25. *Pierce City Empire,* quoted in *Arkansas Sentinel* (Fayetteville), Oct. 13, 1880.
26. *Arkansas Sentinel* (Fayetteville), Nov. 17, 1880.
27. Letter, E. F. Winslow to Directors, April 28, 1880, copied in St. Louis and San Francisco Railway Co., Minutes of the Board of Directors, May 18, 1880, secretary's vault, Frisco Archives.
28. Letter, E. F. Winslow to Jas. A. Williamson, Feb. 15, 1881, box 2, Division "F," Railway Right of Way and Reclamation, Records of the General Land Office, Record Group 49, National Archives. Hereafter cited as Div. "F," R.G. 49, N.A.
29. *New York Tribune,* March 18, 1880, p. 5, col. 4.
30. Ira G. Clark, *Then Came the Railroads: The Century From Steam to Diesel in the Southwest* (Norman: University of Oklahoma Press, 1958), p. 171.
31. *St. Louis Republican,* quoted in *Arkansas Sentinel* (Fayetteville), Feb. 9, 1881.
32. Traffic Agreement dated Sept. 14, 1881, copy in St. Louis and San Francisco Railway Co., Minutes of the Board of Directors, Dec. 6, 1881, secretary's vault, Frisco Archives.
33. Station Agreement dated Sept. 14, 1881, *ibid.*
34. *Neodesha Free Press,* May 28, 1880.
35. *Arkansas Sentinel* (Fayetteville), June 22, 1881.
36. *Ibid.,* June 15, 1881.
37. *Ibid.,* Sept. 7, 1881.
38. *Ibid.,* Oct. 16, 1881.
39. Letter, J. A. Williamson to Britton & Gray, Nov. 4, 1881, Atlantic and Pacific Railroad Co., Records of the Law and Land Dept., 1881–96, Case 36, shelves A and B, Bay 6, Miscellaneous storage, 3rd floor, Santa Fe Archives. Hereafter cited as L&L.
40. *Arkansas Sentinel* (Fayetteville), June 14, 1882.
41. Letter, Thomas Nickerson to James Fish, March 1, 1880, copy in St. Louis and San Francisco Railway Co., Minutes of the Board of Directors, March 16, 1880, secretary's vault, Frisco Archives.
42. St. Louis and San Francisco Railway Co., Minutes of the Board of Directors, May 17, 1881, secretary's vault, Frisco Archives.

43. Letter, Edward F. Winslow to Thomas Nickerson, April 1, 1881, copy inserted loose in St. Louis and San Francisco Railway Co., Book of Record #2, 131, secretary's vault, Frisco Archives.

44. Letter, Thomas Nickerson to Edward F. Winslow, April 6, 1881, *ibid.*

45. U.S. Congress, Senate, *Message . . . in reference to the applications of the Chicago, Texas and Mexican Central, and the Saint Louis and San Francisco Railway Companies, for a Right of Way across the Lands of the Choctaw Nation, in the Indian Territory,* Sen. Ex. Doc. 15, 47th Cong., 1st Sess., 1881, p. 1 (Serial 1986).

46. Letters, J. J. Baxter to S. J. Kirkwood, Oct. 30, Nov. 30, 1881, *ibid.*, pp. 6, 20.

47. Telegram, Jno. T. McCane, D. K. Tripp, Thos. Howard to U. J. Baxter and L. H. Fitzhigh, Oct. 25, 1881, *ibid.*, p. 11.

48. U.S. Congress, Senate, *Message . . . in reference to the bill of Choctaw Council . . . ,* Sen. Ex. Doc. 44, 47th Cong., 1st Sess., 1882, p. 2 (Serial 1987).

49. Letter, U. J. Baxter to S. J. Kirkwood, Oct. 20, 1881, Sen. Ex. Doc. 15, 47th Cong., 1st Sess., 1881, p. 6 (Serial 1986).

50. Telegram, S. J. Kirkwood to U. J. Baxter, Nov. 5, 1881, *ibid.*, p. 14.

51. Letter, B. F. Smallwood, Isham Walker and Joseph P. Folsom to ?, Jan. 9, 1882, Sen. Ex. Doc. 44, 47th Cong., 1st Sess., 1882, p. 12 (Serial 1987).

52. *San Francisco Chronicle,* Jan. 11, 1882, p. 8, col. 4.

53. Angie Debo, *The Rise and Fall of the Choctaw Republic* (Norman: University of Oklahoma Press, 1934), p. 123.

54. Testimony taken before the Senate Committee on Railroads, c. Jan. 1882, transcript is item #19743, Choctaw Railroad File, Indian Archives Division, Oklahoma Historical Society, Oklahoma City. Hereafter cited as IAD.

55. Letter, B. F. Smallwood, Isham Walker, Joseph P. Folsom to ?, Jan. 9, 1882, Sen. Ex. Doc. 44, 47th Cong., 1st Sess., 1882, pp. 10–12 (Serial 1987).

56. Testimony, #19743, Choctaw Railroad File, IAD.

57. U.S. Congress, Senate, 47th Cong., 1st Sess., Jan. 19, 1882, *Congressional Record,* XIII, 503.

58. Speech of Richard Coke of Texas, *ibid.*, p. 504.

59. Letter, J. F. McCurtain to Col. U. J. Baxter, Jan. 3, 1882, Special Case 97, Records of the Office of Indian Affairs, Land Division, Record Group 75, National Archives. Hereafter cited as OIA, R.G. 75, N.A.

60. U.S. Congress, Senate, Speech of Ben Jonas of Louisiana, 47th Cong., 1st Sess., April 11, 1882, *Congressional Record,* XIII, 2761.

61. Testimony, #19743, Choctaw Railroad File, IAD.

62. Biographical information from frontispiece of Fisher letterbook, IAD.

63. Letter, D. O. Fisher to Mattie M. Fisher, Jan. 9, 1882, Fisher letterbook, IAD.

64. *Ibid.*, Jan. 19, 1882.

65. Letter, Jno. D. Miles to Hiram Price, Jan. 3, 1882, Special Case 102, OIA, R.G. 75, N.A.

66. Letter, W. A. Eaton, editor of *The Cheyenne Transporter,* to J. S. Kirkwood, Jan. 9, 1882, *ibid.*

67. Letter, Jno. D. Miles to Hon. Hiram Price, Jan. 7, 1882, *ibid.*

68. Letter, P. Shanahan to W. O. Tuggle, April 16, 1882, *ibid.*; for another view in which Shanahan is regarded as a crackpot see Letter, G. W. Gleason and E. C. Boudinot to D. W. Bushyhead, April 17, 1882, #2663, Cherokee Railroad File, IAD.

69. Letter, John D. Miles to Hiram Price, Jan. 3, 1882, Special Case 102, OIA, R.G. 75, N.A.

70. Telegram, R. Williams to John Pope, Jan. 4, 1882, *ibid.*

71. *New York Tribune,* Jan. 15, 1882, p. 1, col. 5; *San Francisco Chronicle,* Jan. 23, 1882, p. 3, col. 1.

72. Gould/Huntington Agreement dated Nov. 26, 1881, copy in Missouri Pacific Railroad Co., Minutes of the Board of Directors, Dec. 2, 1881, security vault, Missouri Pacific Building, St. Louis, Mo. Hereafter cited as Mo.Pac. Archives.

73. Jan. 24, 1882, p. 5, col. 4.

74. Ross L. Muir and Carl J. White, *Over the Long Term: The Story of J. & W. Seligman & Co.* (New York: J&W Seligman & Co., 1964), p. 97.

75. Julius Grodinsky, *Jay Gould: His Business Career, 1867–1892* (Philadelphia: University of Pennsylvania Press, 1957), p. 380.

76. Muir and White, *Long Term,* p. 97.

77. St. Louis and San Francisco Railway Co., Minutes of the Board of Directors, Jan. 10, 1882, secretary's vault, Frisco Archives.

78. *Ibid.*, Jan. 27, 1882.

79. *St. Louis Republican,* undated clipping in St. Louis and San Francisco Railway Scrapbook, 1886–99, in personal possession of Mr. Andrew Niemeier, St. Louis; the incident was cited in Rogers's obituary.

80. *New York Tribune,* Jan. 26, 1882, p. 1, col. 6.

81. *St. Louis Globe-Democrat,* quoted in *San Francisco Chronicle,* Feb. 2, 1882.

82. *Commercial and Financial Chronicle* (New York), Jan. 28, 1882.

83. *Ibid.*, Jan. 30, 1882, p. 1, col. 4.

84. *Cherokee Advocate* (Talequah, I.T.), Feb. 10, 1882.

85. Cerinda W. Evans, *Collis Potter Huntington,* 2 vols. (Newport News, Va., 1954), I, 93.

86. *New York Times,* Feb. 12, 1882, p. 5, col. 6.

87. *San Francisco Chronicle,* Jan. 28, 1882, p. 3, col. 6.

88. *Ibid.*, Jan. 23, 1882.

89. *Ibid.*, Feb. 1, 1882, p. 3, col. 6.

90. *New York Times,* Jan. 29, 1882, p. 7, col. 3; Gould and Huntington had to buy their twenty thousand shares at par which cost them $2,000,000. Missouri Pacific Railroad Co., Minutes of the Executive Committee, March 2, 1882, Mo.Pac. Archives.
91. *Commercial and Financial Chronicle* (New York), March 4, 1882.
92. *New York Times,* Jan. 31, 1882, p. 1, col. 7.
93. St. Louis and San Francisco Railway Co., Minutes of the Board of Directors, June 21, 1886, secretary's vault, Frisco Archives.
94. U.S. Congress, Senate, 47th Cong., 1st Sess., April 3, 1882, *Congressional Record,* XIII, 2523.
95. Speech of Joseph Hawley of Conn., April 4, 1882, *ibid.,* p. 2570.
96. Speech of George Vest of Missouri, *ibid.,* p. 2576; for the Indian view see Letter, Ward Coachman and Pleasant Porter to Samuel Checote, Feb. 1, 1882, #35735, Creek Railroad File, IAD.
97. U.S. Congress, Senate, Speech of George Vest of Missouri, 47th Cong., 1st Sess., April 12, 1882, *Congressional Record,* XIII, 2803.
98. Speech of April 4, 1882, *ibid.,* p. 2575.
99. *Rolla Weekly Herald,* June 24, 1886.
100. U.S. Congress, Senate, Speech of John Ingalls of Kansas, 47th Cong., 1st Sess., April 11, 1882, *Congressional Record,* XIII, 2567.
101. U.S. Congress, House, *Right of Way to Saint Louis and San Francisco Railroad through the Indian Territory,* H.R. 934, 47th Cong., 1st Sess., 1882, p. 3 (Serial 2067).
102. U.S. Congress, Senate, Speech of Ben Jonas of Louisiana, 47th Cong., 1st Sess., April 11, 1882, *Congressional Record,* XIII, 2762.
103. U.S. Congress, Senate, 47th Cong., 1st Sess., April 13, 1882, *Congressional Record,* XIII, 3857.
104. Letter, J. A. Williamson to Jesse Seligman, May 3, 1882, L&L, Santa Fe Archives.
105. Letter, J. A. Williamson to Britton & Gray, Aug. 10, 1882, *ibid.*
106. *Rolla Weekly Herald,* May 11, 1882.
107. *San Francisco Chronicle,* Jan. 1, 1882, p. 12, col. 5.

CHAPTER 10
THE WESTERN DIVISION

1. Archibald C. E. Sutter, *American Notes 1881* (Edinburgh and London: Wllm. Blackwood and Sons, 1882), pp. vii-ix, 41, 48, 50.
2. *Boston Post,* Dec. 11, 1879, quoted in *Oswego Independent* (Oswego, Kansas), Dec. 20, 1879.
3. *Railroad Gazette* (New York), Feb. 3, 1882.
4. Letter, J. A. Williamson to A. A. Cohen, Feb. 11, 1882, Atlantic and Pacific Railroad Co., Records of the Law and Land Dept., 1881-96, Case

36, shelves A and B, Bay 6, Miscellaneous storage, 3rd floor, unclaimed freight warehouse, Topeka, Kansas. Hereafter cited as L&L, Santa Fe Archives.

5. David F. Myrick, *Railroads of Nevada and Eastern California*, 2 vols. (Berkeley: Howell North, 1963), II, 765.

6. *Kern Weekly Record*, Feb. 9, 1882, quoted in *ibid*.

7. Myrick, *Railroads of Nevada and Eastern California*, II, 769.

8. *Wichita City Eagle* (Wichita, Kansas), Oct. 18, 1883.

9. Atlantic and Pacific Railroad Co., Timetable, July, 1883, Xerox #C-5-27, treasurer's office, Santa Fe Building, Topeka, Kansas.

10. Atchison, Topeka and Santa Fe Railroad Co., Minutes of the Executive Committee, Oct. 9, 1882, in *Atlantic & Pacific R.R. Co. and Atchison, Topeka & Santa Fe R.R. Co. Contracts, Deeds and Other Documents as Between the Two Companies Together with the Charter of the Atlantic & Pacific R.R. Co. and Legislation Subsequent Thereto* (Boston: Alfred Mudge & Son, 1887), p. 136. Hereafter cited as *A&P/AT&SF Documents*.

11. Atlantic and Pacific Railroad Co., Acknowledgment of Loan, Dec. 8, 1883, *ibid.*, 150; St. Louis and San Francisco Railway Co., *Annual Report, 1884*, p. 10, secretary's office, Frisco Building, St. Louis. Hereafter cited as Frisco Archives.

12. Edward Winslow report on Atlantic and Pacific, in St. Louis and San Francisco Railway Co., *Annual Report, 1884*, p. 14, secretary's office, Frisco Archives.

13. Atchison, Topeka and Santa Fe Railroad Co., *Annual Report, 1884*, Xerox #C-5-27, p. 183, treasurer's office, Santa Fe Building, Topeka, Kansas.

14. Edward Winslow report on Atlantic and Pacific, in St. Louis and San Francisco Railway Co., *Annual Report, 1884*, pp. 16–17, secretary's office, Frisco Archives.

15. Atlantic and Pacific Railroad Co., Vote of the Board of Directors, May 10, 1884, *A&P/AT&SF, Documents*, p. 165; *New York Times*, Jan. 23, 1883, p. 1, col. 6.

16. Contract, Atlantic and Pacific Railway Co. with Southern Pacific Railway Co., Aug. 20, 1884 and Traffic Agreement, Aug. 20, 1884, in St. Louis and San Francisco Railway Co., Minutes of the Board of Directors, Aug. 16, 1884, secretary's vault, Frisco Archives.

17. Myrick, *Railroads of Nevada and Eastern California*, II, 788.

18. Letter, J. A. Williamson to F. W. Smith, May 27, 1882, L&L, Santa Fe Archives.

19. Account of E. W. Dike, Oct. 13, 1883, railroad package 333, Lands and Railroads Division, Records of the Department of the Interior, Record Group 48, National Archives.

20. Letter, J. A. Williamson to Lewis Kingman, May 25, 1883, L&L, Santa Fe Archives.

21. Letter, J. A. Williamson to H. C. Nutt, Nov. 18, 1882, *ibid.*

22. Letters, J. A. Williamson to H. C. Nutt, Jan. 7, 1890, and Thomas Sedgwick to J. A. Williamson, June ?, 1882, *ibid.*

23. Letter, T. S. Sedgwick to J. A. Williamson, Oct. 20, 1881, *ibid.*

24. Letter, H. R. Holbrook to Lewis Kingman, March 4, 1883, Lewis Kingman Scrapbook, Kansas State Historical Society.

25. Edward Winslow report on Atlantic and Pacific, in St. Louis and San Francisco Railway Co., *Annual Report, 1884,* p. 19, secretary's office, Frisco Archives.

26. Letter, J. A. Williamson to Col. H. C. Nutt, Nov. 19, 1881, L&L, Santa Fe Archives.

27. Letter, J. A. Williamson to T. S. Sedgwick, March 8, 1882, *ibid.*

28. Letter, J. A. Williamson to W. S. Burke, May 27, 1882, *ibid.*

29. Letter, J. A. Williamson to Hon. Henry L. Waldo, Oct. 6, 1882, *ibid.*

30. Letter, J. A. Williamson to John T. Hogue, Nov. 6, 1882, *ibid.*

31. Letter, T. S. Sedgwick to Major Eugene Techil, June 11, 1883, *ibid.*

32. Letter, T. S. Sedgwick to J. A. Williamson, Sept. 8, 1882, *ibid.*

33. Letter, T. S. Sedgwick to A. J. Hoover, Feb. 16, 1883, *ibid.*

34. Letter, T. S. Sedgwick to J. A. Williamson, Aug. 23, 1885, *ibid.*

35. Letter, T. S. Sedgwick to H. C. Nutt, March 14, 1884, *ibid.*

36. Letter, T. S. Sedgwick to J. A. Williamson, April 5, 1884, *ibid.*

37. Letter, T. S. Sedgwick to G. S. Tuckerman, Oct. 23, 1885, *ibid.*

38. Letter, T. S. Sedgwick to G. S. Tuckerman, Nov. 21, 1881, *ibid.*

39. Letter, G. P. Brene to Editors, July 31, 1884, in *Rolla Weekly Herald,* Aug. 7, 1884.

40. Letter, J. A. Williamson to President and Directors of Atlantic & Pacific R.R. Co., Oct. 17, 1882, L&L, Santa Fe Archives.

41. *Ibid.*

42. Letter, Thomas Sedgwick to J. A. Williamson, Sept. 6, 1883, L&L, Santa Fe Archives.

43. Letter, J. A. Williamson to President and Directors of Atlantic & Pacific R.R. Co., Oct. 17, 1882, *ibid.*

44. Letter, J. A. Williamson to Moore, Bower, & Graffe, July 28, 1886, *ibid.*

45. Leslie Decker, "The Railroads and the Land Office: Administrative Policy and the Land Patent Controversy, 1864–1896," *Mississippi Valley Historical Review,* XLVI, No. 4 (March 1960), 679.

46. Letter, J. A. Williamson to Britton & Gray, April 4, 1882, L&L, Santa Fe Archives.

47. Letter, J. A. Williamson to Hon. Wm. R. Allison, June 6, 1882, *ibid.*

48. Letter, J. A. Williamson to J. Seligman, March 16, 1883, *ibid.*

49. Letter, J. A. Williamson to J. A. Benson, Feb. 7, 1882, *ibid.*

50. Decker, "Land Office," p. 695.

51. Letter, J. A. Williamson to T. S. Sedgwick, Jan. 17, 1882, L&L, Santa Fe Archives.

52. Letter, J. A. Williamson to T. S. Sedgwick, July 7, 1882, *ibid.*

53. Letter, T. S. Sedgwick to J. A. Williamson, Oct. 3, 1882, *ibid.*

54. Letter, J. A. Williamson to W. J. Barnard, undated, *ibid.*

55. Letter, T. S. Sedgwick to J. A. Williamson, Jan. 9, 1882, *ibid.*

56. Letter, J. A. Williamson to Register and Receiver, U.S. Land Office, Los Angeles, Sept. 3, 1885, box 2, Division "F," Right of Way and Reclamation, Records of the General Land Office, Record Group 49, National Archives. Hereafter cited as GLO, R.G. 49, N.A.

57. Letter, T. S. Sedgwick to Edward W. Kinsley, June 13, 1883, L&L, Santa Fe Archives.

58. Letter, J. A. Williamson to O. Ellison, Oct. 31, 1881, *ibid.*

59. Letter, J. A. Williamson to C. G. Megour, Aug. 7, 1883, *ibid.*

60. Letter, T. S. Sedgwick to J. A. Williamson, May 9, 1882, *ibid.*

61. Letter, J. A. Williamson to H. C. Nutt, Jan. 26, 1884, *ibid.*

62. Letter, J. A. Williamson to Dr. J. W. Porter, Aug. 16, 1882, *ibid.*

63. Letter, T. S. Sedgwick to E. W. Kinsley, March 10, 1884, *ibid.*

64. Letter, T. S. Sedgwick to Theo. Wagner, March 26, 1884, *ibid.*

65. *Commercial and Financial Chronicle* (New York), Aug. 15, 1885.

66. Letter, T. S. Sedgwick to J. A. Williamson, Feb. 27, 1884, L&L, Santa Fe Archives.

67. Letter, J. A. Williamson to D. K. Tripp, Aug. 11, 1884, *ibid.*

68. Letters, J. A. Williamson to H. C. Nutt, May 18, 1883, and Dec. 8, 1884, *ibid.*

69. Letters, T. S. Sedgwick to J. A. Williamson, Jan. 28, 1884; T. S. Sedgwick to Theo. Wagner, Jan. 28, 1884; J. A. Williamson to T. L. Bibbons, Jan. 23, 1885, *ibid.*

70. Letter, J. A. Williamson to T. S. Sedgwick, Jan. 29, 1884.

71. Letter, T. S. Sedgwick to J. A. Williamson, Feb. 18, 1884, *ibid.*

72. Letter, J. A. Williamson to T. S. Sedgwick, Dec. 30, 1884, *ibid.*

73. Letter, T. S. Sedgwick to J. A. Williamson, March 21, 1885, *ibid.*

74. *Railroad Gazette* (New York), April 11, 1879.

75. U.S. Congress, Senate, Speech of Ben Martin of W. Virginia, 46th Cong., 3d Sess., Dec. 16, 1880, *Congressional Record,* XI, 205.

76. *Ibid.,* 47th Cong., 1st Sess., XIII, 347, 558, 1838.

77. Letter, J. A. Williamson to H. C. Nutt, Dec. 26, 1883, L&L, Santa Fe Archives.

78. Letter, J. A. Williamson to H. C. Nutt, Dec. 11, 1883, *ibid.*

79. Letter, J. A. Williamson to H. C. Nutt, March 14, 1883, *ibid.*

80. Letter, J. A. Williamson to H. C. Nutt, Dec. 11, 1883, *ibid.*

81. Letter, J. A. Williamson to H. C. Nutt, Jan. 14, 1884, *ibid.*

82. Letter, J. A. Williamson to Preston B. Plumb, Jan. 21, 1884, *ibid.*

83. Letter, J. A. Williamson to H. C. Nutt, Jan. 17, 1884, *ibid.*

84. Letter, J. A. Williamson to H. C. Nutt, Jan. 26, 1884, *ibid.*
85. Letter, J. A. Williamson to H. C. Nutt, Jan. 17, 1884, *ibid.*
86. Letter, J. A. Williamson to H. C. Nutt, July 2, 1885, *ibid.*
87. Letter, J. A. Williamson to H. C. Nutt, July 3, 1885, *ibid.*
88. Letter, T. S. Sedgwick to J. A. Williamson, Jan. 22, 1885, *ibid.*
89. Letter, J. A. Williamson to J. C. D. Atkins, June 18, 1885, special case 102, Records of the Office of Indian Affairs, Land Division, Record Group 75, National Archives.
90. Letter, Citizens of the Cherokee Nation to Commissioner of Indian Affairs, Oct. 31, 1885, *ibid.*
91. Letter, J. A. Williamson to H. C. Nutt, July 2, 1885, L&L, Santa Fe Archives.
92. Letter, J. A. Williamson to H. C. Nutt, Nov. 28, 1885, *ibid.*
93. Letter, J. A. Williamson to H. C. Nutt, Dec. 15, 1885, *ibid.*
94. *New York Tribune,* Dec. 24, 1885, p. 5, col. 3.
95. Letter, J. A. Williamson to H. C. Nutt, Dec. 28, 1885, L&L, Santa Fe Archives.
96. Letter, J. A. Williamson to L. W. Dennis, Dec. 12, 1885, *ibid.*
97. Letter, J. A. Williamson to H. C. Nutt, Feb. 24, 1886, *ibid.*
98. Letters, J. A. Williamson to Edward Winslow, May 26, 1886; J. A. Williamson to Jesse Seligman, June 8, 1886, *ibid.*
99. Letter, L. C. Lamar to Commissioner of General Land Office, Aug. 14, 1887, box 2, Div. "F," GLO, R.G. 49, N.A.
100. *Boston Herald,* Feb. 26, 1888, clipping in St. Louis and San Francisco Railway Scrapbook, 1886–99, in personal possession of Mr. Andrew Niemeir, St. Louis.
101. Atlantic and Pacific Railroad Co. *Annual Report 1887,* box marked "Atlantic and Pacific," records of the A.T. & S.F. Board of Directors, Case 6, Shelf F, Bay 9, Sec. Treas. Floor, Santa Fe Archives. Hereafter cited as A. & P., AR 1887.
102. William S. Creever, *Arid Domain: The Santa Fe Railroad and its Western Land Grant* (Stanford, Calif.: Stanford University Press, 1954), p. 168.
103. A. & P., AR 1887. This report is in MS and not paged.
104. Greever, *Arid Domain,* p. 47.
105. A. & P., AR 1887.
106. Letter, J. A. Williamson to H. C. Nutt, L&L, Santa Fe Archives.

CHAPTER 11
SIEGE AND CAPITULATION

1. *Rolla Weekly Herald* (Rolla, Mo.), Jan. 21, 1886.
2. *Ibid.,* May 13, and May 20, 1886; *St. Louis Republican,* May 13, 1886,

clipping in St. Louis and San Francisco Railway Co., Scrapbook, 1886–99, in personal possession of Mr. Andrew Niemeier, St. Louis. Hereafter cited as Frisco Scrapbook.

3. St. Louis and San Francisco Railway Co., Minutes of the Board of Directors, May 19, 1886, secretary's vault, Frisco Building, St. Louis, Mo. Hereafter cited as Frisco Archives.

4. *St. Louis Post-Dispatch,* Feb. 22, 1887, quoted in *Rolla Weekly Herald,* Feb. 24, 1887.

5. *St. Louis Republican,* March 2, 1887, clipping in Frisco Scrapbook.

6. *Springfield Weekly Herald* (Springfield, Mo.), Feb. 24, 1887, clipping in Frisco Scrapbook.

7. St. Louis and San Francisco Railway Co., Minutes of the Board of Directors, March 7, 1887, Frisco Archives.

8. *Ibid.,* March 1, 1886.

9. Paris and Great Northern Railroad Co., Minutes of the Board of Directors, March 9 and April 13, 1887, basement vault, Frisco Archives.

10. Paris and Great Northern Railroad Co., Minutes of the Stockholders Meeting, Jan. 6, 1886; *Ft. Worth Gazette,* Feb. 24, 1886, clipping in Frisco Scrapbook with notation "sent by James Dun"; Paris and Great Northern Railroad Co., Minutes of the Board of Directors, Feb. 22, 1886, basement vault, Frisco Archives.

11. *Rolla Weekly Herald,* July 22, 1886.

12. *Evans & Howard Fire Brick Company, Appellant,* v. *St. Louis & San Francisco Railway Company, Respondent, Missouri Appeal Reports,* XXI, 651 (1886).

13. *Mary A. Coffin* v. *St. Louis & San Francisco Railway Co., ibid.,* XXII, 606 (1886).

14. *St. Louis Globe-Democrat,* March 12, 1886, clipping in Frisco Scrapbook.

15. *Arkansas Sentinel* (Fayetteville), Feb. 14, 1883.

16. *Wichita City Eagle* (Wichita, Kansas), April 5, 1883.

17. *Albany Evening Journal* (Albany, N.Y.), Sept. 1, 1886, clipping in Frisco Scrapbook.

18. *Rolla Weekly Herald,* Sept. 29, 1892.

19. *Ibid.,* Aug. 4, 1887.

20. *Ibid.,* May 30, 1889.

21. Letter, J. A. Williamson to John D. La Vergne, Feb. 3, 1887, Atlantic and Pacific Railroad Co., Records of the Law and Land Dept., 1881–96, Case 36, shelves A and B, Bay 6, Miscellaneous storage, 3rd floor, unclaimed freight warehouse, Topeka, Kansas. Hereafter cited as L&L, Santa Fe Archives.

22. Letter, J. A. Williamson to H. C. Nutt, Feb. 19, 1887, *ibid.*

23. Clipping undated and untitled labeled "Rec'd from W. L. Frost, Oct. 23, '86," Frisco Scrapbook.

24. Letter, W. B. Strong to A. & P. Directors, June 1, 1887, box marked "Atlantic and Pacific," Records of the A.T. & S.F. Board of Directors, Case 6, Shelf F, Bay 9, Sec. Treas. Floor, Santa Fe Archives.
25. Report, F. W. Bond and A. A. Robinson to E. F. Winslow and W. B. Strong, Feb. 1888, *ibid.*
26. *New York Times,* Oct. 25, 1887, p. 5, col. 3; *Railroad Gazette* (New York), Oct. 28, 1887.
27. Clipping dated March 17, 1887, Frisco Scrapbook.
28. Letter, J. A. Williamson to H. C. Nutt, July 17, 1888, L&L, Santa Fe Archives.
29. Letter, J. A. Williamson to H. C. Nutt, Oct. 17, 1888, *ibid.*
30. Letter, J. A. Williamson to H. C. Nutt, April 2, 1888, *ibid.*
31. *Missouri Republican,* March 12, 1886, clipping in Frisco Scrapbook.
32. *St. Louis Globe-Democrat,* April 14, 1888, clipping in Frisco Scrapbook.
33. *Rolla Weekly Herald,* April 19, 1888.
34. *St. Louis Globe-Democrat,* Dec. 2, 1889, clipping in Frisco Scrapbook; St. Louis and San Francisco Railway Co., *In Re Charges vs. D. H. Nichols, Gen. Supt. Frisco Ry. Evidence,* box 4, Frisco pamphlet collection, Missouri Historical Society, Columbia, Mo. The latter document is packed full of the most embarrassing revelations and was picked up quickly by local newspapers.
35. *St. Louis Republican,* Feb. 28, 1886, clipping in Frisco Scrapbook.
36. St. Louis and San Francisco Railway Co., Minutes of the Board of Directors, March 1, 1886, secretary's vault, Frisco Archives; *St. Louis Republican,* May, 1886, clipping in Frisco Scrapbook.
37. *St. Louis Post-Dispatch,* March 1, 1886, *ibid.*
38. *St. Louis Globe-Democrat,* May 2, 1886, *ibid.*
39. Clipping not dated or titled, notation "Rec'd in C. W. Rogers' letter of Aug. 20, '86," *ibid.*
40. *St. Louis Post-Dispatch,* Aug. 20, 1886, notation "Sent by John O'Day Aug. 21," *ibid.*
41. *Rolla Weekly Herald,* March 10, 1887.
42. *Kansas City Times,* July 1, 1887, clipping in Frisco Scrapbook.
43. *St. Louis Post-Dispatch,* Aug. 20, 1886, *ibid.*
44. *Rolla Weekly Herald,* July 7, 1887.
45. *New York Times,* March 6, 1887, p. 1, col. 3.
46. *Ibid.,* March 17, 1887, p. 5, col. 4.
47. St. Louis and San Francisco Railway Co., Minutes of the Board of Directors, April 14, 1887, secretary's vault, Frisco Archives.
48. *The Financier* (New York), April 16, 1887, clipping in Frisco Scrapbook.
49. *New York Times,* April 23, 1887, p. 8, col. 6.
50. *Ibid.,* April 27, 1887, p. 8, col. 2.

51. *Railroad Gazette* (New York), April 22, 1887; *The People of the State of New York ex rel. Walter Del Mar* v. *The St. Louis and San Francisco Railway Company, New York Reports* (Hun), XLIV, 552 (1887).
52. *New York Commercial,* April 25, 1887, clipping in Frisco Scrapbook.
53. *New York Times,* April 28, 1887, p. 9, col. 6.
54. *Ibid.,* April 24, 1887, p. 3, col. 6.
55. *Ibid.,* May 3, 1887.
56. *Ibid.,* May 13, 1887, p. 5, col. 4.
57. *Ibid.,* May 3, 1887.
58. *Ibid.,* May 5, 1887, p. 5, col. 3.
59. *St. Louis Globe-Democrat,* May 12, 1887, clipping in Frisco Scrapbook.
60. *New York Times,* May 13, 1887, p. 5, col. 4.
61. *Railroad Gazette* (New York), July 8, 1887.
62. *St. Louis Globe-Democrat,* May 12, 1887, clipping in Frisco Scrapbook.
63. *New York Tribune,* May 12, 1887, clipping in Frisco Scrapbook.
64. St. Louis and San Francisco Railway Co., Minutes of the Board of Directors, May 24, 1887, secretary's vault, Frisco Archives.
65. *St. Louis Globe-Democrat,* May 12, 1887.
66. *Springfield Leader* (Springfield, Mo.), Nov. 2, 1889, *ibid.*
67. *Rolla Weekly Herald,* Feb. 22, 1894.
68. Letter, David R. Francis to John R. Wood, Jan. 29, 1890, Francis Letterbooks, Vol. K, p. 326, Missouri Historical Society, St. Louis.
69. *St. Louis Post-Dispatch,* Feb. 12, 1890, clipping in Frisco Scrapbook.
70. *St. Louis Globe-Democrat,* Feb. 19, 1890, clipping in Frisco Scrapbook.
71. *St. Louis Globe-Democrat,* quoted in *Rolla Weekly Herald,* March 6, 1890.
72. *Ibid.,* April 3, 1890.
73. *Kansas Daily State Journal* (Topeka, Kansas), April 15, 1886, clipping in Frisco Scrapbook.
74. *New York Times,* May 4, 1888, p. 2, col. 4.
75. *Rolla Weekly Herald,* April 10, 1890.
76. *Railroad Gazette* (New York), May 30, 1890.
77. *Ibid.,* May 23, 1890; *Rolla Weekly Herald,* May 22, 1890.
78. Letter, Edward F. Winslow to S.L. & S.F. Ry. Directors, May 29, 1890, copied in St. Louis and San Francisco Railway Co., Minutes of the Board of Directors, May 29, 1890, secretary's vault, Frisco Archives.
79. *New York Times,* Oct. 24, 1914, p. 13, col. 6.
80. Letter, Jesse Seligman to S.L. & S.F. Ry. Directors, May 26, 1890, copied in St. Louis and San Francisco Railway Co., Minutes of the Board of Directors, May 26, 1890, secretary's vault, Frisco Archives.
81. *The Financier* (New York), June 28, 1890, clipping in Frisco Scrapbook.
82. *New York Tribune,* June 28, 1896, p. 8, col. 3 and Dec. 20, 1897, p. 12, col. 6.

83. Alphonso A. Hopkins, *The Life of Clinton Bowen Fisk with a Brief Sketch of John A. Brooks* (New York: Funk & Wagnalls, 1888), p. 152.
84. *Rolla Weekly Herald,* Jan. 10, 1895.
85. *Ibid.,* July 4, 1895.
86. *Los Angeles Herald,* Feb. 20, 1888, clipping in Frisco Scrapbook.

BIBLIOGRAPHY

RAILROAD ARCHIVES

Much of the research necessary for reconstructing the history of the thirty-fifth parallel project would not have been possible without the cooperation of the railroad companies which are successors to those involved in the scheme and so hold the relevant corporate records.

Most important in providing a broad base for the narrative were the archives of the St. Louis–San Francisco Railway Co., located at the company offices, 906 Olive St., St. Louis. Only a few pieces of correspondence survived the destruction of many of the old records when the corporation moved out of its St. Louis warehouses some years ago. Many others did not survive the paper drives of two world wars. Almost all the minute books, however, were saved, not only of the Frisco proper but of most of its predecessor and subsidiary companies. The directors and executive committee minutes of the St. Louis and San Francisco Railway Co., 1876–1896, which were a major source for this study, are bound in four handwritten one-thousand-page volumes located in the secretary's vault on the ninth floor of the Frisco Building. Also in the secretary's office may be found several valuable items rescued by Andrew Niemeier, the assistant secretary, from the warehouse destruction: Annual Reports of the St. Louis and San Francisco Railway Co. (bound), 1876–77, 1879–89; Scrapbook of the Southwest Pacific Railroad Co., 1865–70; Scrapbook of the St. Louis and San Francisco Railway Co., 1886–99. The corporate minutes of subsidiaries and predecessors are located in a vault in the basement of the building and are wrapped in brown paper for protection. This collection allowed the author to examine the minutes of all lines of any importance to the thirty-fifth parallel project with the sole exception of the Atlantic and Pacific Railroad Company. Minutes for this company during the Fremont period were included in the minute book of the Southwest Pacific Railroad, but for the later period no railroad company or library knew the location of or could verify the existence of any A. & P. minutes. The A. & P. story was told relying on correspondence collections which fortunately were much more extensive in regard to it than to any other corporation under consideration. Of special use in this study were the following corporate records, found in the Frisco's basement vault:

Joplin Railroad Co. (of Missouri), Minutes of Directors, Nov. 18, 1875–June 3, 1876.

Joplin Railway Co. (consolidated), Minute Book, Dec. 28, 1881–May 24, 1910.

Memphis, Carthage & Northwestern Railroad Co., Minutes, Dec. 20, 1873–Oct. 1, 1874.

213

Paris and Great Northern Railway Co., Minute Books, Jan. 6, 1886–May 15, 1928 (2 vols.).

St. Louis, Arkansas and Texas Railway Co. (of Arkansas), Book of Record, July 15, 1880–Sept. 22, 1881.

———— (of Missouri), Minutes, July 15, 1880–Sept. 22, 1881.

———— (consolidated), Minutes, June 10, 1881–May 10, 1910.

St. Louis, Wichita and Western Railway Co. Book of Record, April 18, 1879–March 24, 1910 (2 vols.).

Springfield and Northern Railway Co., Minute Book, May 3, 1884–May 16, 1903.

Springfield Western and Southern Railroad Co. of Missouri-Springfield and Western Missouri Railroad Co., Minutes, Sept. 6, 1875–March 6, 1888 (2 vols.).

South Pacific Railroad Co. Minutes, March 17, 1868–June 5, 1872.

Southwest Pacific Railroad Co., Minute Book, Sept. 1, 1866–May 18, 1867.

The Missouri Pacific Archives, located in the Missouri Pacific Building in St. Louis, likewise consist almost exclusively of minute books and annual reports. The following were examined in the well-inventoried basement vault of the company:

Missouri Pacific Railway Co. Annual Reports, 1882–1887.

————. Minutes, Oct. 21, 1876–Sept. 22, 1880.

————. Book of Record, Oct. 1, 1880–March 18, 1886.

Pacific Railroad Co. Minutes, 1850–1870. These contain the records of the South-West Branch.

————. Proceedings of the Executive Committee, 1852–1870.

————. Minutes, 1871–1876.

An extremely important body of letters touching on the history of the Western Division in the 1880s is the large collection of records of the Atlantic and Pacific Railroad Company's Law and Land Department, which are now stored in the Atchison, Topeka and Santa Fe unclaimed freight warehouse in Topeka, Kansas. An inventory of the records stored in the warehouse has been compiled by the Kansas State Historical Society. The A. & P. material consists of letterpress copies of about twenty thousand pieces of correspondence between the years 1881 and 1896; these are bound in twenty-three volumes. All the stationery is marked "Atlantic and Pacific. Law and Land Department," but the volumes themselves are marked "Land Commissioner" or "General Solicitor" where the binding covers have survived at all. Most of the letters are from James Williamson, but several volumes contain letters from Thomas Sedgwick. The Sedgwick volumes are handwritten; most of the Williamson volumes are neatly typed. The inventory lists the location of this collection as Case 36, shelves A & B, Bay 6, miscellaneous storage, 3rd floor. The location of thirty boxes of Santa Fe directors records, 1880–1895, which contained useful documents with regard to the A. & P., is Case 6, Shelf B, Bay 9, Sec. Treas. Floor. However, since the warehouse was not intended as a library, the sections are not clearly labeled and the material is being constantly moved. It will be necessary for the researcher to receive aid from the company in locating these materials.

All the railroad archives mentioned are open to researchers only by permission of the company.

OTHER ARCHIVAL MATERIAL

Kansas State Historical Society, Topeka, Kansas

Kingman, Lewis, Scrapbook.

Kingman worked for the A. & P. Western Division. In this book are company publications and a few letters.

Missouri Historical Society, Columbia, Mo.

Pacific Railroad Co. Reports, 1851–1872. Bound in two volumes.

These are the annual reports, engineering reports, speeches, etc., relating to the Pacific Railroad and the South-West Branch.

St. Louis–San Francisco Railroad. Publications. Four boxes.

Pamphlets, advertising and miscellaneous reports of the railroad from the 1870s to the early twentieth century.

Van Sant, R. L. Letter Copy Book, 1879–1882.

Van Sant was assistant engineer on the St. Louis, Wichita and Western. The letters detail construction problems.

Missouri Historical Society, St. Louis, Mo.

Bridge, Hudson E. Papers.

Bridge was an early president of the Pacific of Missouri.

Eads, James B. Papers.

Eads was an early promoter and incorporator of the Atlantic and Pacific.

Francis, David R. Letterbooks.

In this collection was found information concerning the state $300,000 suit against the Frisco in the 1890s. Francis was Missouri governor at the time.

Miller, Ed., to Reeves, Sam J. Oct. 6, 1857, Oct. 27, 1857.

These letters are filed individually.

Southwest Pacific Railroad Co. Account Book, March 1866–Dec. 1867.

The troubles of Fremont are here statistically detailed.

Taylor, George R. Papers.

Taylor was a lobbyist for the Pacific of Missouri and its president in the later 1850s.

National Archives, Washington, D.C.

Department of the Interior. Pacific Railroads. Letters Sent. No. 3. Record Group 48.

Replies from the Interior Department to numerous inquiries regarding the thirty-fifth parallel project are contained in this indexed volume.

————. Lands and Railroads Division. Railroad Packages Nos. 9–14½, 308, 333.

Correspondence from railroad officials to the Interior Department. Package 14½ contains A. & P. mortgages and package 308 contains that railroad's annual reports, 1870–1876 (reports were published only sporadically for the public). All packages deal with A. & P. business. Answers to these letters are found in the volume cited above.

General Land Office. Division "F" Railroad Right of Way and Reclamation. Box 1: Atlantic and Pacific, 1866–1872; Box 2: Southwest Branch Pacific Railroad, 1852–1872, St. Louis and San Francisco Railway Co.; Box 3: Atlantic and Pacific Railroad Co., Relinquishments in Missouri, 1880–81, 1888–92, 1908–16; Box 4: Atlantic and Pacific, 1917–; Box 5: Atlantic and Pacific, 1873–1900. Record Group 49.

These boxes contain letters to the Land Office concerning the problems arising out of the federal land grant to the Atlantic and Pacific and to the state of Missouri for the benefit of the thirty-fifth parallel project.

Office of Indian Affairs. Land Division. Special Cases. No. 97: St. Louis and San Francisco Ry. Co., Rt. of Way, Choctaw and Chickasaw Nations; No. 102: Railroads in Indian Territory. Record Group 75.

Letters and documents deposited in metal file boxes which treat the subject mentioned.

Oklahoma Historical Society, Oklahoma City, Okla.

Cherokee Papers, 1874–1889.

Chickasaw Railroad File.

Cheyenne and Arapahoe, vol. III.

Choctaw Railroad File.

"Copies of Original Letters written by David Osburne Fisher to his wife Mattie McSweeny Fisher," Typescript.

Creek Railroad File.

Hodges, F. S. Reports of Surveys, Atlantic and Pacific R.R. (MSS in library).

Sac and Fox Agency, vol. XI.

Quapaw Railroad File.

All the above materials except as indicated are in the Indian Archives Division. Research is aided by a good card index to the manuscripts.

Offices of J. & W. Seligman & Co., New York, N.Y.

J. & W. Seligman and Co. Private Letter Book, New York Office, Oct. 2, 1868–Sept. 23, 1873.

The company owns a microfilm copy of this document which it kindly made available to the author. The Seligman archives are now being catalogued for the use of scholars.

PRINTED SOURCES

Atlantic and Pacific Railroad Co. *Annual Report. Atlantic and Pacific Railroad Company to the Stockholders, For the Fiscal Year Ending December 31, 1874.* New York: Evening Post Steam Presses, 1875.

————. *Atlantic & Pacific R.R. Co. and Atchison Topeka & Santa Fe R.R. Co. Contracts, Deeds, and Other Documents as Between the Two Companies Together with the Charter of the Atlantic & Pacific R.R. Co. and Legislation Subsequent Thereto.* Boston: Alfred Mudge & Son, 1887.

————. *The Atlantic & Pacific Railroad Co.: The Route and its Advantages; The Congressional Act of Incorporation, and List of Officers.* Boston: for the Company, 1870.

————. *Brochure in Regard to the Atlantic and Pacific Railroad Co. The "New Mexico Southern" or "Thirty Fifth Parallel" Route, and the First Mortgage Bonds of its Western Division.* New York: for the company, 1881.

————. *Circular to the Stockholders of the Atlantic and Pacific Railroad Company.* New York: Geo. F. Nesbitt & Co., 1855.

————. *Laws and Documents. Atlantic & Pacific Railroad and Leased Lines.* St. Louis: Levison & Blythe, 1873.

————. *Route to the Pacific Ocean on the 35th Parallel. Extracts from Reports of E. F. Beale, Esq. and Lieut. Whipple to the War Department Showing the Features of the Route.* New York: Stockholder Job Printing Office, 1867.

————. *The Route for a Railroad to the Pacific Ocean Near the Thirty-Fifth Parallel of Latitude: Its Resources and Advantages.* Boston: for the company, 1870.

————. *A Sectional Map Book of the Atlantic and Pacific Rail-Road Lands. 1,200,000 Acres for Sale.* St. Louis: A. B. Greene [1874].

————. *Southwest Pacific Railroad Company. Atlantic & Pacific Railroad Company. Statutes, Conveyances and Documents.* New York: Stockholder Job Printing Offices, 1867.

Dacus, J. A., and Buel, J. W. *A Tour of St. Louis; or, The Inside Life of a Great City.* St. Louis: Western Publishing Co., 1878.

Davis, C. Wood. "The Farmer, the Investor, and the Railway." *The Arena,* XV (Feb. 1891), 291–313.

Fisk, Clinton B. *Southwest Pacific Railroad. Report of Receipts and Disbursements . . . From June 21, 1867–January 1, 1868.* St. Louis: Missouri Democrat Printing House, 1868.

Hillyer, C. J. *Atlantic and Pacific Railroad and the Indian Territory.* Washington: McGill & Witherow, 1871.

History of Greene County, Missouri. St. Louis: Western History Company, 1883.

Hopkins, Alphonso A. *The Life of Clinton Bowen Fisk with a Brief Sketch of John A. Brooks.* New York: Funk & Wagnalls, 1888.

Miller, Edward. *Address, Delivered by Request, Before a Railroad Meeting of the Citizens of Cooper County . . . April 3, 1858.* St. Louis: George Knapp & Co., 1858.

Mollhausen, Baldwin. *Diary of a Journey from the Mississippi to the Coast of the Pacific with a United States Government Expedition.* Trans. by Mrs. Percy Sinnett. 2 vols. London: Longman, Brown, Green, Longmans & Roberts, 1858.

Pacific Railroad of Missouri. *The Missouri Pacific Railroad. Report of Andrew Peirce General Manager of the Atlantic and Pacific Railroad and Leased Lines, December 1875.* New York: Evening Post Steam Presses, 1875.

————. *Statement Relating to the Southwest Branch, Lands, Bonds, &c.* New York: Geo. F. Nesbitt, 1857.

Peebles, Cornelius Glen. *Exposé of the Atlantic & Pacific Railroad Company (Extraordinary Developments).* New York, 1854.

Peirce, Andrew. *The Atlantic and Pacific Railroad Company. Report of the General Manager to the Directors, December, 1873.* New York: Union Printing House, 1874.

Pictorial and Geneological Record of Greene Co., Mo. Together with Biographies of Prominent Men of Other Portions of the State, Both Living and Dead. Chicago: Goodspeed Brothers, 1893.

Sutter, Archibald C. E. *American Notes 1881.* Edinburgh and London: William Blackwood and Sons, 1882.

Trollope, Anthony. *North America.* 5th Edition. London: Chapman & Hall, 1866.

NEWSPAPERS

Arkansas Sentinel (Fayetteville), 1878–1884.

Arizona Silver Belt (Globe), 1878–1892.

Cherokee Advocate (Talequah, Indian Territory), 1882.

Cheyenne Leader (Cheyenne, Wyo.), 1870–1875.

Commercial and Financial Chronicle (New York), 1873–1893.

Crawford County Clippings Book, Kansas State Historical Soc.

Ellsworth Democrat (Ellsworth, Kansas), 1886–1888.

Jefferson Inquirer (Jefferson City, Mo.), 1854.

Missouri Democrat (St. Louis), 1860–1861, 1866, 1875.

Missouri Republican (St. Louis), 1851.

Missouri Statesman (Columbia), 1862, 1867.
Missouri Weekly Patriot (Springfield), 1865–1876.
Neodesha Free Press (Neodesha, Kansas), 1870–1880.
New York Times, 1853–1897.
New York Tribune, 1875–1898.
Oswego Independent (Oswego, Kansas), 1879–1880, 1882.
Railroad Gazette (New York), 1876–1895.
Rolla Express (Rolla, Mo.), 1860–1863, 1868, 1872–1873.
Rolla Weekly Herald (Rolla, Mo.), 1877–1895.
St. Louis Globe-Democrat, 1876–1877, 1879.
St. Louis Times, 1870.
San Francisco Chronicle, 1880–1883.
Springfield Weekly Patriot-Advertiser (Springfield, Mo.), 1876–1880.
Weekly People's Tribune (Jefferson City, Mo.), 1868, 1870.
Wichita City Eagle (Wichita, Kansas), 1878–1886.

PUBLIC DOCUMENTS

Bailey v. *Atlantic & Pacific R. Co. et al. Federal Cases,* II, 366 (1874).

Evans & Howard Fire Brick Company, Appellant v. *St. Louis & San Francisco Railway Company, Respondent. Missouri Appeal Reports,* XXI, 651 (1886).

Mary A. Coffin v. *St. Louis and San Francisco Railway Co. Missouri Appeal Reports,* XXII, 606 (1886).

The Pacific Railroad v. *the Governor. Missouri Reports,* XXIII, 353–71 (1856).

Pacific Railroad v. *Hughes. Missouri Reports,* XXIII, 291–309 (1855).

Parmley v. *St. Louis I.M. & S.R. Co. Paul* v. *Pacific R. Co. Bailey* v. *Atlantic & P.R. Co. St. John* v. *Missouri K. & T. Ry, Co. Courtright* v. *Clark et al. Federal Cases,* XVIII, 1228 (1874).

The People of the State of New York ex rel. Walter Del Mar v. *The St. Louis and San Francisco Railway Company. New York Reports* (Hun), XLIV, 552 (1887).

U.S. Congress. House. *Forfeited Grants Atlantic and Pacific Railroad Company. May 28, 1884.* House Rpt. 1663, 48th Cong., 1st Sess., 1884 (Serial 2258).

————. *Report of the Secretary of the Interior 1871.* House Exec. Doc. 1, Pt. 5, 42d Cong., 2d Sess., 1872 (Serial 1505).

————. *Report of the Secretary of the Interior 1880.* House Exec. Doc. 1, Pt. 5, 46th Cong., 3rd Sess., 1881.

————. *Report of the Secretary of the Interior 1881.* House Exec. Doc. 1, Pt. 5, 47th Cong., 1st Sess., 1882.

————. *Report of the Secretary of the Interior 1882.* House Exec. Doc. 1, Pt. 5, 47th Cong., 2d Sess., 1882.

————. *Right of Way to Saint Louis and San Francisco Railroad Through the Indian Territory . . . April 6, 1882.* H.R. 934, 47th Cong., 1st Sess., 1882 (Serial 2067).

U.S. Congress. Senate. *Memorial of the Citizens of the Chickasaw Nation Remonstrating Against the Organization of a Territorial Government for the Indian Territory, Jan. 15, 1875.* Sen. Misc. Doc. 34, 42d Cong., 2d Sess., 1875 (Serial 1630).

————. *Memorial of the Citizens of the Cherokee Nation Remonstrating Against the Establishment of a Territorial Government over Them, Feb. 2, 1875.* Sen. Misc. Doc. 66, 42d Cong., 2d Sess., 1875 (Serial 1630).

————. *Memorial of the Citizens of the Creek Nation Remonstrating Against the Organization of a Territorial Government for the Indian Territory.* Sen. Misc. Doc. 71, 42nd Cong., 2d Sess., 1875 (Serial 1630).

————. *Memorial of the Mayor and City Council of Paris, Texas in Favor of the Ratification by Congress of the Act of the Choctaw Nation Granting to the Saint Louis and San Francisco Railroad Company the Right of Way Through that Nation, Dec. 16, 1881.* Sen. Misc. Doc. 18, 47th Cong., 1st Sess., 1881 (Serial 1993).

————. *Message from the President of the United States Transmitting a Communication from the Secretary of the Interior in Reference to the Applications of the Chicago, Texas and Mexican Central, and the Saint Louis and San Francisco Railway Companies, for the Right of Way Across the Lands of the Choctaw Nation, in the Indian Territory, Dec. 15, 1881.* Sen. Exec. Doc. 15, 47th Cong., 1st Sess., 1881 (Serial 1986).

————. *Message from the President of the United States Transmitting a Communication from the Secretary of the Interior with Accompanying Papers in Reference to the Bill of Choctaw Council, Approved November 10, 1881, Granting a Right of Way Through the Choctaw Nation to the Saint Louis and San Francisco Railway Company, &c., Jan. 9, 1882.* Sen. Exec. Doc. 44, 47th Cong., 1st Sess., 1882 (Serial 1987).

————. *Protest of the Osage Nation Against the Establishment by Congress of a Territorial Government of the United States Over the Indian Nations, Feb. 9, 1875.* Sen. Misc. Doc. 72, 42d Cong., 2d Sess., 1875 (Serial 1630).

————. *Reports of Explorations and Surveys to Ascertain the Most Practicable and Economical Route for a Railroad from the Mississippi River to the Pacific Ocean.* Sen. Exec. Doc. 78, 33rd Cong., 2d Sess., 1855 (Serial 758–770).

————. *Resolution of the Legislature of Texas in Favor of A Grant of the Right of Way Through the Indian Territory to the Saint Louis and San Francisco Railway Company, Feb. 21, 1881.* Sen. Misc. Doc. 46, 46th Cong., 3rd Sess., 1881 (Serial 1944).

————. *Testimony Taken Before a Subcommittee of the Committee on Territories.* Sen. Rept. 744, 45th Cong., 3rd Sess., 1879 (Serial 1839).

U.S. *Congressional Globe,* Vols. XXII, XXVIII, XXXII, XXXVI.

U.S. *Congressional Record.* Vols. XI, XIII.

U.S. Interstate Commerce Commission. "Valuation Docket No. 400. St Louis–San Francisco Railway Company et al., Sept. 20, 1928." *Valuation Reports,* XLI, 139–879.

U.S. *Statutes at Large.* Vols. XIV, XV, XVII, XXII.

U.S. War Department. *The War of the Rebellion: A Compilation of the Official Records of the Union and Confederate Armies.* Series I. Vol. XXXIV. Washington: G.P.O., 1891.

BOOKS

Anderson, George L. *Kansas West.* San Marino, Calif.: Golden West Books, 1963.

————. *Official Explorations for Pacific Railroads 1853–1855.* Berkeley: University of California Press, 1921.

Bancroft, Hubert Howe. *History of California, 1860–1890.* Vol. XXIV of *The Works of Hubert Howe Bancroft.* San Francisco: The History Company, 1890.

Bashford, Herbert, and Wagner, Harr. *A Man Unafraid: The Story of John Charles Fremont.* San Francisco: Harr Wagner Publishing Co., 1927.

Belcher, Wyatt Winton. *The Economic Rivalry Between St. Louis and Chicago, 1850–1880.* New York: Columbia University Press, 1947.

Birmingham, Stephen. *Our Crowd: The Great Jewish Families of New York.* New York: Harper & Row, 1967.

Brownlee, Richard. *Gray Ghosts of the Confederacy: Guerrilla Warfare in the West, 1861–1865.* Baton Rouge: Louisiana State University Press, 1958.

Bruce, Robert V. *1877—Year of Violence.* New York: Bobbs-Merrill, 1959.

Clark, Ira. G. *Then Came the Railroads: The Century from Steam to Diesel in the Southwest.* Norman: Oklahoma University Press, 1958.

Cleveland, Frederick A., and Powell, Fred Wilbur. *Railroad Promotion and Capitalization in the United States.* New York: Longmans, Green & Co., 1909.

Cochran, Thomas C. *Railroad Leaders, 1845–1890: The Business Mind in Action.* Cambridge: Harvard University Press, 1953.

Conrad, Howard L. *Encyclopedia of the History of Missouri.* 6 vols. New York: The Southern History Company, 1901.

Daggett, Stuart. *Railroad Reorganization.* Vol. IV of Harvard Economic Studies. Boston: Houghton, Mifflin and Co., 1908.

Debo, Angie. *The Rise and Fall of the Choctaw Republic.* Norman: Oklahoma University Press, 1961.

Decker, Leslie. *Railroads, Land and Politics: The Taxation of the Railroad Land Grants, 1864–1891.* Providence, R.I.: Brown University Press, 1964.

Erickson, Charlotte. *American Industry and the European Immigrant, 1860–1885.* New York: Russell & Russell, 1957.

Evans, Cerinda W. *Collis Potter Huntington.* 2 vols. Newport News, Va., 1954.

Eyre, Alice. *The Famous Fremonts and Their America.* Boston: The Christopher Publishing House, 1961.

Federal Writers' Project. *Missouri: A Guide to the "Show Me" State.* New York: Hastings House, 1954.

Foreman, Grant, ed. *A Pathfinder in the Southwest: The Itinerary of Lieutenant A. W. Whipple During his Explorations from Fort Smith to Los Angeles in the Years 1853 and 1854.* Norman: Oklahoma University Press, 1941.

French, Bryant Morey. *Mark Twain and The Gilded Age.* Dallas: Southern Methodist University Press, 1965.

Gates, Paul W. *Fifty Million Acres: Conflicts Over Kansas Land Policy, 1854–1890.* Ithaca: Cornell University Press, 1954.

George, Preston, and Wood, Sylvan. *The Railroads of Oklahoma.* Boston: The Railway and Locomotive Historical Society, 1943.

Goetzmann, William H. *Army Exploration in the American West, 1803–1863.* New Haven: Yale University Press, 1959.

————. *Exploration and Empire: The Explorer and the Scientist in the Winning of the American West.* New York: Alfred A. Knopf, 1966.

Goodwin, Cardinal. *John Charles Fremont: An Explanation of His Career.* Stanford: Stanford University Press, 1930.

Greever, William S. *Arid Domain: The Santa Fe Railway and its Western Land Grant.* Stanford: Stanford University Press, 1954.

Grodinsky, Julius. *Jay Gould: His Business Career, 1867–1892.* Philadelphia: University of Pennsylvania Press, 1957.

————. *Transcontinental Railway Strategy, 1869–1893: A Study of Businessmen.* Philadelphia: University of Pennsylvania Press, 1962.

Jackson, W. Turrentine. *Wagon Roads West: A Study of Federal Surveys and Construction in the Trans-Mississippi West, 1846–1869.* Berkeley and Los Angeles: University of California Press, 1952.

Johnson, Arthur E., and Supple, Berry E. *Boston Capitalists and Western Railroads.* Cambridge: Harvard University Press, 1967.

Kaplan, Justin. *Mr. Clemens and Mark Twain.* New York: Simon & Schuster, 1966.

Malone, Dumas, ed. *Dictionary of American Biography.* New York: Charles Scribners Sons, 1936.

Masterson, V. V. *The Katy Railroad and the Last Frontier.* Norman: Oklahoma University Press, 1952.

Marshall, James. *Santa Fe: The Railroad that Built an Empire*. New York: Random House, 1945.

Million, John W. *State Aid to Railways in Missouri*. Vol. IV of Economic Studies of the University of Chicago. Chicago: University of Chicago Press, 1896.

Missouri Pacific Lines. *The First 112 Years*. n.p.: for the company, [1966].

Muir, Ross L., and White, Carl J. *Over the Long Term: The Story of J. & W. Seligman & Co*. New York: J. & W. Seligman & Co., 1964.

Myrick, David F. *Railroads of Nevada and Eastern California*. 2 vols. Berkeley: Howell North, 1963.

Nevins, Allan. *Fremont: Pathmarker of the West*. New York: D. Appleton–Century Co., 1939.

Primm, James Neal. *Economic Policy in the Development of a Western State. Missouri, 1820–1860* Cambridge: Harvard University Press, 1954.

Reed, S. G. *A History of the Texas Railroads and of Transportation Conditions under Spain and Mexico and the Republic and the State*. Houston, Texas: The St. Clair Publishing Co., 1941.

Riegel, Robert E. *The Story of the Western Railroads: From 1852 Through the Reign of the Giants*. New York: Macmillan, 1926.

Shenton, James P. *Robert John Walker: A Politician from Jackson to Lincoln*. New York and London: Columbia University Press, 1961.

Wardell, Morris L. *A Political History of the Cherokee Nation, 1838–1907*. Norman: Oklahoma University Press, 1938.

Waters, L. L. *Steel Trails to Santa Fe*. Lawrence, Kans.: University of Kansas Press, 1950.

ARTICLES

Allhands, James L. "History of the Construction of the Frisco Railway Lines in Oklahoma." *Chronicles of Oklahoma*. III (1925), 229–39.

Cotterill, Robert S. "The National Railroad Convention in St. Louis 1849." *Missouri Historical Review*. XII (July 1918), 203–15.

Decker, Leslie E. "The Railroads and the Land Office: Administrative Policy and the Land Patent Controversy, 1864–1896." *Mississippi Valley Historical Review*, XLVI (March 1960), 679–99.

Ehrlich, Walter. "Was the Dred Scott Case Valid?" *Missouri Historical Review*. LXIII (April 1969), 317–28.

Ellis, David M. "The Forfeiture of Railroad Land Grants, 1867–1894." *Mississippi Valley Historical Review*. XXXIII (June 1946), 27–60.

McLear, Patrick E. "The St. Louis Cholera Epidemic of 1849." *Missouri Historical Review*. LXIII (Jan. 1969), 171–81.

Miner, Craig. "The Colonization of the St. Louis and San Francisco Railway Company, 1880–1882: A Study of Corporate Diplomacy." *Missouri Historical Review*. LXIII (April 1969), 345–63.

————. "Hopes and Fears: Ambivalence in the Anti-Railroad Movement at Springfield, Missouri, 1870–1880." *Bulletin of the Missouri Historical Society,* XXVII (Jan. 1971), 129–46.

————. "The Struggle for an East-West Railway into the Indian Territory, 1870–1882." *Chronicles of Oklahoma.* XLVII (Spring 1969), 560–81.

Riegel, Robert E. "The Missouri Pacific Railroad to 1879." *Missouri Historical Review."* XVIII (Oct. 1923), 3–26.

Stoddard, Francis R. "Amiel Weeks Whipple." *Chronicles of Oklahoma.* XXVIII (Autumn 1950), 226–30.

Wright, Muriel H., and Shirk, George H., eds. "The Journal of Lieutenant A. W. Whipple." *Chronicles of Oklahoma.* XXVIII (Autumn, 1950), 235–83.

OTHER

Fitzsimmons, Margaret Louise. "Railroad Development in Missouri, 1860–1870." Unpublished Ph.D. dissertation. Washington University, St. Louis, June, 1931.

Mann, Clair V., ed. "Frisco First: A Source Materials History of the St. Louis & San Francisco Railroad, 1845–1945." 4 vols. Unpublished typescript. Phelps Co. Historical Society, Rolla, Mo.

Miner, Craig. "The Border Tier Line: A History of the Missouri River, Fort Scott and Gulf Railroad, 1865–1870." Unpublished Masters thesis. Wichita State University, 1967.

INDEX

Adair, William: debate with Baker, 104

Alabama claims: depress bond market, 83

Albert, Anselm: 55

Albuquerque, N. M.: 2, 27, 51, 65, 107, 109, 113, 121, 122, 135, 138, 139; surveyors at, 10, 11; A.&P. land office at, 142–43, 157

Allen, Thomas: 178 n. 17; speech at Pacific celebration, 20; fails to sell bonds, 22

American Emigrant Aid and Homestead Co.: imports Danes, 54–55

Ames, Oliver: 94; buys A.&P. land, 93

Anderson, Bill: 32

Antelope Hills: 8

Arapahoe Indians. *See* Indians

Arena: 110

Arizona: 138, 141, 144, 146

Arizona Cattle Co.: 153

Arizona Lumber Co.: 153

Arizona Mineral Belt Railway: 157

Arkansas: 107, 116, 129; railroad survey at, 6, 7; lands withdrawn, 84; Arkansas division of Frisco, 114, 120, 121, 122, 124, 125

Arkansas Industrial University: 124, 137

Arkansas River: 5, 46; bridge at Van Buren, 125

Arlington, Mo.: 71

Ash Grove, Mo.: 108

Atchison, Topeka and Santa Fe Railroad Co.: 109, 135, 146, 150, 158; and antibond movement, 110; Tripartite Agreement, 113, 120–24; and rebates, 125–26; and Gould-Huntington purchase, 130, 131, 132, 133; A.&P. Western Division finance, 139, 140, 141, 143, 157; operates A.&P., 156; and Frisco

stock fight, 161; takes control of Frisco, 166, 167

Atlantic and Pacific Railroad Co. (1853): 47

Atlantic and Pacific Railroad Co. (1866): 58, 64, 69, 98, 134; charter, 40, 45–47, 49–51; predictions concerning, 45–46, 50, 51–52, 59, 63, 116, 138; route, 51, 64–65, 71, 82, 86, 109; land policy Central Division (Indian Territory), 51, 57, 78, 79, 82, 84, 92, 103–05, 116, 125; mergers, 56, 65, 72, 75, 85; town policy, 56, 71, 72, 77, 78, 79, 145; ground-breaking, 68–69; finance Missouri and Central Divisions, 69, 71, 83, 84, 85, 86, 87, 89; land policy Missouri Division, 75–76; rates, 76, 109; taxation, 77, 148; construction, 78–79, 116, 135, 138, 140, 157; relations with M.K.&T., 80, 81, 86; lease of Pacific, 82, 83, 85–86, 87; excursion, 88, 89; receivership of, 91–93; sale of Missouri Division 1876, 95–96; land policy Western Division, 105, 124, 135, 139, 140, 141, 143–47, 153; Tripartite Agreement 1880, 113, 120–24; rebate issue, 125–26; Gould-Huntington purchase 1882, 130–33; finance Western Division, 139, 152, 157, 161; Southern Pacific lease, 140; land grant forfeiture, 145, 148–52, 156; foreclosure sale 1896, 167, 168

Attorneys: local papers criticize, 96

Atwood Car Wheel Co.: 99

Aztec Land and Cattle Co.: 152

Baker, James: 97, 100, 105, 109, 115; advocates home company, 62–66; background, 62, 63; to New York for capital, 64; and Southwest Missouri Co., 65–66; salary for South

225